CAMBRIDGE SURVEYS OF ECONOMIC LITERATURE

CAPITAL THEORY AND DYNAMICS

CAMBRIDGE SURVEYS OF ECONOMIC LITERATURE

Editors:

Miss Phyllis Deane, University of Cambridge and
Professor Mark Perlman, University of Pittsburgh

Editorial Advisory Board:

Professor A. B. Atkinson, University College, London
Professor M. Bronfenbrenner, Duke University
Professor K. D. George, University College, Cardiff
Professor C. P. Kindleberger, Massachusetts Institute of Technology
Professor T. Mayer, University of California, Davis
Professor A. R. Prest, London School of Economics and Political
    Science

The literature of economics is expanding rapidly and many subjects
have changed out of recognition within the space of a few years.
Perceiving the state of knowledge in fast-developing subjects is
difficult for students and time-consuming for professional economists.
This series of books is intended to help with this problem. Each
book will be quite brief, giving a clear structure to and balanced
overview of the topic and written at a level intelligible to the senior
undergraduate. The books will therefore be useful for teaching, but will
also provide a mature yet compact presentation of the subject for the
economist wishing to update his knowledge outside his own
specialism.

First books in the series:

E. Roy Weintraub: Microfoundations: The compatibility of
microeconomics and macroeconomics
Dennis C. Mueller: Public choice
Robert L. Clark and Joseph J. Spengler: The Economics of individual
and population aging
Edwin Burmeister: Capital theory and dynamics
Mark Blaug: The methodology of economics or how economists
explain

Capital theory and dynamics

EDWIN BURMEISTER

Commonwealth Professor of Economics
University of Virginia

CAMBRIDGE UNIVERSITY PRESS
CAMBRIDGE
LONDON NEW YORK NEW ROCHELLE
MELBOURNE SYDNEY

Published by the Press Syndicate of the University of Cambridge
The Pitt Building, Trumpington Street, Cambridge CB2 1RP
32 East 57th Street, New York, NY 10022, USA
296 Beaconsfield Parade, Middle Park, Melbourne 3206, Australia

First published 1980

Printed in the United States of America
Typeset by Progressive Typographers, Inc., Emigsville, Pa.
Printed and bound by The Murray Printing Co., Westford, Mass.

Library of Congress Cataloging in Publication Data

Burmeister, Edwin.

   Capital theory and dynamics.

   (Cambridge surveys of economic literature)

   Includes bibliographical references.

   1. Capital–Mathematical models.
   2. Saving and investment–Mathematical models.
   3. Economic development–Mathematical models.
   4. Statics and dynamics (Social sciences)
   I. Title.
HB501.B8469   332′.041   79–28412
ISBN 0 521 22889 1   hard covers
ISBN 0 521 29703 6   paperback

To Curt, Carl, Eva, and Craig

CONTENTS

PREFACE

Capital theory and dynamics are primary cornerstones for almost every branch of economics. Indeed, except in a fictional world in which events replicate themselves–where the economies of yesterday, today, and tomorrow are identical–issues of capital formation and dynamic behavior must always arise.

Unfortunately, the relevant literature is often technically formidable, if not incomprehensible, to nonspecialists. Still, most of the important results in capital theory and dynamics can be understood and used even though their proofs may not be understood fully. This book exploits this fact and thereby makes the subject accessible to students and economists who might not possess the mathematical background required to prove theorems. Some mathematical literacy is a prerequisite, but the reader familiar with the techniques taught in a standard ''mathematics for economists'' course (such as constrained maximization problems, simple differential equations, and elementary matrix algebra) will encounter few technical difficulties. The focus here is upon economic significance and interpretation; references to the appropriate proofs are provided for those who are interested in more advanced discussions.

Three categories of readers are envisioned. First, undergraduate economics majors interested in economic theory and unable to find suitable upper-level courses will find that this book provides such an option; the text has been used successfully in an undergraduate seminar at the University of Virginia. Second, graduate students wishing an overview of capital theory and dynamics will find this text appropriate. Third, this book will serve as a survey for those economists in other fields who want a better background in capital theory and dynamics. The concluding chapter, in particular, should be of interest to macroeconomists, for there it is shown that rational-expectations models and heterogeneous-capital-good models share similar dynamic structures.

The ultimate objective of this book is to stimulate discussion of issues relevant to the question of how economies evolve over time. The topics addressed offer solutions to some questions and indicate the directions of current research on others, but many fundamental problems remain. It is my hope that this book will provide a framework within which new questions may be formulated, and that it will inspire future work to broaden our understanding of economics.

I am grateful to the Center for Advanced Studies at the University of Virginia for supporting my research, and special thanks is extended to John Atkins, Elizabeth Wright, and Alessandro Zanello for their careful scrutiny of preliminary drafts and help in the preparation of the final version.

Edwin Burmeister
Charlottesville, Virginia

1

Introduction and overview

Uncertainty is pervasive in economics. It is difficult to determine even the *current* state of actual economies, let alone to forecast *future* economic states with certainty. Moreover, expectations about future economic events affect the observed current economic state. For example, under standard economic assumptions, the current competitive price of an asset is equal to the discounted value of the future earnings that asset is expected to produce, where in general the proper discounting procedure depends upon expected future interest rates and attitudes toward risk. If expectations about future earnings change, so does the current price, and one can never construct a theory of current asset price determination without some assumption – implicit or explicit – about the future.

All too often this essential feature is superficially treated in introductory and intermediate-level microeconomics courses. Students learn about expectations in macroeconomics, but microeconomic theory typically is presented within a static framework. This approach is valid if each economic event replicates itself every time period so that there is no distinction between today, tomorrow, and any other future day. Such an unrealistic assumption is necessary to justify common behavioral assumptions such as "maximizing utility," because obviously to maximize today's utility with no regard for the future implies consumption binges that make sense only if there *is* no tomorrow.

Upon reflection it is evident that time plays two distinct roles:

(1) Even if future events are certain, current rational economic behavior must reflect the existence of a future that will generally differ from the present. This influence is called the *pure role of time*.

(2) Recognizing that future events influence the current economic state, the fact that future events are not known with certainty adds another complexity. This influence is called the *role of uncertainty*.

For the most part, our focus in this book will be on problems involving the pure role of time. Of course, such problems are generally easier to analyze than those involving uncertainty, but for pedagogical reasons alone, it is preferable to study the pure role of time prior to examining the effects of uncertainty. Moreover, for many important economic problems, an equilibrium time path derived under the assumption that the values of future variables are known with certainty is identical to that arising in an uncertain world if the variables that were assumed to be known are replaced by their expected values. Indeed, this convenient feature is present in most "rational expectations models," such as the simple ones we will study in Chapter 7.

Our study begins in Chapter 2 by introducing basic concepts such as *discounted prices* and *own discount factors*. If we have n distinct types of commodities and T time periods, it is evident that there is an exact correspondence to a static model having different commodities equal in number to nT. New technical difficulties arise when the time horizon is infinite ($T = +\infty$), so that any analogous static model must admit an infinite number of distinct commodities.

Even within this limited framework, however, we are able to introduce and study the important concept of *dynamic efficiency*. This criterion is the intertemporal analog of the well-known *static efficiency* concept: given fixed productive inputs, no more of any one commodity can be produced without producing less of at least one other commodity. The result that any competitive equilibrium is static efficient also generalizes; we demonstrate that a competitive equilibrium path also meets the dynamic efficiency criterion, a result that we refer to as "the dynamic invisible hand."

If every static result generalized to a dynamic context, our study of the pure role of time would appear economically vacuous. The following simple example serves to dispel such fears and, we hope, to convince students that the effort they must put forth in working through this book will result in significant economic insights.

An economy is said to be *Pareto optimal* (or *Pareto efficient*) if no economic agent can be made better off without making another agent worse off; moreover, it is a standard result that every static competitive equilibrium is also Pareto optimal.[1] In Section 3.4 we present a simple example proving that this result *does not generalize* to an intertemporal world. In this example economic agents maximize their utility function, which depends upon consumption in the first and second periods of their two-period life cycles, and perfect competition prevails. Nevertheless, competitive equilibria paths exist which are dynamically *Pareto inefficient* in the sense that there exists a technologically feasible alternative which makes every economic agent better off in every time period! This result serves as a dramatic counterexample to anyone who asserts that maximizing behavior and perfect competition *necessarily* results in economically desirable outcomes.

Capital goods play an especially important role in intertemporal economics, for it is the past decisions concerning investment in various capital goods that determine the quantities of those goods available for production today. Thus by producing capital rather than consumption goods today, future consumption possibilities are increased. Were *no* new capital goods ever produced, existing capital stocks would deteriorate through depreciation, and eventually consumption possibilities would be limited to those producible using only labor and other primary factors.

When only one type of capital good exists, the analysis is especially straightforward, for two reasons:

First, if the single type of capital good is the only asset in the economy, then whatever portion of disposable income that is not consumed (i.e., net investment) must be channeled into the accumulation of this single asset. In these circumstances there does not exist any *portfolio problem,* namely the problem of allocating a given volume of net investment among several alternative assets. Such a portfolio problem is examined in Section 3.7, where there is a single capital good and money serves as an alternative means of holding wealth. It obviously also arises when there are many different types of capital goods.

Second, when there are several types of capital goods, we must either find a suitable index for "aggregate capital" or else study a technically more complex disaggregated model. Except under extraordinarily restrictive conditions, it is impossible to aggregate *any* group of heterogeneous commodities into a well-behaved index that has the economic properties of a single commodity. This statement, of course, applies with equal validity to the aggregation of heterogeneous labor, but traditionally the problem of "capital aggregation" has received the most attention (perhaps misplaced) in the literature.

Common one-capital-good models are surveyed in Chapter 3, including the standard two-sector model with one pure capital good and one pure consumption good (Section 3.6) and a simple monetary growth model (Section 3.7). The same basic subject material is covered, in considerably more detail, by the first six chapters of Burmeister and Dobell (1970).

In Chapter 4 we turn to models admitting many heterogeneous capital goods and discuss numerous aspects of the so-called "Cambridge controversy," including reswitching, paradoxical consumption behavior, the labor theory of value, Sraffa's "Standard Commodity," and the neo-Austrian indices of "roundaboutness." In *every* instance we find that the "controversial" nature of the results stems from a superficial view of the economic problem. For example, suppose that a particular steady-state (i.e., dynamic) equilibrium, say equilibrium *A*, possesses certain properties, while a different steady-state equilibrium, call it B, possesses other properties. More concretely, suppose that at A, per capita consumption is C_A and the steady-state equilibrium interest rate is r_A; analogously, at B we have C_B and r_B. One then may conclude that it is "paradoxical" if $C_B > C_A$ and $r_A < r_B$. However, given that an economy is at A, the properties of B, whatever they might be, are *economically irrelevant*. Given that an economy is at A, the *only* economically significant facts concern the properties of the set of technologically feasible dynamic paths emanating from A as an initial condition. There may not even exist a feasible time path along which it is possible to move from A to B, and (except in trivial cases) it is *never* possible to move instantaneously from A to B. Thus, comparisons of only A and B necessarily involve the wrong economic questions.

Similarly, tricks such as the labor theory of value or Sraffa's "Standard Commodity," even in those special cases in which they can be made to "work" in some meaningful sense, are predicated upon the assumption that steady-state equilibrium always prevails; this assumption precludes most of the economically feasible options. Unfortunately, many ill-conceived economic questions have received extensive attention in the literature; the purpose of Chapter 4 is to acquaint students with some of the common mistaken approaches so that they can avoid wasting their time on dead-end roads.

In Chapter 5 we turn to the relevant question just posed, namely: Given a technology and a specified starting point, what are the properties of the feasible dynamic paths that an economy might follow? As a first step, we introduce the concept of a *competitive path,* and we see that, under reasonable assumptions, a competitive path maximizes the present value of consumption (Theorem 5.2).

Next, we turn to *intertemporal rates of transformation,* relating how much additional future consumption is possible in a future time period if current consumption is reduced by a certain amount. These ideas are illustrated by a simple, comprehensive numerical example, which also serves to highlight the fact that the "paradoxical results" discussed in Chapter 4 are based upon economic misunderstandings. We then prove a general result illustrated by the previous numerical example: marginal rates of intertemporal transformation, which are determined by the technology, are always related by an inequality to a ratio of competitive present value prices.

Finally, Solow's rate of return concept is discussed, and we present the necessary and sufficient Cass conditions for a dynamic path to be *consumption efficient*. This concept of consumption efficiency was previously introduced and defined in Section 2.5. Loosely speaking, a dynamic path is consumption efficient if there exists no other feasible path that always gives as much consumption and sometimes gives more consumption. Both with or without the presence of heterogeneous capital goods, a competitive path need not be consumption efficient. This idea, called the problem of ''capital overaccumulation,'' again confirms the conclusion stated previously that perfect competition does not necessarily imply Pareto optimality in a dynamic world.

Having studied the fundamental properties of the set of feasible paths in Chapter 5, we turn in Chapter 6 to the subset of paths that actual economies will follow under specified rules. These rules fall into two categories:

(1) We may select a particular technologically feasible path by finding that path (or those paths) which maximizes a specified criterion function (e.g., the present discounted value of future consumption). This approach defines *optimal economic growth problems,* which we survey briefly in Section 6.4. The subject is so extensive that several books would be needed to cover it thoroughly. Some topics, such as various stability issues and the problem of exhaustible resources, are discussed in the text, but readers interested in comprehensive treatments are referred to the references cited.

(2) A feasible path may be determined by specifying behavioral rules for economic agents. Such *descriptive economic models* (as opposed to *optimal economic models* or, equivalently, *planning models*) are intended to capture features of the actual dynamic

paths observable in economies. For example, most of the formulations in the one-capital-good setting of Chapter 3 involve the assumption that consumption is a constant fraction of disposable income, and this specification is justified on the grounds that it is ''consistent with'' (or at least not obviously inconsistent with) empirical observations.

As already noted, there is a portfolio problem when more than one asset exists. In particular, when there are heterogeneous capital goods, that constant fraction of disposable income which is not consumed must be allocated, during every time period, to determine net investment in each of the different types of capital goods. This allocation is assumed to satisfy the competitive equilibrium condition that the rates of return on every asset, including capital gains or losses, be equalized every time period. In general, the resulting descriptive heterogeneous capital good model exhibits *saddlepoint instability*. That is, given arbitrary initial capital stocks, the economy will converge over time to a steady-state (dynamic) equilibrium only if very special initial prices are specified; for ''almost all'' values of initial prices, the economy will be unstable. This so-called *Hahn problem* is discussed in Sections 6.2 and 6.3.

Actual economies apparently are not featured by this dramatic type of dynamic instability, and thus we are forced to look for ''more realistic'' descriptive models. One promising theoretical attack involves the concept of a *perfect-foresight competitive equilibrium* (PFCE), as discussed in Section 6.3. A PFCE entails maximization of an intertemporal utility function on the part of consumers and maximization of the present discounted value of profits on the part of firms. Then, under reasonable assumptions, only one path is consistent with equality of demand and supply for every commodity during every time period, and this particular equilibrium path is not unstable in the sense that it either converges to a steady-state equilibrium point or eventually remains in a region ''near'' the steady-state point. Moreover, a remarkable *equivalence theorem* (Theorem 6.1) asserts that a perfect foresight competitive equilibrium is the solution to an optimizing or planning problem, and vice versa. This equivalence theorem, discussed in Section 6.4, reveals the close connection between optimal paths and PFCEs and, by so doing, casts doubt upon the concept of a PFCE as an appropriate *descriptive* assumption.

First steps toward introducing uncertainty are taken in Chapter 7. Roughly speaking, one may generalize the concept of a PFCE to that of a *rational expectations competitive equilibrium* simply by replacing every perfect foresight variable with its rational expectation. This interpretation makes evident the strength of a common assumption used in rational expectations modeling: the *assumption* that rational expectations paths converge. This assumption, and issues regarding its legitimacy, are discussed in Section 7.2, and in Section 7.3 a disequilibrium model is presented. This disequilibrium example – in which supply and demand need not always be equal – serves to prove that the common assumption of convergent rational expectations can sometimes lead to a logical contradiction.

We are left, therefore, with the conclusion that many fundamental economic questions remain unanswered. Foremost among these are (1) the question of how finite-lived economic agents determine the length of their planning horizons which presumably may vary with economic conditions; and (2) the question of which "disequilibrium mechanisms" are consistent with maximizing behavior in the presence of transactions costs, and how such "frictions" affect the dynamic stability properties of economic models. A "best answer" to these questions probably does not exist, but the intent of this book is to provide readers with important economic insights so that, given a particular economic issue for investigation, they will be better able to construct an appropriate model that reflects our uncertain world with heterogeneous assets.

2

The pure role of time

2.1. Pricing and definitions

In this chapter we isolate the pure role of time from issues of uncertainty by considering only the very special subset of dynamic paths for which expectations are always realized. Such paths of self-fulfilling expectations are called *perfect-foresight paths*. To achieve this end we examine an economy in which binding contracts for all future commodity exchanges are written at the beginning of the first period, thus eliminating any uncertainty about future events. The model is extremely limited, applicable to only issues of "the pure role of time," as opposed to issues relating to the fact that in reality the future always is uncertain.[1]

There are distinct commodities of types $i = 1, 2, \ldots$ exchanged at the beginning of time periods $t = 1, 2, \ldots$. The price determined at the beginning of period 1 for 1 unit of the ith-type commodity to be delivered at the beginning of period t is denoted by

$$p_i^t.$$

If there are n distinct commodities (chocolates, popcorn, hammers, etc.) and T time periods, the prices p_i^t to be determined at the beginning of period 1 are nT in number. For each of these nT goods we assume the existence of a market and a competitive

9

market price. Because all binding contracts for future commodity exchanges are written at the beginning of period 1, the markets that determine the prices of commodities for future delivery are called *future markets,* and the prices p_i^t are called *present* or *discounted prices. Current* or *undiscounted prices* will be defined later.

We can see that our intertemporal model with nT prices to be determined is analogous to a one-period static model with nT commodities. This analogy between our intertemporal model and a static (one-period) model makes it evident that only relative prices can be determined, and we must select some price normalization rule if our p_i^t values are to be unique. (Otherwise, if p_i^t are equilibrium prices, so are the prices λp_i^t, where λ is any positive number.) We shall arbitrarily select 1 unit of commodity 1 delivered at the beginning of period 1 as the *numéraire* good,[2] that is,

$$p_1^1 \equiv 1.$$

Accordingly, we shall interpret the p_i^t's as prices relative to the *numéraire* good, giving the following definition for discounted prices:

p_i^t = quantity of the *numéraire* good, namely 1 unit of commodity 1 delivered at the beginning of period 1, that (at the beginning of period 1) must be guaranteed in exchange for 1 unit of commodity i delivered at the beginning of period t.

More generally, the price ratio

$\dfrac{p_i^t}{p_j^\tau}$ = quantity of the commodity of type j that must be given up at the beginning of period τ in exchange for 1 unit of commodity i at the beginning of period t.

When both commodities are the same but have different guaranteed delivery dates, we can define "own discount factors" and "own interest rates" as in Definitions 2.1 and 2.2. We shall assume that there are no free goods in any time period ($p_i^t > 0$ for all i, t), in which case the definitions are always economically meaningful. We then have:

DEFINITION 2.1

$\beta_i^t = \dfrac{p_i^t}{p_i^1} = $ *own discount factor* for commodity i from periods 1 to t.

$ = $ pure number denoting the quantity of commodity i that must be delivered now (the beginning of period 1) in exchange for the guaranteed delivery of 1 unit of the same commodity, type i, at the beginning of the future period t.

DEFINITION 2.2

$r_i^t = \dfrac{p_i^t}{p_i^{t+1}} - 1 = $ *own interest rate* for commodity i for period t, that is, over the time interval from the beginning of period t to the beginning of period $t + 1$[3].

Clearly,

$$\beta_i^{t+1} = \frac{p_i^{t+1}}{p_i^1} = \frac{p_i^{t+1}}{p_i^t} \cdot \frac{p_i^t}{p_i^1} = \frac{\beta_i^t}{1 + r_i^t}. \tag{2.1.1}$$

In the special case when the values of r_i^t are independent of t, the own rate of interest for commodity i is a constant r_i with a corresponding own discount factor

$$\beta_i^t = \frac{1}{(1 + r_i)^{t-1}},$$

from which we find that the discounted price p_i^t is given by

$$p_i^t = \beta_i^t p_i^1 = \frac{p_i^1}{(1 + r_i)^{t-1}}. \tag{2.1.2}$$

We can interpret own interest rates by considering commodity loans.[4] A person making a loan provides 1 unit of commodity i to some other person at the beginning of period t. This 1 unit of commodity i has a value of p_i^t at the beginning of period 1, the time when all contracts are written. At the beginning of period $t + 1$ (or at the end of period t since the end of one period and the beginning of the next are equivalent for our purposes), the loan must be repaid. The payment consists of principal (1 unit of commodity i) plus interest (r_i^t units of commodity i). Hence the total loan repayment consists of $(1 + r_i^t)$ units of commodity i delivered at the beginning of period $t + 1$.

What is the value of these $(1 + r_i^t)$ units of commodity i at the time the loan contract is written (the beginning of period 1)? Clearly, its value then is

$$p_i^{t+1}(1 + r_i^t).$$

But recall that the value (at the beginning of period 1) of 1 unit of commodity i delivered at the beginning of period t is by definition p_i^t. If markets are perfect and no profits can be made by arbitrage, in equilibrium the value of the amount loaned and the value of the amount paid back (including interest) must be equal when both are viewed from the beginning of period 1:

$$p_i^t = p_i^{t+1}(1 + r_i^t). \tag{2.1.3}$$

Note that (2.1.3) also follows from the definition of r_i^t (see Definition 2.2), so that we have *defined* own interest rates in such a way that no profits can be reaped from arbitraging loans. Clearly, this feature is consistent with a competitive model having all binding contracts written at the beginning of period 1, all future markets in competitive equilibrium, and no transactions costs.

We have assumed that there are no free goods, so that

$$p_i^t > 0 \qquad \text{for all time periods } t \text{ and all commodities } i.$$

This assumption implies that:

(1) All own discount factors are positive ($\beta_i^t > 0$).
(2) All own interest rates are larger than minus 1 ($r_i^t > -1$).

There is no reason at this point to suppose that own interest rates are positive.

In much of the capital theory literature, some commodity, which we may identify by the index 1 (perhaps a single pure consumption good), is designated as the *numéraire,* having an undiscounted price equal to unity *in every time period.* Such undiscounted or current prices are denoted by P_i^t, with $P_1^t \equiv 1$ being the current price of the *numéraire.* Since $p_1^1 = P_1^t = 1$ for all t, we have

$$\beta_1^t = \frac{p_1^t}{p_1^1} = \frac{p_1^t}{1} = p_1^t, \qquad (2.1.4)$$

and the *relative* prices between commodity i and commodity 1 in every time period satisfy

$$\frac{p_i^t}{p_1^t} = \frac{P_i^t}{P_1^t} = \frac{P_i^t}{1} = P_i^t. \qquad (2.1.5)$$

To better understand (2.1.5), note that the relative price

$\dfrac{p_i^t}{p_1^t} =$ amount of the *numéraire* good that must be given up at the beginning of period t in exchange for 1 unit of commodity i at the same time

$\quad =$ current price at time t of commodity i in terms of commodity 1

$\quad = P_i^t/P_1^t = P_i^t \qquad$ since $P_1^t \equiv 1$ for all t

Then, using (2.1.4) and (2.1.5), we have

$$p_i^t = \beta_1^t P_i^t; \qquad (2.1.6)$$

and, finally, when r_1^t is independent of t,

$$p_i^t = \beta_1^t P_i^t = \frac{P_i^t}{(1 + r_1)^{t-1}}. \qquad (2.1.7)$$

2.2. Dynamic efficiency

It is well known that perfect competition leads to economic efficiency in static models; given fixed total quantities of productive inputs, under competitive conditions more of one commodity cannot be produced without producing less of some other commodity, a situation we refer to as *static efficiency*. What kinds of economic efficiency should we look for in a dynamic economy where the outputs of this period can be used to change the available total quantities of productive inputs next period? Suppose that we consider two alternative paths (both feasible) for the quantities of commodities in our economic system. Since initial quantities are taken as exogenously given, the two paths we consider have identical initial positions at the beginning of period 1. Let us designate these paths as A and B.

Suppose that:

(1) Both paths A and B yield *identical* consumption streams.
(2) Both paths end at some terminal period T with exactly the same stocks of all commodities but one (which we may as well identify as commodity 1).
(3) Path A has a larger terminal stock (at the end of period T) of commodity 1 than does path B.

Under conditions (1) through (3), path B is then said to be *dynamically inefficient*. On the other hand, if *no* feasible path A satisfies (1) through (3), "one cannot do better" than path B, and it is said to be *dynamically efficient*. We will now illustrate the concept of dynamic efficiency more precisely by considering a specific economic model.[5]

We postulate that the technological conditions governing production in the tth period are described by a neoclassical production function[6] (or, as some may prefer, a production possibilities frontier)

$$y_1^{t+1} = F^t(y_2^{t+1}, \ldots, y_n^{t+1}; k_1^t, \ldots, k_n^t, \ell_1^t, \ldots, \ell_m^t) \qquad (2.2.1)$$

where y_i^{t+1} = net output of the ith type commodity at the end of period t (and hence available for use during period $t + 1$), $i = 1, \ldots, n$.

k_i^t = input of the ith commodity at the beginning of period t, $i = 1, \ldots, n$.

ℓ_i^t = input of the ith-type primary (nonproduced) factor at the beginning of period t,
$i = 1, \ldots, m$.

Because y_i^{t+1} is a *net* output (taking into account the input k_i^t), the amount of the ith commodity available as an input during the period $t + 1$ simply equals this net output less any consumption at the beginning of period $t + 1$; that is,

$$y_i^{t+1} = k_i^{t+1} + c_i^{t+1} \tag{2.2.2}$$

where c_i^{t+1} = consumption of the ith-type commodity
at the beginning of period $t + 1$, $i = 1, \ldots, n$.

Thus, if we interpret any of the inputs as capital goods, this formulation accommodates complicated patterns of depreciation, including cases in which depreciation rates for various capital goods vary from period to period. And if there is any pure consumption good (i.e., any good never used as a productive input), say a commodity of type h, we simply define $k_h^t \equiv 0$ for all t; such commodities could be dropped from the list of inputs in (2.2.1).

To illustrate the concept of dynamic efficiency, we employ a consumptionless two-capital good model without primary factors; that is, $n = 2$, $m = 0$, and $c_1^t = c_2^t = 0$. It suffices to consider only two production periods, $t = 1, 2$. We also assume that no corner solutions exist so that we can safely ignore inequalities.

At the beginning of period 1 the initial capital stocks of types 1 and 2 are given:

$$k_1^1 = \bar{k}_1^1, \qquad k_2^1 = \bar{k}_2^1. \tag{2.2.3}$$

With these initial conditions, the inputs available for use in the next period, $t = 2$, must satisfy the production conditions imposed by the technology in period 1; that is, k_1^2 and k_2^2 must satisfy the first-period production function

$$y_1^2 = k_1^2 = F^1(k_2^2; \bar{k}_1^1, \bar{k}_2^1). \tag{2.2.4}$$

Similarly, whatever the values of k_1^2 and k_2^2 satisfying (2.2.4), the terminal capital stocks left at the end of period 2 (the beginning of period 3) must satisfy the second-period production function

$$y_1^3 = k_1^3 = F^2(k_2^3; k_1^2, k_2^2). \tag{2.2.5}$$

Suppose that we set an arbitrary feasible target for the terminal capital stock of type 2, say

$$k_2^3 = \bar{k}_2^3. \tag{2.2.6}$$

Equation (2.2.6) can be satisfied for many dynamic sequences

$$\{(\bar{k}_1^1, \bar{k}_2^1), (k_1^2, k_2^2), (k_1^3, \bar{k}_2^3)\} \tag{2.2.7}$$

which are possible because they are consistent with the technological restrictions imposed by (2.2.4) and (2.2.5). However, only a sequence that provides the maximum feasible quantity of the terminal capital stock of type 1, k_1^3, is *dynamically efficient*, because any other value of k_1^3 would mean that a different time allocation of resources could have resulted in *more* of the terminal stock of type 1 while yielding the same terminal stock of type 2 $(k_2^3 = \bar{k}_2^3)$.

The requirement that the sequence (2.2.7) be dynamically efficient in this sense implies that certain conditions necessarily must hold along the accumulation path, and we now turn to deriving these *dynamic efficiency conditions*.

The formal problem is to maximize (2.2.5) or $k_1^3 = F^2(k_2^3; k_1^2, k_2^2)$ subject to (2.2.4) and (2.2.6). The constraint (2.2.6) can be eliminated by substitution into (2.2.5), and as noted above, we shall presume interior solutions so that no constraints are binding. A more general result involving inequalities can be derived using Kuhn–Tucker methods, but it does not yield significant economic insights and is best left as an exercise for mathematically inclined readers. We also observe that the production function (2.2.1) as we have written it already embodies the ordinary static efficiency property; that is, with every quantity in parentheses on the right-hand side of (2.2.1) fixed, the quantity

y_1^{t+1} given by the function F^t is the *maximum* amount that can be produced.

To solve our intertemporal maximization problem, we form the Lagrangian expression

$$L(k_1^2, k_2^2, \lambda_1) = F^2(\bar{k}_2^3; k_1^2, k_2^2) + \lambda_1[F^1(k_2^2; \bar{k}_1^1, \bar{k}_2^1) - k_1^2].$$
$$(2.2.8)$$

The necessary conditions for a constrained maximum are

$$\frac{\partial L}{\partial k_1^2} = \frac{\partial F^2}{\partial k_1^2} - \lambda_1 = 0 \qquad (2.2.9a)$$

$$\frac{\partial L}{\partial k_2^2} = \frac{\partial F^2}{\partial k_2^2} + \lambda_1 \frac{\partial F^1}{\partial k_2^2} = 0 \qquad (2.2.9b)$$

$$\frac{\partial L}{\partial \lambda_1} = F^1(k_2^2; \bar{k}_1^1, \bar{k}_2^1) - k_1^2 = 0, \qquad (2.2.9c)$$

implying that

$$\lambda_1 = \frac{\partial F^2}{\partial k_1^2} = -\frac{\partial F^2/\partial k_2^2}{\partial F^1/\partial k_2^2}. \qquad (2.2.10)$$

Our desired dynamic efficiency condition is (2.2.10); of course, with more types of capital goods and more time periods, there will be many analogous conditions.

Condition (2.2.10) has a simple interpretation. The partial derivative $\partial F^2/\partial k_1^2$ tells us how much more of k_1^3 we could obtain with more k_1^2 and therefore is a gross own rate of return for capital of type 1. On the other hand, the reciprocal of $(-\partial F^1/\partial k_2^2)$ measures how much more k_2^2 would have been available if *less* k_1^2 had been produced, while $\partial F^2/\partial k_2^2$ tells us the extra k_1^3 that could be produced with this extra k_2^2. Thus the ratio

$$-\frac{\partial F^2/\partial k_2^2}{\partial F^1/\partial k_2^2}$$

gives the additional k_1^3 producible from extra k_2^2 freed by reducing k_1^2. To maximize k_1^3, at the margin the two alternative means of producing extra k_1^3 must be equalized, which is the meaning of equation (2.2.10).

2.3. **Dynamic efficiency and the "dynamic invisible hand"**

Every individual endeavors to employ his capital so that its produce may be of greatest value. He generally neither intends to promote the public interest, nor knows how much he is promoting it. He intends only his own security, his own gain. And he is in this led by an *invisible hand* to promote an end which was no part of his intention. By pursuing his own interest he frequently promotes that of society more effectively than when he really intends to promote it. Adam Smith, *The Wealth of Nations*[7]

Adam Smith's concept of an invisible hand is a cornerstone of economics. In its modern form the proposition asserts that a free private-enterprise economy, operating under conditions of perfect competition, results in a static equilibrium that is optimal in a certain sense. More precisely, an equilibrium position of a perfectly competitive laissez-faire economy has the property that no one individual can be made better off, as judged by that individual's own tastes and preferences, without making at least one other individual worse off. Such an equilibrium is termed *Pareto optimal*.

This is a remarkable proposition. It implies that under free competition, resources will be allocated to their most profitable uses and that in equilibrium the rates of return to all resources will be equalized. Stigler (1976, p. 1201) writes that the latter idea "was the crown jewel of *The Wealth of Nations,* and it became, and remains to this day, the foundation of the theory of the allocation of resources. . . . [It] is still the most important substantive proposition in all of economics."

A perfectly competitive economy, through the workings of the ordinary invisible hand, achieves a Pareto optimal equilibrium which is *static*. That is, in equilibrium all prices and quantities are unchanging over time, so that tomorrow is an exact replication of today and yesterday. But clearly, we do not live in such a static world; prices and quantities do change from one period to the next. What remains of Adam Smith's proposition in such a dynamic economy? The answer to this question provides a remarkable "dynamic invisible hand" principle – that perfect competition and profit maximization in each time period considered separately imply conditions that are *equivalent* to the dynamic efficiency conditions derived in the last section on the basis of purely technological considerations.[8] We now turn to a proof of this principle for our simple model.

The profit for the tth period, denoted by π^t, is equal to the value of net output at the end of period t (taking into account the value of inputs at the beginning of period t). Let us suppose first that all inputs are paid for at the end of the production period, and we will introduce the subscript $i = 0$ to denote the unit of account ("money") in terms of which all current output and factor prices are expressed.[9] Thus from equation (2.1.3) we see that

$$\frac{P_i^{t+1}}{P_i^t} = \frac{p_i^{t+1}/p_0^{t+1}}{p_i^t/p_0^t} = \frac{p_0^t/p_0^{t+1}}{p_i^t/p_i^{t+1}} = \frac{1 + r_0^t}{1 + r_i^t} \tag{2.3.1}$$

where r_0^t is the "money" rate of interest during period t and r_i^t is the ith own rate of interest for period t.

If the capital stocks (machines) k_1^t and k_2^t are rented at the beginning of period t, they must be returned at the end; hence the value of net output with $c_1^{t+1} = c_2^{t+1} = 0$ is

$$P_1^{t+1}(k_1^{t+1} - k_1^t) + P_2^{t+1}(k_2^{t+1} - k_2^t). \tag{2.3.2}$$

The current factor price or rental rate (again in terms of "money") for use of the ith capital stock during period t, but paid at the end of period t, is denoted by W_i^t, and the cost of production incurred at the end of period t is

$$W_1^t k_1^t + W_2^t k_2^t. \tag{2.3.3}$$

From (2.3.2), (2.3.3), and the tth period production function

$$k_1^{t+1} = F^t(k_2^{t+1}; k_1^t, k_2^t),$$

we find that current profit in period t is

$$\pi^t = P_1^{t+1}[F^t(k_2^{t+1}; k_1^t, k_2^t) - k_1^t]$$
$$+ P_2^{t+1}(k_2^{t+1} - k_2^t) - (W_1^t k_1^t + W_2^t k_2^t). \qquad (2.3.4)$$

Maximization of π^t implies the necessary conditions

$$\frac{\partial \pi^t}{\partial k_2^{t+1}} = P_1^{t+1} \frac{\partial F^t}{\partial k_2^{t+1}} + P_2^{t+1} = 0 \qquad (2.3.5a)$$

$$\frac{\partial \pi^t}{\partial k_1^t} = P_1^{t+1} \left(\frac{\partial F^t}{\partial k_1^t} - 1 \right) - W_1^t = 0 \qquad (2.3.5b)$$

$$\frac{\partial \pi^t}{\partial k_2^t} = P_1^{t+1} \frac{\partial F^t}{\partial k_2^t} - P_2^{t+1} - W_2^t = 0 \qquad (2.3.5c)$$

or, equivalently,

$$\frac{P_2^{t+1}}{P_1^{t+1}} = - \frac{\partial F^t}{\partial k_2^{t+1}} \qquad (2.3.6a)$$

$$\frac{W_1^t}{P_1^{t+1}} + 1 = \frac{\partial F^t}{\partial k_1^t} \qquad (2.3.6b)$$

$$\frac{W_2^t}{P_1^{t+1}} + \frac{P_2^{t+1}}{P_1^{t+1}} = \frac{\partial F^t}{\partial k_2^t}. \qquad (2.3.6c)$$

Now consider an investor facing perfectly competitive asset markets without uncertainty. One dollar can purchase

$$\frac{1}{P_i^t}$$

units of the ith asset at the beginning of period t. At the end of period t the investor receives a rental return of W_i^t dollars per unit, or a total return of

$$\frac{W_i^t}{P_i^t}.$$

But now, at the end of period t (which, remember, coincides with the beginning of period $t + 1$), the investor can also sell units of the ith asset at the price of P_i^{t+1} per unit, and the total capital gain (or loss) is

$$\frac{P_i^{t+1}}{P_i^t} - 1.$$

Thus an investor with \$1 worth of the ith asset receives a total net return equal to the sum of the last two expressions, namely a rental return plus the capital gain:

$$\frac{W_i^t}{P_i^t} + \frac{P_i^{t+1}}{P_i^t} - 1.$$

Alternatively, \$1 invested in a "bank" yields a net return of r_0^t dollars, where r_0^t is the "money" rate of interest over period t. Because there is no uncertainty, in equilibrium investors must be *indifferent* among the various assets and the "bank" as alternative means of holding wealth.[10] This fact leads us to the *portfolio equilibrium condition* consistent with perfectly competitive asset markets:

$$\frac{W_1^t}{P_1^t} + \frac{P_1^{t+1}}{P_1^t} - 1 = \frac{W_2^t}{P_2^t} + \frac{P_2^{t+1}}{P_2^t} - 1 = \cdots$$
$$= \frac{W_n^t}{P_n^t} + \frac{P_n^{t+1}}{P_n^t} - 1 = r_0^t. \tag{2.3.7}$$

Arbitrage ensures that this equal yield condition will be satisfied for every time period t.

For our simple model with two assets, namely capital goods of types 1 and 2, the portfolio equilibrium condition (2.3.7) is

$$\frac{W_1^t}{P_1^t} + \frac{P_1^{t+1}}{P_1^t} = \frac{W_2^t}{P_2^t} + \frac{P_2^{t+1}}{P_2^t}. \tag{2.3.8}$$

Equations (2.3.6a)–(2.3.6c) and (2.3.8) must hold for all t if there are to be profit maximization and portfolio equilibrium in every time period under the assumption of perfect competition.

In particular, let $t = 1$ in (2.3.6a) and $t = 2$ in (2.3.6b) and (2.3.6c); then the dynamic efficiency condition (2.2.10) can be written as

$$\frac{\partial F^2}{\partial k_1^2} = -\frac{\partial F^2/\partial k_2^2}{\partial F^1/\partial k_2^2}$$

or

$$\frac{W_1^2}{P_1^3} + 1 = -\frac{W_2^2/P_1^3 + P_2^3/P_1^3}{-P_2^2/P_1^2}.$$ (2.3.9)

Simplifying the latter expression yields

$$W_1^2 + P_1^3 = P_1^2 \left(\frac{W_2^2}{P_2^2} + \frac{P_2^3}{P_2^2}\right)$$

or

$$\frac{W_1^2}{P_1^2} + \frac{P_1^3}{P_1^2} = \frac{W_2^2}{P_2^2} + \frac{P_2^3}{P_2^2}.$$ (2.3.10)

But the latter is simply the portfolio equilibrium condition (2.3.8) for $t = 2$.

> *Conclusion:* Under perfect competition in the production and asset markets, myopic maximization of current profits π^1 and π^2 in both periods 1 and 2 implies that the necessary dynamic efficiency condition (2.2.1) is satisfied by means of a "dynamic invisible hand"!

It was already noted that $\partial F^2/\partial k_1^2$ is a gross own rate of interest for commodity 1 and hence, by (2.2.10), the Lagrangian multiplier associated with the technological maximization problem of Section 2.2 is

$$\lambda_1 = 1 + r_1^2.$$ (2.3.11)

We may see how this result relates to prices by using (2.2.10) and (2.3.6b) to write

$$\lambda_1 = \frac{\partial F^2}{\partial k_1^2} = \frac{W_1^2}{P_1^3} + 1 = \frac{P_1^2}{P_1^3}\left(\frac{W_1^2}{P_1^2} + \frac{P_1^3}{P_1^2}\right).$$ (2.3.12)

Now, from (2.3.7) and (2.3.10) we see that the yield on an investment in a capital good of type 1 or 2 over the time period 2 must equal the corresponding yield over period 2 on the *numéraire* unit of account; that is, the common (net) yields are equal to the "money" rate of interest:

$$\frac{W_1^2}{P_1^2} + \frac{P_1^3}{P_1^2} - 1 = \frac{W_2^2}{P_2^2} + \frac{P_2^3}{P_2^2} - 1 = r_0^2$$

or

$$\frac{W_1^2}{P_1^2} + \frac{P_1^3}{P_1^2} = \frac{W_2^2}{P_2^2} + \frac{P_2^3}{P_2^2} = 1 + r_0^2. \tag{2.3.13}$$

Thus (2.3.12) and (2.3.13) imply that

$$\lambda_1 = \frac{P_1^2}{P_1^3} (1 + r_0^2), \tag{2.3.14}$$

while (2.3.1) with $t = 2$ and $i = 1$ tells us that the capital gain measured in *current* prices is

$$\frac{P_1^3}{P_1^2} - 1 = \frac{1 + r_0^2}{1 + r_1^2} - 1. \tag{2.3.15}$$

Equations (2.3.14) and (2.3.15) imply (2.3.11) and confirm that the Lagrangian multiplier λ_1 equals the gross own rate of return for commodity 1 over the second time period. Since λ_1 is associated with the constraint for capital of type 1 available at the beginning of period 2, a relaxation of this constraint by adding a small amount $\epsilon > 0$ to the input k_1^2 increases the terminal k_1^3 which is to be maximized by $\epsilon(1 + r_1^2)$.

An alternative form of economic organization is one in which firms own, rather than rent, the capital goods used as productive inputs, eliminating the portfolio equilibrium condition (2.3.7) because there are no pure investors whose economic role is simply to hold capital stocks as assets in this model.[11] The profits in period t discounted to the beginning of period 1 are denoted by $\hat{\pi}^t$. Clearly, discounted profits are simply equal to the discounted values of outputs minus the discounted values of inputs, and as the firms now own all the capital stocks, they retain all of the output. This means that

$$\hat{\pi}^t = p_1^{t+1} F^t(k_2^{t+1}; k_1^t, k_2^t) + p_2^{t+1} k_2^{t+1} - (p_1^t k_1^t + p_2^t k_2^t) \tag{2.3.16}$$

where, as in Section 2.1, p_i^t are prices discounted to the beginning of period 1.

Maximization of $\hat{\pi}^t$ necessitates

$$\frac{\partial \hat{\pi}^t}{\partial k_2^{t+1}} = p_1^{t+1} \frac{\partial F^t}{\partial k_2^{t+1}} + p_2^{t+1} = 0 \tag{2.3.17a}$$

$$\frac{\partial \hat{\pi}^t}{\partial k_1^t} = p_1^{t+1} \frac{\partial F^t}{\partial k_1^t} - p_1^t = 0 \tag{2.3.17b}$$

$$\frac{\partial \hat{\pi}^t}{\partial k_2^t} = p_1^{t+1} \frac{\partial F^t}{\partial k_2^t} - p_2^t = 0 \tag{2.3.17c}$$

or, equivalently,

$$\frac{p_2^{t+1}}{p_1^{t+1}} = -\frac{\partial F^t}{\partial k_2^{t+1}} \tag{2.3.18a}$$

$$\frac{p_1^t}{p_1^{t+1}} = \frac{\partial F^t}{\partial k_1^t} \tag{2.3.18b}$$

$$\frac{p_2^t}{p_1^{t+1}} = \frac{\partial F^t}{\partial k_2^t}. \tag{2.3.18c}$$

The foregoing conditions for profit maximization must hold in all t. In particular, using (2.3.17a) with $t = 1$ and (2.3.17b) and (2.3.17c) with $t = 2$, the dynamic efficiency condition (2.2.10) is

$$\lambda_1 = \frac{p_1^2}{p_1^3} = -\frac{p_2^2/p_1^3}{-p_2^2/p_1^2}, \tag{2.3.19}$$

implying our "dynamic invisible hand" principle that independent maximization of profits $\hat{\pi}^1$ and $\hat{\pi}^2$ is equivalent to the necessary dynamic efficiency condition (2.2.10). Moreover, (2.3.19) provides an immediate interpretation of the Lagrangian multiplier λ_1, since the definition of the own interest rate for commodity i (Definition 2.2) is

$$r_i^t = \frac{p_i^t}{p_i^{t+1}} - 1,$$

and thus

$$\lambda_1 = 1 + r_1^2$$

as in the previous case.[12]

Several observations can be made:

(1) It should be clear that the "dynamic invisible hand" principle generalizes to many types of capital goods $(i = 1, \ldots, n)$ over a multiperiod time horizon $(t = 1, \ldots, T)$. The portfolio equilibrium condition (2.3.7) is already expressed for the case of n assets, and it is clear how the profit-maximization conditions generalize. Generalization of the dynamic efficiency condition (2.2.10) is a bit more difficult, though straightforward. Moreover, given the concavity of our neoclassical production functions $F^t(\cdot)$, these necessary conditions will also be sufficient for a finite planning horizon.

(2) The issue of dynamic efficiency for an infinite horizon with $T = \infty$ is complex, a problem to which we shall return in Chapter 5. Suffice it to say at this point that we must modify our concept of efficiency, because it makes no sense to prescribe terminal values of the capital stocks $k_j^\infty = \bar{k}_j^\infty$, $j = 2, \ldots, n$, and to maximize the remaining "terminal" capital stock k_1^∞; there is no terminal time period! Similarly, the operation of the "dynamic invisible hand" in an infinite time model becomes treacherous, and the possibility arises of "speculative fevers" or "tulip manias" in which self-fulfilled price expectations, always satisfying our portfolio equilibrium condition, may not correspond to an appropriate definition of dynamic efficiency in infinite time.

(3) The concept of dynamic efficiency, even in a model with a finite time horizon, is a rather weak restriction. One would like to select accumulation paths that are "good" according to some optimality criterion for consumption paths. Nevertheless, provided that every capital good is productive in the production of a desired consumption good, dynamic efficiency with respect to capital accumulation is clearly necessary for any sensible definition of consumption optimality. If the actual capital path of an economy were not efficient, an efficient capital accumulation path could provide more capital stocks, and these in turn could produce ad-

ditional consumption. The obvious case is when every capital good also serves as a consumption good. These vague remarks will be made more precise later.

(4) It should be noted that there are an infinite number of dynamically efficient capital accumulation paths starting from fixed initial conditions. Which path will in fact be followed under laissez-faire perfect competition depends upon knowing either initial prices p_i^1 or, alternatively, terminal prices p_i^{T+1}. This fact lies at the heart of a serious stability problem encountered in Chapter 6, where we examine a descriptive economy with many types of capital goods. And we still must address the issue of uncertainty.

2.4. **A Fisherian one-commodity, two-period model of production and exchange**[13]

The issue of dynamic efficiency discussed in Sections 2.2 and 2.3 arises only because there are two or more different inputs (different types of capital goods or machines) which can be produced in the economy. Since the stocks of inputs are fixed at the beginning of any time period t, the production and consumption decisions determine the pattern of inputs available for use at the beginning of the *next* period, time $t + 1$. The consumption decisions for every time period are taken as exogenous to define dynamic efficiency, and clearly no such issue would arise if there were only one commodity; then static efficiency entails producing as much as possible of that one commodity in every time period, and whatever is left over after consumption becomes the available input for the next period.

Now, however, we wish to study how consumption decisions are made in the context of our "pure role of time" model, and to do this it is convenient to assume that there is only one type of commodity which serves as both a consumption good and a production input. Accordingly, in this section we shall drop the subscripts that denote different commodities.

A "representative consumer" is taken to have a well-behaved intertemporal utility function

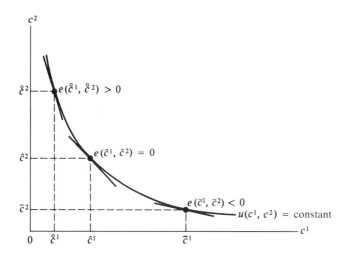

Figure 2.1. Positive, zero, and negative marginal time preferences along an indifference curve.

$$u(c^1, c^2) \qquad\qquad\qquad (2.4.1)$$

where c^t denotes the consumption of the (single) commodity at the beginning of period t.[14] Define

$$e(c^1, c^2) \equiv -\left.\frac{dc^2}{dc^1}\right|_{u=\text{constant}} - 1. \qquad\qquad (2.4.2)$$

If $e(c^1, c^2) > 0$, the representative consumer values a unit of current consumption, c^1, more than a unit of future consumption, c^2, and is said to exhibit *positive marginal time preference* at the point (c^1, c^2). Similarly, $e(c^1, c^2) < 0$ and $e(c^1, c^2) = 0$ are associated with *negative* and *zero marginal time preference* at the point (c^1, c^2).

Frequently, the intuitive notion of impatience – the notion that consumers systematically prefer current to future consumption – is used to justify positive marginal time preference, but such an association between positive marginal time preference, as we have defined it, and "impatience" is wrong. This fact is evident from Figure 2.1, for whereas impatience pre-

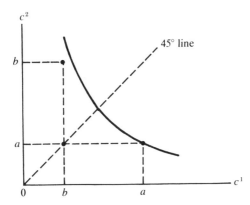

Figure 2.2. Positive absolute time preference is illustrated with $u(a, b) > u(b, a)$ for a particular choice of a and b with $a > b$. A person's tastes exhibit positive absolute time preference if $u(a, b) > u(b, a)$ for *all* $a > b$.

sumably should be a property of the utility function, the same indifference curve may have points exhibiting positive, zero, and negative marginal time preference. What in fact we shall subsequently prove is that if the own interest rate (for the single commodity between the beginning of period 1 and the beginning of period 2) is positive, then $e(\bar{c}^1, \bar{c}^2) > 0$ in the neighborhood of an equilibrium point $(\bar{c}^1, \bar{c}^2)$. But this result is not inconsistent with $e(\bar{c}^1, \bar{c}^2) \leq 0$ at nonequilibrium points.

An alternative concept is called *absolute time preference*. Consider any two points

$$(c^1, c^2) = (a, b) \quad \text{and} \quad (c^1, c^2) = (b, a) \qquad \text{with } a > b > 0.$$

If for *all* such a, b we have $u(a, b) > u(b, a)$, a person's tastes are said to exhibit *positive absolute time preference* (see Figure 2.2); $u(a, b) = u(b, a)$ is *time indifference* and $u(a, b) < u(b, a)$ is *negative absolute time preference*. One could assume that positive absolute time preference is a property of tastes – a property of the representative consumer's utility function – but this assumption requires justification in terms of empirical evidence or a theoretical argument based upon other axioms of rational intertemporal behavior.

The problem of the representative consumer is to maximize the intertemporal utility function $u(c^1, c^2)$ subject to the consumer's given endowments of the commodity at the beginning of each period, x^1 and x^2, respectively, and subject to a production function

$$y^2 = f(k^1) \tag{2.4.3}$$

> where k^1 = input of the single commodity at the beginning of period 1
>
> y^2 = net output of the commodity at the beginning of period 2 (or end of period 1).

Since there are now exogenous endowments at the beginning of each period, the amount of commodity used as an input at the beginning of period 1 equals

(1) the endowment at the beginning of period 1, minus
(2) the consumption at the beginning of period 1, minus
(3) the (net) quantity loaned to another individual at the beginning of period 1.

The contract, made at the beginning of period 1, to loan someone else 1 commodity unit at the beginning of period t in exchange for payment of principal plus interest at the beginning of period $t + 1$ we shall call a *bond,* and the quantity of such bonds is denoted by b^t. Thus we have

$$k^1 = x^1 - c^1 - b^1. \tag{2.4.4}$$

The output resulting from this input is given by (2.4.3), and the total amount of the commodity available to the representative consumer at the beginning of period 2 is

$$y^2 + x^2 + (1 + r)b^1 \tag{2.4.5}$$

where r is the own rate of interest (from the beginning of period 1 to the beginning of period 2) on the single commodity. If the model were extended for another period, we would have

$$k^2 = y^2 + x^2 + (1 + r)b^1 - c^2 - b^2, \qquad (2.4.6)$$

but in fact we postulate that the end of period 2 is a terminal time and impose the terminal conditions

$$k^2 = b^2 = 0. \qquad (2.4.7)$$

Accordingly, from (2.4.6) and (2.4.7), consumption at the beginning of period 2 is simply

$$c^2 = y^2 + x^2 + (1 + r)b^1. \qquad (2.4.8)$$

We first consider the production decision of our representative consumer faced with the production function (2.4.3) having the usual regularity properties

$$f(0) = 0, \qquad \text{and } f'(k^1) > 0, \quad f''(k^1) < 0 \quad \text{for } k^1 \geq 0$$

where, as usual, primes denote total differentiation.

The *present discounted value of profits* for production during period 1 is

$$\begin{aligned} \hat{\pi}^1 &= p^2 y^2 - p^1 k^1 \\ &= p^2 f(k^1) - p^1 k^1. \end{aligned} \qquad (2.4.9)$$

See equation (2.3.16) for an analogous result. Maximization of $\hat{\pi}^1$, given competitive prices p^1, p^2 regarded as fixed, necessitates the condition

$$\frac{d\hat{\pi}^1}{dk^1} = p^2 f'(k^1) - p^1 = 0 \qquad (2.4.10)$$

or

$$f'(k^1) = \frac{p^1}{p^2} = 1 + r \qquad \text{(using Definition 2.2).} \quad (2.4.11)$$

Thus the value of k^1 satisfying

$$f'(k^1) = 1 + r \qquad (2.4.12)$$

gives the optimal (profit-maximizing) input, provided that

$$f'(0) > 1 + r. \qquad (2.4.13)$$

We shall assume for simplicity that (2.4.13) holds; if it does not, the best optimal input is $k^1 = 0$ and no production takes place. Accordingly, in profit-maximizing equilibrium, the *net* marginal product of the input ("capital"), $f'(k^1) - 1$, is equal to the own interest rate, r.

From (2.4.4), (2.4.8), and $p^1/p^2 = 1 + r$, we see that

$$c^2 = x^2 + \frac{p^1}{p^2}(x^1 - c^1 - k^1) + y^2$$

or

$$p^2(x^2 - c^2) + p^1(x^1 - c^1) + (p^2y^2 - p^1k^1) = 0 \quad (2.4.14)$$

or

$$p^2(x^2 - c^2) + p^1(x^1 - c^1) + \hat{\pi}^1 = 0. \quad (2.4.15)$$

Equation (2.4.14) or (2.4.15) is a budget constraint that our representative consumer must satisfy. Alternatively, if we identify the discounted value of endowments ($p^1x^1 + p^2x^2$) plus discounted profits ($\hat{\pi}^1$) as "wealth" and denote it by W, then W must equal the discounted value of consumption:

$$W = p^1c^1 + p^2c^2. \quad (2.4.16)$$

Rather than use the profit-maximization condition (2.4.11), we shall treat the consumption and production decisions simultaneously. We thus set up the problem:

$$\underset{c^1,c^2,k^1}{\text{maximize}} \ u(c^1, c^2) \quad \text{subject to equation (2.4.14).}$$

The necessary conditions for this constrained maximization problem are derived by constructing the Lagrangian expression

$$\begin{aligned} L(c^1, c^2, k^1, \lambda) = u(c^1, c^2) &+ \lambda\{p^2(x^2 - c^2) \\ &+ p^1(x^1 - c^1) + [p^2f(k^1) - p^1k^1]\}. \end{aligned}$$
$$(2.4.17)$$

The first-order necessary conditions for a constrained maximum are

$$\frac{\partial L}{\partial c^1} = \frac{\partial u}{\partial c^1} - \lambda p^1 = 0 \tag{2.4.18a}$$

$$\frac{\partial L}{\partial c^2} = \frac{\partial u}{\partial c^2} - \lambda p^2 = 0 \tag{2.4.18b}$$

$$\frac{\partial L}{\partial k^1} = \lambda[p^2 f'(k^1) - p^1] = 0 \tag{2.4.18c}$$

$$\frac{\partial L}{\partial \lambda} = p^2(x^2 - c^2) + p^1(x^1 - c^1) + [p^2 f(k^1) - p^1 k^1] = 0. \tag{2.4.18d}$$

Manipulation of (2.4.18a)–(2.4.18c) gives the condition

$$\frac{\partial u/\partial c^1}{\partial u/\partial c^2} = \frac{p^1}{p^2} = 1 + r = f'(k^1) \tag{2.4.19a}$$

or

$$e(c^1, c^2) = -\frac{dc^2}{dc^1}\bigg|_{u=\text{constant}} - 1 = \frac{\partial u/\partial c^1}{\partial u/\partial c^2} - 1.$$
$$= r = f'(k^1) - 1 \tag{2.4.19b}$$

Thus a utility-maximizing consumer taking $r = (p^1/p^2) - 1$ as given selects a point (c^1, c^2, k^1) where the marginal rate of time preference and the net marginal product of capital are both equal to the own interest rate. Note that discounted profits $\hat{\pi}^1$ are maximized, because (2.4.19) implies (2.4.11) (and because the first-order necessary conditions are sufficient under the regularity conditions that we have imposed on the intertemporal utility and production functions).[15]

So far we have considered only a simple representative consumer, and we now wish to aggregate over *different* consumers to obtain market equations. Consider first the *current market* for commodities actually exchanged at the beginning of period 1, and define

$$C^1 \equiv \sum c^1, \qquad K^1 \equiv \sum k^1, \qquad X^1 \equiv \sum x^1 \tag{2.4.20}$$

where the summation is taken over all individuals. Each individual faces his or her own exogenously given endowments x^1, x^2, and every individual satisfies condition (2.4.19) for his or her utility function, treating the relative price $p^1/p^2 = 1 + r$ as given. Thus the equilibrium quantities selected by individuals are functions of the own interest rate, r, and we will denote this fact by writing the aggregate quantities as

$$C^1 = C^1(r), \qquad K^1 = K^1(r), \qquad \text{etc.} \tag{2.4.21}$$

Competitive equilibrium in the current market requires that

$$C^1(r) + K^1(r) = X^1. \tag{2.4.22}$$

Similarly, competitive equilibrium in the *future market* – the market for commodities actually delivered at the beginning of period 2 – necessitates that

$$C^2(r) = Y^2(r) + X^2 \tag{2.4.23}$$

where

$$C^2(r) \equiv \sum c^2, \qquad Y^2(r) \equiv \sum y^2 \equiv \sum f(k^1). \tag{2.4.24}$$

Finally, under the assumption that default is possible, we have the following condition for the clearing of the *bond market:*

$$B(r) = X^1 - C^1(r) - K^1(r) = 0 \tag{2.4.25}$$

where

$$B(r) \equiv \sum b^1. \tag{2.4.26}$$

The three equations (2.4.22), (2.4.23), and (2.4.25) involve only one unknown, r. However, equilibrium in the current market obviously implies equilibrium in the bond market [i.e., (2.4.22) implies (2.4.25)]. Moreover, if we aggregate (2.4.8) over individuals, we obtain

$$C^2(r) = Y^2(r) + X^2 + (1 + r)B^1(r), \tag{2.4.27}$$

so that (2.4.25) and (2.4.27) imply (2.4.22). Accordingly, we have an example of Walras's law: *only one* of the three market clearing equations is independent. In principle, this one independent

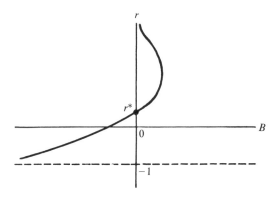

Figure 2.3. Excess demand function $B(r)$.

equation suffices to determine the one unknown own interest rate.

Of course, nothing we have said assures us that a meaningful equilibrium value of r exists. [Remember that we must have $r > -1$. Also note that *if* the equilibrium value of r is positive, (2.4.19) implies that every consumer exhibits positive marginal time preferences in equilibrium.] Moreover, even if an equilibrium exists, further restrictions may be needed for uniqueness. These technical problems involve issues in general equilibrium theory and are beyond the scope of this book. However, it is clear that, in general, existence and uniqueness properties will depend upon both (1) the properties of the individual utility and production functions, and (2) the *distribution* of x^1, x^2 endowments among individuals.

Finally, let us briefly consider the dynamics of the bond market. As noted, only one of the three markets is independent, and consequently we need only study the dynamics for one of them. The relationship between aggregate excess demand for bonds, $B(r)$, and the own interest rate, r, is depicted in Figure 2.3 with a unique equilibrium at $r = r^*$. Assuming a Walrasian price adjustment process (which takes place at the beginning of period 1) of the conventional form – one for which r falls in response to excess supply of goods or, equivalently, falls in response to excess demand for bonds – stability of the bond market requires that the slope of the excess demand function $B(r)$ be positive in a (deleted) neighborhood of equilibrium where $B(r^*) = 0$; that is,

$$\frac{dB(r^*)}{dr} > 0 \quad \text{for all } r \text{ in a (deleted) neighborhood of } r^*,$$

as illustrated in Figure 2.3.   (2.4.28)

If (2.4.28) holds, the conventional price adjustment process (at the beginning of period 1) is locally stable, so that if an "auctioneer" calls off an initial r sufficiently close to r^*, the assumed disequilibrium adjustment mechanism for r is dynamically stable. Indeed, it can be proved that the stability condition (2.4.28) does hold provided different individuals have wealth effects that are "sufficiently close." In general, though, such dynamic stability need *not* prevail, even in this most simplified model of an intertemporal economy. As we shall see in subsequent chapters, various types of dyamic stability questions recur throughout capital theory.

2.5. Concluding remarks

In this chapter we explored the pure role of time in the context of extremely simplified models and introduced concepts such as the own discount factor and the own interest rate, which will be used throughout the book. We saw that the criterion of static efficiency in timeless models generalizes to that of *dynamic efficiency* in intertemporal models. Moreover, we saw that a "dynamic invisible hand" assures that every competitive equilibrium path is also dynamically efficient. In Section 2.4, a Fisherian one-commodity, two-period model of production and exchange is examined, and it is shown that firms maximizing their discounted profits and representative consumers maximizing their intertemporal utility functions will result in one independent market clearing equation that suffices to determine the one unknown variable – the interest rate, r, between periods 1 and 2. In Chapter 6 we see how this simple model of production and exchange generalizes to allow for many types of commodities and many time periods. The type of intertemporal equilibrium illustrated by this example in Section 2.4 also generalizes to the important concept of a *perfect-foresight competitive equilibrium*.

Indeed, for the most part our subsequent investigations represent generalizations of the basic ideas introduced in this chapter. For example, we must allow for the fact that there exist produced factors of production, called *capital goods*, which may be accumulated over time. The role of these capital goods is essential in understanding intertemporal economics, and in Chapter 3 we begin by studying models having one type of capital good.

Exercises

2.1 Define the own rate of interest on commodity i from the beginning of period t to the beginning of period $t + \tau$ as

$$r_i^{t,t+\tau} \equiv \frac{p_i^t}{p_i^{t+\tau}} - 1.$$

Prove that the relationship between long and short (i.e., one-period) interest rates is given by

$$1 + r_i^{t,t+\tau} = (1 + r_i^t)(1 + r_i^{t+1}) \cdots (1 + r_i^{t+\tau-1}).$$

2.2 Consider a T-period program with the technology

$$k_1^{t+1} = F^t(k_2^{t+1}, \ldots, k_n^{t+1}; k_1^t, \ldots, k_n^t).$$

Given initial capital stocks $k_1^1 = \bar{k}_1^1, \ldots, k_n^1 = \bar{k}_n^1$ and feasible terminal stocks (at the end of period T) $\bar{k}_2^{T+1}, \ldots, \bar{k}_n^{T+1}$, maximize the remaining terminal stock k_1^{T+1}. Show that the Lagrangian for this problem may be written as

$$L = F^T(\bar{k}_2^{T+1}, \ldots, \bar{k}_n^{T+1}; k_1^T, \ldots, k_n^T)$$
$$+ \sum_{t=1}^{T-1} \lambda_t[F^t(k_2^{t+1}, \ldots, k_n^{t+1}; k_1^t, \ldots, k_n^t) - k_1^{t+1}],$$

and derive the necessary conditions

$$\lambda_{t+1} \frac{\partial F^{t+1}}{\partial k_1^{t+1}} - \lambda_t = 0$$

$$\lambda_{t+1} \frac{\partial F^{t+1}}{\partial k_j^{t+1}} + \lambda_t \frac{\partial F^t}{\partial k_j^{t+1}} = 0$$

for $j = 2, \ldots, n$, $t = 1, \ldots, T - 1$, and with $\lambda_T \equiv 1$. Show that the latter imply that

$$\frac{\lambda_t}{\lambda_{t+1}} = \frac{\partial F^{t+1}}{\partial k_1^{t+1}} = -\frac{\partial F^{t+1}/\partial k_j^{t+1}}{\partial F^t/\partial k_j^{t+1}},$$

and prove that $\lambda_t/\lambda_{t+1} = 1 + r_1^{t+1}$.

2.3 Prove that positive absolute time preference implies positive marginal time preference for all points such that $(c^1, c^2) = (a, a) > (0, 0)$.

2.4 Prove that the equilibrium value of the Lagrangian multiplier in equation (2.4.17) is equal to the marginal utility of discounted endowments plus discounted profits; that is,

$$\lambda = \frac{du}{dW}.$$

2.5 Assume that $u(c^1, c^2)$ is homothetic. Prove that if $c^1 = c^2 = c$, the marginal rate of time preference is a constant for all values of $c > 0$.

3

Introduction to dynamic economics

3.1. Introduction to one-sector, two-sector, and monetary growth models

One- and two-sector growth models have only one type of capital good, a feature that we shall discover is essential for many of the results we derive. In most of these models short-run Keynesian problems are ignored, and we follow this tradition here. The focus of attention is on the time path of an evolving economy always in momentary (static) full-employment equilibrium, a situation that has become known as *equilibrium dynamics*. Decisions made this period (or at this instant in a continuous-time formulation) determine the flow of investment and hence the stock of the single type of capital good available for use in the next period (or the next instant in continuous time). At every point in time the stocks of the two productive inputs – homogeneous labor and homogeneous capital – are taken as given to determine a static competitive equilibrium.

The central question of dynamic stability concerns the circumstances under which the capital–labor ratio will converge over time toward some constant steady-state value. Closely related issues are (1) the existence and (2) the uniqueness of such a steady-state equilibrium value for the capital–labor ratio.

The rate of growth of the labor force is usually taken as an exogenously determined nonnegative constant, $g \geq 0$. If the rate of

growth of the labor force is positive ($g > 0$), the rate of growth of
the capital stock must also be positive in a steady-state equilibrium if the capital–labor ratio is to be constant. Moreover, since
gross investment must provide for both depreciation of the existing capital stock and the equipping of new workers with new
capital, it, too, must be growing over time.

Until we reach Section 3.7, where money is introduced, there is
only one way in which wealth can be held, because there is only
one asset: the one type of capital good (homogeneous "machines"). Thus the gross-saving decision (together with the depreciation rate on capital and the rate of growth of labor) completely determines the change in the capital–labor ratio every
time period (or every instant in continuous time). Often, some
simple gross-saving rule is specified (e.g., a constant fraction of
gross national product is saved), thereby identifying the time path
along which the model economy will evolve from any initial stock
of capital and any initial size of the labor supply.

We make the common simplifying assumption that capital need
not be identified by current or past usage and that it can be trans-
ferred instantaneously and costlessly from one production
process to any other. Under such conditions we say that capital is
malleable. Note that when the malleable capital assumption is not
satisfied [i.e., when capital once installed for a particular use
must be distinguished from capital put to other uses (as, e.g., in
the so-called "putty-clay" models)], it is no longer true that there
exists only a single *type* of homogeneous capital. We do not have
space to deal with such complications here.

The remaining sections of Chapter 3 each contain an analysis of
the most typical problems arising in one-capital-good models. In
Section 3.2 we examine the standard one-sector model in which a
single commodity serves as both the capital good and the consumption good. The specification is altered in Section 3.3 to allow
for technological change, and other generalizations are examined
in Section 3.4. In Section 3.5 we turn to the concept of *consumption efficiency* and provide a characterization of dynamic paths
that meet this criterion. In Section 3.6 we study a two-sector

model with two commodities, a pure consumption good (i.e., a commodity that is only consumed) and a pure capital good (i.e., one that is used only as a factor of production and is never consumed), each of which is produced in a separate industry or sector of the economy. Finally, in Section 3.7 we introduce a model having both a single commodity, which is both consumed and used as a capital good, and a new asset called "money," which serves as an alternative means of holding wealth over time.

3.2. The one-sector model

As with the Fisherian model of production and exchange that we studied in Section 2.4, our first step is to consider an economy with a single type of commodity. There are at least two justifications for this endeavor.

(1) It is obvious that the dynamic behavior of a one-commodity economy will be easier to analyze than one with many types of commodities, because there will exist no relative price changes to affect the composition of "aggregate output" and "aggregate demand." In other words, by postulating a one-commodity economy, we can avoid all the complex aggregation problems which, as we shall discover, constitute one of the most fundamental issues in capital theory.

(2) In much of the macroeconomic literature, one finds the assumption of an "aggregate production function," which, for fixed capital stocks, gives the maximum "output" at each level of employment. However, since output consists of both "consumption" and "investment," except in freak cases (when net investment in *every* type of capital good is exactly zero), the capital stock is always changing over time. Accordingly, the "short run," defined as the length of time for which capital stocks are fixed, generally is of one-period duration at most in a discrete-time model, and such a short run lasts only an instant in continuous-time models. It is not only reasonable, then, but absolutely crucial, to ask how changing capital stocks may affect our analyses of traditional macroeconomic problems such as unemployment and inflation in "longer runs." This being the ultimate

objective of our research strategy, we first ignore both unemployment and aggregation problems so as to isolate those properties of a dynamic economy which rest solely on the fact that saving and investment today alters the future production-possibility options. (This feature arises simply because saving and investment today determines how much the capital available for production tomorrow will differ from today's.) It should be stressed, though, that by focusing upon such a narrow question, we can at least hope to gain some generally valid economic insights. In particular, by examining the simplest case first, we will be able to see how modification of the model to encompass more realistic features (such as the introduction of many commodities) alters dynamic behavior in some respects while leaving other conclusions intact (such as the possibility of capital overaccumulation). It must be remembered that the simple one-commodity model discussed below is appropriate only for the simple question at hand. One should always be cognizant of the observation expressed by Mark Kac:

> Models are, for the most part, caricatures of reality, but if they are good, then, like good caricatures, they portray, though perhaps in distorted manner, some of the features of the real world.
>
> The main role of models is not so much to explain and to predict – though ultimately these are the main functions of science – as to polarize thinking and to pose sharp questions. Above all, they are fun to invent and to play with, and they have a peculiar life of their own. The "survival of the fittest" applies to models even more than it does to living creatures. They should not, however, be allowed to multiply indiscriminately without real necessity or real purpose.
>
> Unless, of course, we all follow the dictum, attributed to Oswald Avery, that "you can blow all the bubbles you want provided *you* are the one who pricks them." (1969, p. 699)

We will formulate our one-commodity economy in continuous time, although exactly parallel results can be obtained in discrete time. To avoid notational complexity the time parameter, t, is indicated only when it is essential for clarity, and it should be understood that all variables depend upon time. The technology is described completely by a neoclassical production function giving total output:[1]

$$\text{gross national product} = Q = F(K, L). \tag{3.2.1}$$

Because constant returns to scale are assumed, we may define a per capita production function by

$$\text{per capita GNP} = \frac{Q}{L} = \frac{F(K, L)}{L} = F\left(\frac{K}{L}, 1\right)$$
$$= F(k, 1) \equiv f(k) = q \tag{3.2.2}$$

where $k \equiv K/L$ = the capital–labor ratio. As there is only one commodity, gross output equals the sum of consumption and gross investment:

$$\text{GNP} = \text{consumption} + \text{gross investment}$$

or

$$Q = C + I. \tag{3.2.3}$$

Net investment, which here is equal by definition to the change in the capital stock, equals gross investment minus depreciation, and we assume that capital depreciates at the exponential rate δ.[2] Thus, as noted in Chapter 1, no portfolio problem exists in this one-asset model, and accordingly, net investment = gross investment – depreciation, which is equivalent to[3]

$$\dot{K} = I - \delta K. \tag{3.2.4}$$

Combining (3.2.1), (3.2.3), and (3.2.4), we have

$$\dot{K} = F(K, L) - C - \delta K. \tag{3.2.5}$$

Labor is assumed to grow at the exogenous rate $g \geq 0$, and thus from the definition of k, we obtain

$$\frac{\dot{k}}{k} = \frac{\dot{K}}{K} - \frac{\dot{L}}{L} = \frac{\dot{K}}{K} - g$$

or

$$\dot{k} = \frac{\dot{K}}{L} - gk. \tag{3.2.6}$$

If we divide (3.2.5) by L and use (3.2.2) and (3.2.6), we obtain the fundamental equation for the dynamic behavior of the capital–labor ratio:

$$\dot{k} = f(k) - c - (g + \delta)k \tag{3.2.7}$$

where the lowercase letter c denotes per capita consumption ($c \equiv C/L$).

It is evident from (3.2.7) that the dynamic behavior of this one-commodity model is characterized by an ordinary differential equation in k provided that we can express per capita consumption as a function of the capital–labor ratio, for then we would be able to write (3.2.7) as

$$\dot{k} = \dot{k}(k) = f(k) - c(k) - (g + \delta)k. \tag{3.2.8}$$

We shall postulate that consumption is a linear function of GNP, that is,

$$C = \beta F(K, L)$$

where $0 < \beta < 1$, or in per capita form,

$$c = \beta f(k) = (1 - s)f(k), \qquad \beta \equiv 1 - s. \tag{3.2.9}$$

Thus from (3.2.8) and (3.2.9) we finally arrive at the desired result:

$$\dot{k} = sf(k) - (g + \delta)k. \tag{3.2.10}$$

The latter accumulation equation for the capital–labor ratio can be analyzed to answer three basic questions:

(1) Does there *exist* a steady-state capital–labor ratio $k^* > 0$ such that $\dot{k} = 0$ when $k = k^*$?
(2) Is such a k^* *unique?*
(3) Starting at time $t = 0$ from any initial capital–labor ratio $k(0) = k^0 > 0$, is the economy *stable* in the sense that $\lim_{t\to\infty} k(t) = k^*$?

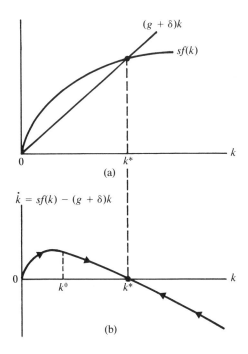

Figure 3.1. Stability of the point k^*. For positive values of k less than k^*, $\dot{k}$ is positive and k must rise, whereas for values of k larger than k^*, k must fall.

The answers to questions (1) through (3) depend upon the properties of $f(k)$, the limiting values of $f'(k)$ as $k \to 0$ and $k \to \infty$, and the magnitude of $(g + \delta)/s$. However, these details are not of essential economic significance, and we will avoid distracting complications by assuming the following regularity conditions for the per capita production function:

$$f(0) = 0; \qquad\qquad f(k) > 0 \quad \text{for } k > 0;$$
$$f'(k) > 0 \quad \text{for } 0 \leqslant k < \infty; \qquad f''(k) < 0 \quad \text{for } 0 \leqslant k < \infty;$$
$$\lim_{k \to 0} f'(k) = \infty; \qquad\qquad \lim_{k \to \infty} f'(k) = 0.$$

For example, these properties are satisfied for Cobb–Douglas production functions $Q = F(K, L) = K^\alpha L^{1-\alpha}$ or $q = f(k) = k^\alpha$, where $0 < \alpha < 1$.

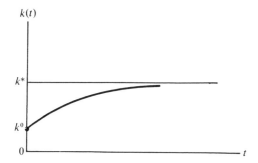

Figure 3.2. Behavior of $k(t)$ starting from the initial condition $k(0) = k^0$.

Given these regularity conditions, the curve $sf(k)$ has the shape depicted in Figure 3.1a. It starts at the origin because $f(0) = 0$, has a steeper slope than $g + \delta$ at $k = 0$ because $\lim_{k \to 0} f'(k) = \infty$, can intersect the line $(g + \delta)k$ at most once because $f''(k) < 0$, and *must* intersect the line $(g + \delta)k$ at least once because $\lim_{k \to \infty} f'(k) = 0$. Obviously, then, a unique steady-state capital–labor ratio $k^* > 0$ exists; it is the value of k at which the curve $sf(k)$ and the line $(g + \delta)k$ intersect in Figure 3.1a.

The dynamic behavior of $k(t)$ is shown in Figure 3.1b. Whenever the curve $sf(k)$ lies above the line $(g + \delta)k$, $\dot{k}$ is positive and hence $k(t)$ is growing. On the other hand, whenever the line $(g + \delta)k$ lies above the curve $sf(k)$, $\dot{k}$ is negative and $k(t)$ is falling. The arrows on the $\dot{k}$ curve in Figure 3.1b indicate this movement of k. Since every arrow points toward k^*, it is evident that $k(t)$ becomes very close to k^* for large enough values of t.

For example, suppose that the model economy starts at time $t = 0$ with a capital–labor ratio equal to k^0, as indicated in Figures 3.1b and 3.2; then $k(t)$ will grow toward k^*, and the system is stable; that is,

$$\lim_{t \to \infty} k(t) = k^*.$$

Clearly, the same stability conclusion is true for any positive value of k^0. Also note that $k = 0$ is another dynamic equilibrium point where $\dot{k} = 0$, but it is of no economic interest since at $k = 0$ we have a consumptionless world without any output.

This stability result is very strong indeed. However, one implication is that per capita consumption approaches a constant; that is,

$$\lim_{t \to \infty} c(t) = c^* = (1 - s)f(k^*). \tag{3.2.11}$$

It is natural to ask whether or not we can modify the model to admit a dynamic equilibrium in which per capita consumption is rising over time, and we now turn to this question.

3.3. Technological change and the "stylized facts" of industrialized economies

Again ignoring all the aggregation problems that we will explore in subsequent chapters, we may question whether or not a simple one-commodity model is capable of explaining widely believed empirical observations about the dynamic behavior of industrialized economies operating at or near full employment. Although no one would argue that the "stylized facts" listed below hold in any exact sense, they do deserve serious consideration as a set of propositions that may be roughly consistent with long-run trends.[4] For this reason alone, we should like to modify our one-sector model so that its long-run behavior does not necessarily contradict the following observations.

(1) The investment–output ratio is constant.
(2) The capital–output ratio is constant.
(3) The capital–labor and output–labor ratios are rising at a constant rate.
(4) The rate of interest is constant.
(5) The real wage rate is rising at a constant rate.
(6) The relative shares of capital and labor are constant.

Clearly, "facts" (3) and (5) are inconsistent with the model described in Section 3.2, for there the capital–labor ratio is equal to a constant k^* in dynamic equilibrium with $\dot{k} = 0$, and the corresponding real wage rate

$$w^* = f(k^*) - k^*f'(k^*)$$

is also constant. Common sense suggests that one crucial factor that we have ignored is technological change, for no one would reasonably expect that technological conditions remain constant over very long time periods.

For the most part, changes in technology do not "just happen," but result from various research and development programs. Completely satisfactory theories of technological change that model research and development activities in the context of uncertain future discoveries simply do not exist. Such theories would have to be very complicated indeed; they necessarily would involve the *expected* present discounted value of future profit streams in a stochastic world. Moreover, the processes by which new technological knowledge is diffused through the economy would have to be modeled.

However important such issues may be, our task is to construct a simple one-commodity model that allows us to tell a story that is at least consistent in some important ways with the extremely complex economic world we observe. For such objectives it is useful to postulate that technological changes – for whatever underlying reasons they occur – can be described by a technology for which the unit isoquant $1 = F(K, L)$ moves inward over time. Such technological changes are called *disembodied,* because output will rise over time even if factor inputs are kept constant.[5]

In general, therefore, we shall assume that the production function (3.1.1) is modified to

$$Q(t) = F[K(t), L(t), t] \qquad (3.3.1)$$

with the property that

$$\left.\frac{\partial F}{\partial t}\right|_{K,L} > 0.$$

That is, $Q(t)$ rises over time even if $K(t)$ and $L(t)$ are held fixed. It can be proved that the stylized facts (1)–(6) hold only if (3.3.1) ultimately approaches the form[6]

$$Q(t) = F[K(t), \alpha(t)L(t)] \qquad \text{where } \alpha(0) = 1, \ \frac{\dot{\alpha}(t)}{\alpha(t)} = \gamma > 0.$$

$$(3.3.2)$$

Such disembodied change is termed *purely labor augmenting* or, equivalently, *Harrod neutral;* it has the property that the relative shares of capital and labor remain constant along paths for which the capital–output ratio remains constant. Since the stylized facts are long run in nature, and since to explain them disembodied technological change must be of the Harrod neutral type described by (3.3.2), we may as well assume that (3.3.2) holds from the outset. Of course, such an assumption means that we must ignore various processes of "induced technological change" by which (3.3.1) converges to (3.3.2), but it does not affect our answers to long-run questions.[7]

One simple trick enables us to replace (3.2.1) by (3.3.2): we shall now define a new variable $\ell(t)$ termed *labor efficiency units* by

$$\ell(t) \equiv \alpha(t)L(t). \tag{3.3.3}$$

Furthermore, we now define corresponding variables:

$$\textit{capital–labor efficiency unit ratio} = \frac{K}{\ell(t)} \equiv \bar{k}$$

$$\textit{output–labor efficiency unit ratio} = \frac{Q}{\ell(t)} \equiv \bar{q},$$

etc.

Because we postulate that (3.3.2) exhibits constant returns to scale in $K(t)$ and $\ell(t)$, we have that

$$\bar{q} = F\left[\frac{K(t)}{\ell(t)}, 1\right] \equiv f(\bar{k}). \tag{3.3.4}$$

Moreover, since

$$\frac{\dot{\ell}}{\ell} = \frac{\dot{\alpha}}{\alpha} + \frac{\dot{L}}{L} = \gamma + g, \tag{3.3.5}$$

replacing g in the previous analysis by $\bar{g} \equiv g + \gamma$ renders the two models mathematically identical. We conclude, therefore, that the model is stable in the new variables; that is,

$$\lim_{t \to \infty} \hat{k}(t) = \hat{k}^*. \tag{3.3.6}$$

This result – (3.3.6) – enables us to explain the six stylized facts for our model economy in dynamic equilibrium where $\hat{k} = \hat{k}^*$.

(1) The investment–output ratio

$$\frac{sQ}{Q} = \frac{sQ/\ell}{Q/\ell} = s$$

is constant by assumption.

(2) The capital–output ratio

$$\frac{K}{Q} = \frac{K/\ell}{Q/\ell} = \frac{\hat{k}}{\hat{q}} = \frac{\hat{k}^*}{f(\hat{k}^*)}$$

is constant.

(3) The capital–labor ratio

$$\frac{K}{L} = \frac{\alpha(t)K}{\ell} = \alpha(t)\hat{k}^*$$

and the output–labor ratio

$$\frac{Q}{L} = \frac{\alpha(t)Q}{\ell} = \alpha(t)\hat{q}^* = \alpha(t)f(\hat{k}^*)$$

are both rising at the rate $\gamma = \dot{\alpha}/\alpha$.

(4) The net rate of interest

$$r = f'(\hat{k}^*) - \delta$$

is constant.

(5) The real wage

$$w = \frac{\partial F[K, \alpha(t)L]}{\partial L} = \alpha(t)[f(\hat{k}^*) - \hat{k}^*f'(\hat{k}^*)]$$

is rising at the rate $\gamma = \dot{\alpha}/\alpha$.

(6) The relative shares of capital

$$\frac{(r + \delta)K}{Q} = \frac{(r + \delta)\hat{k}^*}{\hat{q}^*} = \frac{\hat{k}^*f'(\hat{k}^*)}{f(\hat{k}^*)}$$

and labor

$$\frac{wL}{Q} = \frac{w}{Q/L} = \frac{w}{\alpha(t)\hat{q}^*} = 1 - \frac{\hat{k}^*f'(\hat{k}^*)}{f(\hat{k}^*)}$$

are constant.

Moreover, we also have:

(7) Per capita consumption

$$c^* = \alpha(t)(1 - s)f(\tilde{k}^*)$$

is rising over time at the rate $\gamma = \dot\alpha/\alpha$.

Although we have successfully constructed a model exhibiting long-run behavior that is consistent with the list of stylized facts, one should not make too much of this accomplishment. We have merely identified a form of technological change that "works," with no consideration of any underlying microeconomic mechanisms to explain *why* it is that (3.3.2) is ultimately an appropriate description of technological opportunities. In particular, even if (3.3.2) does prevail eventually, we should want a theory that predicts how the rate of technological change, $\dot\alpha(t)/\alpha(t)$, is determined, rather than assuming that $\dot\alpha(t)/\alpha(t) = \gamma$ is an exogenous constant. However, before examining the underlying microeconomic determinants of technological change, one should consider disaggregated models with many heterogeneous commodities. This need is obvious once it is recognized that changes in technological production conditions often depend upon the particular commodity being produced, and many technological advances involve the introduction of *new* commodities (e.g., transistors) which were not even imagined until the time of their "discovery" or "invention" was near.

3.4. Some variations on the standard one-sector theme

The standard one-sector model can be modified in a number of ways, and in this section we shall briefly discuss three representative modifications: (1) the introduction of a distinction between the labor force and population, (2) Harrod's interpretation of the investment decision, and (3) life-cycle utility maximization.

a. *Population and labor supply*

Suppose that the total population grows according to

$$\text{population} = N(t) = N(0)e^{gt}, \tag{3.4.1}$$

but that the labor force is given by

$$\text{labor} = L(t) = \phi(w)N(t) \tag{3.4.2}$$

where the function $\phi(w)$ denotes the *labor-force participation rate*, and the real wage rate is

$$w = f(k) - kf'(k) = \frac{\partial F(K, L)}{\partial L}. \tag{3.4.3}$$

It is then a matter of straightforward calculation (left as Exercise 3.1) to derive the new accumulation equation,

$$\dot{k} = \frac{sf(k) - (g + \delta)k}{1 + \eta_\phi \eta_w} \tag{3.4.4}$$

where η_ϕ = elasticity of the participation rate with respect to the wage rate

η_w = elasticity of the wage rate with respect to the capital–labor ratio.

When $d\phi/dw > 0$ as we normally would expect (and since dw/dk is always positive), the *qualitative* behavior of $k(t)$ is unaltered by this modification, allowing the stability conclusions to remain valid. More complex hypotheses concerning endogenous population growth as well as questions of optimal population size can also be considered; the interested reader is referred to Pitchford's *Population in Economic Growth* (1974).

b. *Harrod's interpretation of the investment decision*

Consider an initial positive capital–labor ratio at time $t = 0$ which is less than the steady-state value, $k(0) = k^0 < k^*$. Because of diminishing returns $[f''(k) < 0]$ the net profit rate $r \equiv f'(k) - \delta$ must *fall* from its initial value $r^0 = f'(k^0) - \delta$ toward $r^* = f'(k^*) - \delta$ if capital accumulation results in a rising capital–labor ratio with $k(t)$ approaching k^*.

Now suppose that per capita consumption decisions are accurately reflected by the linear consumption function

$$c = (1 - s)f(k), \tag{3.4.5}$$

as before; desired saving is then

$$\dot{k} + (g + \delta)k = sf(k). \tag{3.4.6}$$

Will *actual* investment always match the desired saving given by (3.4.6)?

If, in fact, there is only one way to hold wealth, then actual investment in the single capital good must match desired saving simply because there is no alternative. Realistically, however, there do exist alternative assets; suppose that there is some other riskless asset yielding a fixed net return r_0. Obviously, then, capital accumulation will take place only if

$$r \geq r_0.$$

But what if

$$r_0 > f'(k^*) - \delta? \tag{3.4.7}$$

Under these circumstances the capital–labor ratio will rise to a value $\bar{k}$ satisfying

$$\bar{r} = f'(\bar{k}) - \delta = r_0, \tag{3.4.8}$$

but it can rise no further if r_0 remains unchanged. The *warranted rate of growth,* for this value of r_0, is determined by treating s and $\bar{k}$ as parameters, and we define

$$\frac{s}{\bar{v}} \equiv warranted\ rate\ of\ growth \tag{3.4.9}$$

where $\bar{v} \equiv \bar{k}/f(\bar{k})$ = capital–output ratio at r_0. The *natural rate of growth* is simply g, and when $g > s/\bar{v}$, there is not sufficient capital accumulation to keep pace with the growth in the labor force with increasing levels of unemployment resulting. If, on the other hand, the warranted rate of growth exceeds the natural rate – that is, if $g < s/\bar{v}$ – then the warranted growth rate cannot be achieved.

In both instances the stability conclusion that $\lim_{t\to\infty} k(t) = k^*$ no longer holds. We thus see that, except in the razor's-edge case when the warranted and natural rates of growth are equal, the introduction of an alternative asset results in *instability*. And even though we have neither rigorously considered the portfolio-choice problem faced by economic agents in a multiasset economy, nor indicated how the relative prices of assets influence investment decisions, we shall find that this instability result does provide an economic insight: in Section 3.6, where money is introduced, and in subsequent chapters with many assets, the stability properties exhibited by one-commodity models no longer prevail.

c. *Life-cycle utility maximization*

A conspicuous shortcoming of many models, including those examined thus far in this chapter, is the absence of explicit utility maximization on the part of economic agents.[8] Although it is possible that a linear consumption function of the form $c = (1 - s)f(k)$ is consistent with intertemporal utility maximization, such a circumstance is the exception rather than the rule.[9] We now shall consider a discrete-time life-cycle model in which economic agents live for exactly two periods and maximize their two-period utility functions.[10] During the first period of their lives, the workers' only source of income is wages, and they earn a wage rate w^t which depends upon the capital–labor ratio at that time:

$$w^t = f(k^t) - k^t f'(k^t). \tag{3.4.10}$$

Consider an economic agent, designated by the subscript i, who during the tth period is in the first stage of his or her life cycle. This economic agent consumes c_i^t and saves s_i^t, so that we have

$$s_i^t = w^t - c_i^t. \tag{3.4.11}$$

This saving is invested and earns a yield equal to the marginal product of capital during the next time period, $f'(k^{t+1})$. Bequest motives are ignored, and the ith consumer's consumption at the end of his or her second life-cycle period, c_i^{t+1}, equals total income in that period. It is assumed that no wage income is earned during this second life-cycle stage, and thus we have

$$c_i^{t+1} = s_i^t f'(k^{t+1}). \tag{3.4.12}$$

There is no uncertainty, and the ith economic agent faces the intertemporal utility maximization problem: max $u_i(c_i^t, c_i^{t+1})$ *subject to* (3.4.10)–(3.4.12). The solution to this standard problem entails the necessary condition

$$\frac{\partial u_i/\partial c_i^t}{\partial u_i/\partial c_i^{t+1}} = f'(k^{t+1}). \tag{3.4.13}$$

For simplicity, let us postulate that individuals' preferences are identical and that the utility and production functions are of the Cobb–Douglas forms

$$u(c_i^t, c_i^{t+1}) = (c_i^t)^\beta (c_i^{t+1})^{1-\beta}, \qquad 0 < \beta < 1, \quad \text{all } i \tag{3.4.14}$$

and

$$k^{t+1} + c^{t+1} = f(k^t) = (k^t)^\alpha, \qquad 0 < \alpha < 1, \tag{3.4.15}$$

respectively. We then have a special case of (3.4.13):

$$\frac{\beta c_i^{t+1}}{(1-\beta)c_i^t} = f'(k^{t+1}). \tag{3.4.16}$$

But, in view of (3.4.10), (3.4.11), and (3.4.12), we see that (3.4.16) implies

$$\beta s_i^t = (1-\beta)(w^t - s_i^t)$$

or

$$s_i^t = (1-\beta)w^t. \tag{3.4.17}$$

We postulate that (1) L^t persons are at stage 1 of their lives during the tth period, and (2) the growth rate of population is g, that is,

$$L^{t+1} = (1+g)L^t. \tag{3.4.18}$$

Accordingly, total saving in period t is simply

$$\sum_i s_i^t = L^t(1-\beta)w^t. \tag{3.4.19}$$

This saving can take only the form of capital used during period

$t + 1$, and thus the capital–labor ratio during period $t + 1$ is given by

$$k^{t+1} \equiv \frac{K^{t+1}}{L^{t+1}} = \frac{\sum_i s_i^t}{L^{t+1}} = \frac{L^t}{L^{t+1}} (1 - \beta)w^t$$

or, using (3.4.18),

$$k^{t+1} = \frac{1 - \beta}{1 + g} w^t. \tag{3.4.20}$$

Finally, using (3.4.10), we arrive at the capital accumulation equation,

$$k^{t+1} = \frac{1 - \beta}{1 + g} [f(k^t) - k^t f'(k^t)],$$

or, from the Cobb–Douglas assumption (3.4.15),

$$k^{t+1} = \frac{(1 - \beta)(1 - \alpha)}{1 + g} (k^t)^\alpha. \tag{3.4.21}$$

Equation (3.4.21) is a simple nonlinear difference equation in k^t for this perfectly competitive model with perfect foresight and intertemporal utility maximization by economic agents. As illustrated by Figure 3.3, the capital-accumulation process is stable with

$$\lim_{t \to \infty} k^t = k^* = \left[\frac{(1 - \beta)(1 - \alpha)}{1 + g} \right]^{1/1-\alpha} \tag{3.4.22}$$

starting from any initial condition $k^0 > 0$.

As in Section 2.4, the interest rate during the tth period equals the net marginal product of capital:[11]

$$r^t = f'(k^t) - 1. \tag{3.4.23}$$

Because the model is stable, the interest rate converges to its steady-state value with

$$\lim_{t \to \infty} r^t = r^* = f'(k^*) - 1 = \frac{\alpha(1 + g)}{(1 - \beta)(1 - \alpha)} - 1. \tag{3.4.24}$$

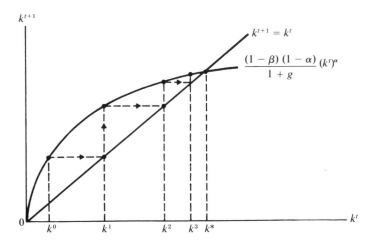

Figure 3.3. Convergence of k^t to k^* starting from the initial condition k^0.

Now, as we shall see in Section 3.5, an economy for which

$$r^* < g$$

is *consumption inefficient* in the sense that *everyone* can be made better off in terms of having higher consumption in *every* time period. Inspection of (3.4.24) shows that such dynamic inefficiency occurs in this model whenever

$$\frac{\alpha}{(1 - \beta)(1 - \alpha)} < 1. \tag{3.4.25}$$

For example, if $\alpha = \frac{1}{4}$, the inequality of (3.4.25) holds for all values of $\beta < \frac{2}{3}$.

The economic reason for this inefficiency is that, given any value of α, sufficiently small values of β result in "too much saving." Then "too much" capital is accumulated, and eventually the interest rate is driven down below the growth rate g. The no-growth case of $g = 0$ is clearest: then we have $r^* < 0$, and the economy accumulates so much capital that the net marginal return on capital becomes negative.

The somewhat startling conclusion is that perfect competition and intertemporal utility maximization do not necessarily imply Pareto optimality in a dynamic sense. Of course, in actuality there exist forms of wealth other than holdings of a physical capital stock, and it may be true that excessive capital accumulation is not a realistic problem in economies for which there are alternative paper assets (e.g., money and government bonds). Nevertheless, in general one must recognize the theoretical possibility of such intertemporal Pareto inefficiency, *despite* perfect competition and intertemporal utility maximization in a perfect foresight world. Obviously, then, the ordinary conclusions concerning Pareto optimality in a static world do not generalize to dynamic economies, at least not to ones with finite-lived economic agents, as above.

We now turn to this problem of capital accumulation in a more general context.

3.5. The Golden Rule, capital overaccumulation, and consumption-inefficient capital paths

Questions of efficiency are fundamental to economics: how should scarce resources be allocated to achieve a maximum value for some appropriate "output" measure? In Chapter 2 we introduced the concept of *dynamic efficiency,* which arises in economies with more than one type of capital good. However, we considered only intertemporal problems with finite time horizons, and the consumption paths were taken as exogenously given. In models with only one capital good, no such dynamic efficiency issue arises because only one type of output is produced, and capital accumulation is always determined by output minus consumption. That is, in a one-commodity world, if we are given (1) an initial capital stock, and (2) a time profile of consumption, the capital-accumulation path is completely determined. By contrast, suppose that we are given initial stocks of different types of capital in a multicommodity world. Even if one also takes the time profile of consumption as given, in general there will exist many feasible time paths for the capital stocks; the dynamic efficiency criterion selects a subset of these feasible paths.

Another concept of economic efficiency which involves comparison of alternative (feasible) consumption paths over infinite time horizons merits examination. In this chapter we shall retain the one-commodity framework, thereby avoiding any need to consider the previous issue of dynamic efficiency. Although we could work in continuous time, most of the literature dealing with this problem is written with discrete-time formulations, and we shall do the same here. Thus, with notation analogous to that employed in Chapter 2, we postulate an economy with a discrete-time technology described by[12]

$$K^{t+1} + C^{t+1} = F(K^t, L^t)$$

or

$$\frac{L^{t+1}}{L^t}\left(\frac{K^{t+1}}{L^{t+1}} + \frac{C^{t+1}}{L^{t+1}}\right) = F\left(\frac{K^t}{L^t}, 1\right) \equiv f\left(\frac{K^t}{L^t}\right). \qquad (3.5.1)$$

a. *The Golden Rule*

As a first step toward discussing intertemporal economic efficiency in terms of consumption paths, we will study the so-called *Golden Rule*. Assume that labor grows exogenously at the rate $g \geq 0$ with

$$L^{t+1} = (1 + g)L^t, \qquad (3.5.2)$$

and suppose that we restrict our attention only to steady states for which the capital–labor ratio and per capita consumption are constant over time with

$$\frac{K^t}{L^t} \equiv k^t = \bar{k} \qquad \text{for all } t \qquad (3.5.3)$$

and

$$\frac{C^t}{L^t} \equiv c^t = \bar{c} \qquad \text{for all } t. \qquad (3.5.4)$$

The technologically feasible steady states are determined from (3.5.1) and (3.5.2):

$$(1 + g)(\bar{k} + \bar{c}) = f(\bar{k})$$

or

$$\bar{c} = \frac{f(\bar{k})}{1 + g} - \bar{k}. \tag{3.5.5}$$

What steady-state value of the capital–labor ratio would you select if you were given the option to do so costlessly? Ignoring any questions of income distribution, it is clear that one would want to select that value of $\bar{k}$ which yields the maximum per capita consumption; that is, $\bar{k}$ is selected such that

$$\frac{d\bar{c}}{d\bar{k}} = \frac{f'(\bar{k})}{1 + g} - 1 = 0$$

or

$$f'(\bar{k}) - 1 = g. \tag{3.5.6}$$

Recalling that $f'(k^t) - 1$ is the net marginal product of capital which must in competitive equilibrium equal the commodity own interest rate r^t, the Golden Rule condition (3.5.6) may be written as

$$\tilde{r} = g \tag{3.5.7}$$

where $\tilde{r} = f'(\hat{k}) - 1$ denotes the steady-state interest rate at the Golden Rule level of the steady-state capital–labor ratio (i.e., at $\bar{k} = \hat{k}$).

An alternative characterization of the Golden Rule for this model can be stated in terms of saving and consumption functions. If we assume that $\tilde{r} = g$, then from (3.5.5) and (3.5.6) we have

$$\begin{aligned}
\tilde{c} &= \frac{f(\hat{k})}{f'(\hat{k})} - \hat{k} \\
&= \frac{f(\hat{k}) - \hat{k}f'(\hat{k})}{f'(\hat{k})} .
\end{aligned} \tag{3.5.8}$$

But, again using (3.5.6), this implies that

$$(1 + g)\tilde{c} = f(\hat{k}) - \hat{k}f'(\hat{k}) = \tilde{w}$$

where $\tilde{w}$ is the real wage rate at $\bar{k} = \hat{k}$. Hence

$$\tilde{w} = (1 + g)\tilde{c} = \frac{L^{t+1}}{L^t} \cdot \frac{C^{t+1}}{L^{t+1}}$$

or

$$C^{t+1} = \tilde{w}L^t. \tag{3.5.9}$$

That is, *at the Golden Rule capital–labor ratio, consumption is equal to total real labor income.*[13] Similarly, one may derive

$$K^{t+1} = f'(\hat{k})K^t. \tag{3.5.10}$$

That is, *at the Golden Rule capital–labor ratio, total saving (equal to K^{t+1}) is equal to total profit income.* The derivation of (3.5.10) is left to the reader as Exercise 3.2.

Upon reflection, then, it should be evident that for models such as the one at hand, if all wage income is always consumed and all profit income is saved (invested in capital accumulation), the capital–labor ratio, starting from any initial magnitude, will converge to its Golden Rule value (see Exercise 3.3).

The Golden Rule condition that the interest rate equal the rate of growth of labor is a very robust result, having efficiency implications in far more general models. For example, it is a condition for the maximization of a utility function defined over per capita consumption of different commodities in models with many capital goods. Consider also the life-cycle model discussed in Section 3.4c and suppose that we confine our attention to steady states with a constant capital–labor ratio. A representative consumer has a lifetime utility function defined over consumption in each of the consumer's two life-cycle stages, and assuming identical preferences and a constant time pattern of consumption, we may write

$$u(c_1, c_2) \tag{3.5.11}$$

where

$$c_1 \equiv \sum_i c_i^t \quad \text{and} \quad c_2 \equiv \sum_i c_i^{t+1} \quad \text{for all } t \text{ (and where}$$
$$c_i^t, c_i^{t+1} \text{ are defined in Section 3.4c).}$$

The steady-state path along which every individual has the highest feasible utility level is found by solving the problem

$$\max u(c_1, c_2) \quad \text{subject to } f(k)$$
$$- (1 + g)k - \left(c_1 + \frac{c_2}{1 + g}\right) = 0. \tag{3.5.12}$$

The solution to this problem, left as Exercise 3.4, implies that

$$\frac{\partial u}{\partial c_1} = (1 + g)\frac{\partial u}{\partial c_2} \quad \text{and} \quad f'(k) - (1 + g) = 0. \tag{3.5.13}$$

The latter condition of (3.5.13) is, of course, the Golden Rule.

For models with only one primary factor (provided that joint production is excluded[14] and constant returns to scale prevail), the steady-state equilibrium value of every economic variable may be regarded as a function of the steady-state commodity interest rate, r. This result follows from Samuelson's *Nonsubstitution Theorem*, which asserts that, under our stated assumptions, relative prices are functions of the interest rate in steady-state equilibria. Given these equilibrium prices, every physical magnitude is also determined.[15] Thus in a world of identical, well-behaved preferences, it is quite a general proposition that we may write per capita utility as a function of the interest rate:

$$u = u(r). \tag{3.5.14}$$

In preparation for our discussion in Chapter 4 of a "paradox" arising in heterogeneous capital good models, it is instructive to consider the behavior of this function. The Golden Rule theorem holds under our stated assumptions, so we already know that $u(r)$ attains its global maximum at $r = g$. For now let us postulate a one-commodity model with

$$k^{t+1} - k^t = f(k^t) - c - (1 + g)k^t. \tag{3.5.15}$$

In steady states with $k^{t+1} = k^t = k$ we may write

$$u(c) = u[f(k) - (1 + g)k] \tag{3.5.16}$$

where $u(c)$ is a "well-behaved" utility function having the properties $u'(c) > 0$, $u''(c) < 0$. The behavior of $u(r)$ is seen by calculating

$$
\begin{aligned}
\frac{du[c(r)]}{dr} &= u'(c) \left[f'(k)\frac{dk}{dr} - (1 + g)\frac{dk}{dr} \right] \\
&= u'(c)[f'(k) - 1 - g]\frac{dk}{dr}.
\end{aligned}
\tag{3.5.17}
$$

But since

$$
\begin{aligned}
r &= f'(k) - 1, \\
\frac{dk}{dr} &= \frac{1}{f''(k)},
\end{aligned}
\tag{3.5.18}
$$

and thus

$$\frac{du}{dr} = (r - g)\frac{u'(c)}{f''(k)}. \tag{3.5.19}$$

The regularity conditions $u'(c) > 0$ and $f''(k) < 0$ imply that

$$\text{sgn}\,\frac{du}{dr} = \text{sgn}\,(g - r) \textit{ across steady-state equilibria.}$$

$$\tag{3.5.20}$$

That is, per capita steady-state utility always rises with decreases in the steady-state interest rate, provided that the steady-state interest rate exceeds the rate of growth of labor; otherwise, it falls. This "well-behaved" case is illustrated in Figure 3.4.

When there is only one type of capital good, saving and capital accumulation are identical, and lower values of r are unambiguously associated with higher values of the steady-state capital–labor ratio, k. Thus for $r > g$, smaller values of r, which always imply larger values of k and more saving, also imply higher levels of utility. But for r *below* g, there is *too much* saving. Additional saving, with the associated still lower r and

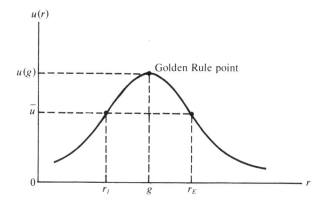

Figure 3.4. The steady-state level of utility is maximized at the Golden Rule point where $r = g$.

larger k, results in *decreases* in the steady-state utility level: there is *capital overaccumulation*. For example, in Figures 3.4 and 3.5 the steady-state utility level $u = \bar{u}$ can be attained with a capital–labor ratio of either k_E or k_I. But at k_I, the interest rate is $r_I = f'(k_I) - 1 < g$ and hence it is consumption inefficient – there is capital overaccumulation at the steady state with $k = \bar{k}_I$.

It is, of course, obvious that such overaccumulation always can occur, for suppose that *all* of output were devoted to capital accumulation. The steady-state value of k satisfying

$$0 = f(k) - (1 + g)k \tag{3.5.21}$$

could then be maintained, but consumption would be zero. At the opposite extreme, if nothing is saved, the only maintainable capital–labor ratio is $k = 0$, and again consumption is zero. The Golden Rule point $r = g$ characterizes the steady state between these two extremes where per capita steady-state consumption (and hence utility) is maximized. The name "Golden Rule" is appropriate if one views the problem as that of selecting the steady-state world one would like to live in under the constraint that "generations living before us shall save for us as we shall save for future generations yet to be born."

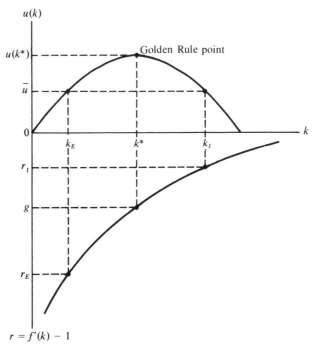

Figure 3.5. The Golden Rule point is at $r = g$, where the capital-labor ratio is k^*.

Even when we do not compare only steady-state equilibria, the Golden Rule point provides a crucial benchmark for identifying certain consumption-inefficient capital-accumulation paths. Suppose, for example, that we consider a path for which

$$k(t) \geq k^* + \epsilon, \qquad \text{some } \epsilon > 0, \quad \text{all } t \geq t_0, \qquad (3.5.22)$$

where now k^* denotes the Golden Rule value of the capital–labor ratio. It is then always possible to find another feasible path, starting at the same capital–labor ratio at time $t = t_0$, which provides *more* consumption at some time $t = \tau \geq t_0$ and never less consumption than the original path.[16] Thus a path for which the inequality (3.5.22) holds is termed *consumption inefficient*.

Note that this type of inefficiency arises because the capital–labor ratio is bounded above its Golden Rule value *forever* after time $t = t_0$. Such inefficiency cannot be deduced if the inequality in (3.5.22) holds only over a finite time horizon, say $t_0 \leq t \leq T$, for then the "excessive capital" accumulated up to time $t = T$ always could be consumed at some *future* times $t > T$. Our task now is to make these ideas more precise by providing a rigorous definition of consumption inefficiency, as well as a necessary and sufficient condition for its existence.

b. *Capital overaccumulation and consumption inefficiency*

Preliminary to our discussion of consumption efficiency with an infinite time horizon, we must introduce a few definitions. We shall continue to use a one-commodity model in discrete time,[17] and the technologically feasible choices available in the tth period are described by a production function $f(k^t)$, where k^t is the ratio of capital to labor inputs in the tth period. The output from production in the tth period is used next period with

$$c^{t+1} + k^{t+1} = f(k^t). \tag{3.5.23}$$

At this point it should be noted that (3.5.23) is equivalent to numerous other technological specifications. For example, consider the familiar alternative

$$C^{t+1} + I^{t+1} = F(K^t, L^t) \tag{3.5.24a}$$

$$K^{t+1} - K^t = I^{t+1} - \delta K^t \tag{3.5.24b}$$

$$L^{t+1} = (1 + g)L^t. \tag{3.5.24c}$$

Equation (3.5.24a) says that consumption plus gross investment equals gross output, (3.5.24b) says that net investment ($K^{t+1} - K^t$) equals gross investment minus depreciation (assumed equal to δK^t), while (3.5.24c) gives the exogenous labor supply. The equivalence between (3.5.23) and (3.5.24a)–(3.5.24c) is proved by setting

$$k^t \equiv \frac{K^t}{L^t}, \qquad c^{t+1} \equiv \frac{C^{t+1}}{L^{t+1}},$$

$$f(k^t) \equiv \frac{F(K^t/L^t,\ 1) + (1 - \delta)K^t/L^t}{1 + g}, \tag{3.5.25}$$

as the reader is asked to do in Exercise 3.5. Note also that the Golden Rule point for (3.5.24a)–(3.5.24c) occurs where the net marginal product of capital is equal to the labor growth rate, that is, where

$$\frac{\partial F}{\partial K^t} - \delta = g. \tag{3.5.26}$$

But, from (3.5.25), the analogous Golden Rule point for (3.5.23) occurs where

$$f'(k^t) = 1. \tag{3.5.27}$$

Since we have shown that the interest rate is

$$r^t = f'(k^t) - 1 \tag{3.5.28}$$
$$= \text{net marginal productivity of capital,}$$

the Golden Rule point for the economy described by (3.5.23) occurs at a zero interest rate. Essentially, we have eliminated labor from the system by reducing (3.5.24a)–(3.5.24c) to (3.5.23), and the signal of an inefficient steady state with capital overaccumulation now is a steady-state interest rate satisfying $-1 \leq r < 0$.

We assume that the production function satisfies the regularity conditions

$$f(0^t) = 0, \quad f'(k^t) > 0, \quad f''(k^t) < 0 \qquad \text{for all } k^t.$$

A *program* is a technologically feasible infinite sequence of non-negative inputs

$$\{k^t\} = \{k^0, k^1, k^2, \ldots \}. \tag{3.5.29}$$

Any program has an associated infinite sequence of consumption levels given by

$$c^{t+1} = f(k^t) - k^{t+1} \geqslant 0, \qquad t = 0, 1, 2, \ldots, \quad \text{with } c^0 \equiv 0.$$
$$(3.5.30)$$

Similarly, the *price sequence* associated with any program $\{k^t\}$ is defined by

$$p^{t+1} = \frac{p^t}{f'(k^t)}, \qquad p^0 \equiv 1, \quad t = 0, 1, 2, \ldots \qquad (3.5.31)$$

The prices given by (3.5.31) are precisely those which maximize profits in each period; that is, if prices are given by (3.5.31) for any program $\{k^t\}$, then for all t,

$$p^{t+1}f(k^t) - p^t k^t \geqslant p^{t+1}f(k') - p^t k', \qquad \text{any } k' \geqslant 0.$$
$$(3.5.32)$$

As before, the commodity own interest rate over period t is

$$r^t = f'(k^t) - 1. \qquad (3.5.33)$$

The *capital-value* sequence $\{v^t\}$ associated with the program $\{k^t\}$ is defined by

$$v^t = p^t k^t. \qquad (3.5.34)$$

We now introduce two crucial definitions:

DEFINITION 3.1
A program $\{\hat{k}^t\} = \{\hat{k}^0, \hat{k}^1, \hat{k}^2, \ldots\}$ with an associated consumption sequence $\{\hat{c}^t\} = \{\hat{c}^0, \hat{c}^1, \hat{c}^2, \ldots\}$ is termed *consumption efficient* if there exists *no* other program $\{k^t\}$ with an associated consumption sequence $\{c^t\}$ such that

(1) $k^0 = \hat{k}^0$ (so that both programs have the same starting point);
(2) $c^t \geqslant \hat{c}^t$ for all t (so that there does not exist another program with consumption bigger than or equal to, for all t, the consumption associated with the program $\{\hat{k}^t\}$); and
(3) $c^\tau > \hat{c}^\tau$ for some time period $t = \tau$ (so that there does not exist another program which gives more consumption in some time period).

A *consumption-inefficient* program is one that is not efficient.

DEFINITION 3.2

An infinite sequence of positive numbers $\{n^0, n^1, n^2, \ldots\}$ is said to *grow too fast* if

$$\sum_{t=0}^{\infty} \frac{1}{n^t} < \infty.$$

For example, the sequence $\{1, 2, 3, \ldots\}$ has the property that

$$\frac{1}{1} + \frac{1}{2} + \frac{1}{3} + \cdots = \infty,$$

and hence does *not* grow too fast, while the sequence $\{1, 2, 4, 8, \ldots\}$ has a convergent sum given by

$$\frac{1}{1} + \frac{1}{2} + \frac{1}{4} + \cdots = \frac{1}{1 - \frac{1}{2}} = 2,$$

and hence does grow too fast.

The fundamental consumption-efficiency theorem proved by Cass (1972b) can now be stated.[18]

THEOREM 3.1

Suppose that we consider only programs for which capital stocks are bounded away from zero and infinity; that is, assume that there exist positive numbers m and M such that

$$m < k^t < M \qquad \text{for all } t.$$

Suppose further that $f''(k^t) < a < 0$ for all k^t. Such a program is consumption efficient if and only if its associated price sequence $\{p^t\}$ grows too fast.

The theorem states a necessary and sufficient condition and consequently provides a complete characterization of consumption efficiency. The previous result – that a program for which

$$k^t \geq k^* + \epsilon, \qquad \text{some } \epsilon > 0, \quad \text{all } t, \tag{3.5.35}$$

(where k^* denotes the Golden Rule value of the capital–labor ratio) is consumption inefficient – is but a special case of the general theorem. To see this fact, merely observe that when (3.5.35) holds, from (3.5.31) we have that

$$p^0 = 1, \quad p^1 = \frac{p^0}{f'(k^* + \epsilon)} = \frac{1}{f'(k^* + \epsilon)},$$

$$p^2 = \frac{p^1}{f'(k^* + \epsilon)} = \frac{1}{[f'(k^* + \epsilon)]^2}, \quad \cdots, \tag{3.5.36}$$

while $f''(k^t) < 0$ and (3.5.27) imply that

$$f'(k^* + \epsilon) < 1. \tag{3.5.37}$$

Thus letting $f'(k^* + \epsilon) = \theta$,

$$\sum_{t=0}^{\infty} \frac{1}{p^t} = 1 + \theta + \theta^2 + \cdots = \frac{1}{1 - \theta} < \infty \qquad \text{since } 0 < \theta < 1.$$

Hence we conclude that the price sequence associated with the program given by (3.5.35) grows too fast, and therefore by the Cass theorem it is consumption inefficient.

The question of consumption efficiency is historically rooted in the paper by Malinvaud, written over 25 years ago.[19] Malinvaud proved, for a somewhat different model, that the convergence of the *value of capital* to zero implies consumption efficiency; that is,

if $\lim_{t \to \infty} v^t = 0$, then the associated program is consumption efficient. (3.5.38)

However, clearly this criterion is not completely satisfactory, for in an economy starting and remaining at the Golden Rule capital–labor ratio (k^*), $v^t = p^0 k^*$ for all t, and

$$\lim_{t \to \infty} v^t = k^* \neq 0 \qquad \text{(since } p^0 \equiv 1\text{)}.$$

However, such a program is clearly consumption efficient.

The Cass theorem is restricted to capital paths that are bounded from above and below with

$$m < k^t < M \quad (m, M > 0) \qquad \text{for all } t, \tag{3.5.39}$$

and thus it is evident that the price sequence $\{p^t\}$ grows too fast if, and only if, the capital-value sequence $\{v^t\}$ does. What if the assumption (3.5.39) is dropped? For example, the model with technological change analyzed in Section 3.3 has an unbounded capital–labor ratio in natural units. The capital–efficiency unit ratio does converge to $\bar{k}^*$, but

$$k^t = \alpha(t)\bar{k}^*$$

becomes infinite as $t \to \infty$, because we assumed that the rate of technological change was a positive constant ($\dot{\alpha}/\alpha = \gamma > 0$).

Generalizations of the Cass theorem by Benveniste and Gale (1975) allow consideration of such cases with technological change and unbounded capital–labor ratios. In particular, $f(k^t)$ is replaced by a production function allowing technological change, $f^t(k^t)$. The boundedness condition (3.5.39) is dropped, replaced by the assumption that there exist positive numbers m, M, q, and Q such that, for all t,

$$q \leq \frac{x}{f(x)} \frac{df^t(x)}{dx} \leq Q \quad \text{and} \quad -m \leq \frac{x^2}{f(x)} \frac{d^2 f^t(x)}{dx^2}$$
$$\leq -M \text{ for } 0 \leq x \leq k^t. \tag{3.5.40}$$

Benveniste and Gale prove that, under assumption (3.5.40), a program $\{k^t\}$ is consumption inefficient if, and only if, the associated capital-value sequence $\{v^t\}$ grows too fast.

The latter result enables us to apply the concept of consumption efficiency to models with technological change and unbounded capital stocks. However, assumption (3.5.40), which is an elasticity-type condition independent of measuring units, does play a crucial role in eliminating some programs from consideration. In particular, the assumption is violated if either

$$(1) \lim_{k^t \to 0} \frac{df^t(k^t)}{dk^t} < \infty, \quad \text{or} \quad (2) \lim_{k^t \to \infty} \frac{df^t(k^t)}{dk^t} > 0.$$

If (1) holds, there exist programs for which

$$\lim_{t \to \infty} k^t = 0$$

and the capital-value sequence $\{v^t\}$ grows too fast, but nevertheless they are efficient. If (2) holds, there exist consumption-inefficient programs having an associated capital-value sequence that does not grow too fast.[20]

These remarks should serve as ample warning that the subject under discussion is of treacherous difficulty, and assumption-insensitive results are illusive. Of course, matters only become more complex when the model is generalized to allow for many heterogeneous commodities, and often the economic meaning of various sets of assumptions becomes obscure. When there are many capital goods, say $k_1^t, \ldots, k_n^t$ with associated (competitive) present-value prices $p_1^t, \ldots, p_n^t$, the value of capital is simply

$$v^t = \sum_{i=1}^{n} p_i^t k_i^t.$$

Various theorems about consumption efficiency involve the behavior of the capital-value sequence $\{v^t\}$. For example, under certain assumptions about the technology, Mitra and Majumdar (1976) have established that the so-called *transversality condition*,

$$\lim_{t \to \infty} v^t = 0, \tag{3.5.41}$$

is both necessary and sufficient for consumption efficiency. On the other hand, Benveniste (1976a), generalizing the seminal work of Cass on multisector models (1972a), specifies an alternative model for which the necessary and sufficient condition is that the capital-value sequence $\{v^t\}$ does not grow too fast. Observe that the transversality condition (3.5.41) implies, but is not implied by, the condition that $\{v^t\}$ does not grow too fast.[21]

The question of the relationship between Samuelson's dynamic efficiency (discussed in Section 2.2) and consumption efficiency does arise in models with many capital goods. However, as is evident from Section 2.3, dynamic efficiency is implied by intertemporal profit maximization on the part of both firms and wealth holders. In the literature on consumption efficiency, it is generally implicitly assumed that firms own (rather than rent) their capital inputs, and thus the assumption of profit maximization in every period *implies* dynamic efficiency [see, e.g., the derivation of equation (2.3.19)]. The two approaches are therefore equivalent for our purposes. Note, however, that when firms own their capital, they must take capital gains and losses into account when reckoning their profits, whereas in models where firms rent capital goods and maximize profits subject to given rental rates for the capital inputs, it is the owners of the capital goods who must take into account capital gains in their portfolio equilibrium calculations.

Accordingly, starting with the set of all technologically *feasible* intertemporal paths (*F*), the set of dynamically efficient paths is a subset (*D*), and this subset is taken as the beginning in the search for consumption-efficient paths which constitute another subset (*E*), that is,

$$E \subseteq D \subseteq F. \tag{3.5.42}$$

The set *E* (the set of consumption-efficient paths) has the property of *intertemporal Pareto optimality* defined as follows:

> An economy is said to exhibit *intertemporal Pareto optimality* if, given consumption sequences for every individual, no individual can be made better off (can be given more consumption) in any time period without making either that same or some other individual worse off (by having less consumption) in some other period.

The economic significance of the results on consumption efficiency – and our justification for having devoted so much space to it – is that even when every assumption about perfect competition is satisfied in a perfect-foresight model, there exist intertemporal paths that are not Pareto optimal in this sense. We have seen that paths along which the capital–labor ratio is forever bounded above its Golden Rule value constitute one example of such intertemporal Pareto inefficiency. This phenomenon was first observed in another context by Samuelson (1958); the reason a competitive price system can fail is that, with an *infinite* time horizon, there is no economic mechanism to signal capital overaccumulation. In other words, there does not exist any *market* signal in response to a capital-overaccumulation condition such as

$$\sum_{t=0}^{\infty} \frac{1}{v^t} < \infty.$$

It is less clear what policy conclusions, if any, one should draw from this fundamental theoretical proposition about the efficient allocation of resources over time. We have already noted that no path can be judged consumption inefficient in finite time, for one could always consume in the future. Nevertheless, if an economy is on a consumption-inefficient path along which *every* agent is obeying maximizing rules of competition, presumably it would take some kind of intervention to attain consumption efficiency; but no single individual agent, acting alone, can ever achieve this desired result. For certain parameter values the life-cycle model discussed in Section 3.4 exemplifies this type of behavior.

Of course, even intertemporal Pareto optimality is a rather weak criterion, and presumably in general economic agents would have a preference for one particular Pareto optimal path over another. Thus it sometimes has been suggested that we further restrict our attention to programs that are *optimal* in the sense of maximizing some intertemporal utility function defined over consumption paths. The set of such optimal paths, O, constitutes a further subset, so that (3.5.42) is extended to

$$O \subseteq E \subseteq D \subseteq F. \tag{3.5.43}$$

If, then, agents do, in fact, always select a path that is optimal, obviously we could observe only intertemporally Pareto efficient paths (since $O \subseteq E$).

However, whether or not this device is acceptable depends upon our willingness to define a utility function over the *infinite* consumption sequences $\{c^t\}_{t=0}^{\infty}$; for if not, the previously mentioned life-cycle example serves to demonstrate that even with competitive prices, perfect foresight, *and* intertemporal utility maximization on the part of agents over their two-period lives, *consumption-inefficient* (i.e., *intertemporally Pareto inefficient*) *paths can occur.*

Moreover, when we do define optimality by the solution(s) to the problem

$$\max u(c^0, c^1, c^2, c^3, \dots) \equiv \sum_{t=0}^{\infty} \frac{u(c^t)}{(1 + \rho)^t}$$

(where $\rho \geq 0$ is the rate of time preference),

as we shall do in Chapter 6, there exists a related question as to the class of economic models for which the transversality condition

$$\lim_{t \to \infty} v^t = 0$$

constitutes one of the *necessary* conditions for optimality. Thus even if one dismisses the problem of capital overaccumulation as irrelevant, the theoretical concepts we have introduced are of fundamental significance in dynamic economics and will be encountered again.

3.6. **A two-commodity model with a single capital good**

While the one-commodity model examined thus far in this chapter can be rationalized in terms of examples such as corn – corn can both be consumed and used as an input to produce more corn – in general it is obviously a drastic oversimplification to suppose that a single type of output can be used both as a capital good and as a consumption good (i.e., machines cannot be eaten). As a first step toward disaggregation, we shall now consider the conventional two-sector model consisting of two commodities: a single pure consumption good (which is never used as a productive input and cannot be stored) and a single type of capital good (which is never consumed, but which is used as a productive input to produce both more of itself and the consumption good).

One essential feature of the one-commodity model remains:

there is only one form in which wealth can be held because we have stipulated that the pure consumption good be nonstorable, and accordingly the only existing asset is the single type of capital good.

Production of the consumption good, the output of which is C, depends upon the quantities of the capital and the labor used to produce it:

$$C = F_c(K_c, L_c). \tag{3.6.1}$$

Since the production function $F_c(K_c, L_c)$ is assumed to exhibit constant returns to scale, as before we may write

$$c \equiv \frac{C}{L_c} = F_c\left(\frac{K_c}{L_c}, 1\right) = F_c(k_c, 1) \equiv f_c(k_c) \tag{3.6.2}$$

where k_c is the ratio of capital to labor *in the consumption-good sector*. Also note that now c *does not* denote per capita consumption, but rather it equals the ratio of total consumption to the number of workers in the consumption-good sector (i.e., the average productivity of labor in this sector).

Analogously, the output from the investment-good sector is equal to gross investment and depends upon the capital and labor allocated to the production of the capital or investment good:[22]

$$\dot{K} + \delta K = F_I(K_I, L_I). \tag{3.6.3}$$

We may express the latter in terms of the workers in the investment-good sector by writing

$$\frac{\dot{K}}{L_I} + \delta \frac{K}{L_I} = F_I\left(\frac{K_I}{L_I}, 1\right) = F_I(k_I, 1) \equiv f_I(k_I). \tag{3.6.4}$$

Now we define

$$\beta \equiv \frac{L_I}{L} = \text{ratio of workers in the investment-good sector to total labor,}$$

and we have

$$\frac{\dot{K}}{L_I} + \delta \frac{K}{L_I} = \frac{1}{\beta}\left(\frac{\dot{K}}{L} + \delta \frac{K}{L}\right) = \frac{1}{\beta}[\dot{k} + (g + \delta)k] = f_I(k_I)$$

$$(3.6.5)$$

where $\dot{L}/L = g \geq 0$ is exogenous and where the overall capital–labor ratio in the economy is

$$k \equiv \frac{K}{L} = \frac{K_I + K_c}{L_I + L_c}. \tag{3.6.6}$$

In writing (3.6.6) we have assumed full employment of both capital and labor; equivalently,

$$k = \beta k_I + (1 - \beta)k_c. \tag{3.6.7}$$

For simplicity, the production functions are assumed to satisfy the following regularity conditions for both $i = I$ and $i = c$:

$$f_i(0) = 0$$
$$f_i'(k_i) > 0, \quad f_i''(k_i) < 0 \qquad \text{for } 0 < k_i < \infty$$
$$\lim_{k_i \to 0} f_i'(k_i) = \infty$$

and

$$\lim_{k_i \to \infty} f_i'(k_i) = 0.$$

The analysis may now take a number of directions. The three equations (3.6.2), (3.6.5), and (3.6.7) involve the six variables c, k_c, $\dot{k}$, k_I, β, and k. However, we still must impose the following marginal conditions for $i = I$ and $i = c$:

$$P_i \frac{\partial F_i(K_i, L_i)}{\partial K_i} = R = \text{gross rental rate for} \atop \text{the capital good} \tag{3.6.8}$$

$$P_i \frac{\partial F_i(K_i, L_i)}{\partial L_i} = W = \text{wage rate} \tag{3.6.9}$$

(where P_I and P_c are the prices of the respective outputs). Letting $\omega \equiv W/R$ denote the wage–rental rate ratio, (3.6.8) and (3.6.9) imply that

$$\frac{f_i(k_i) - k_i f_i'(k_i)}{f_i'(k_i)} = \omega, \qquad i = I, c. \tag{3.6.10}$$

Finally, the system is completed with the addition of a consumption function, and for simplicity let us suppose for now that the value of per capita consumption is a constant fraction $(1 - s)$ of per capita GNP; that is,

$$\frac{P_c C}{L} = (1 - s) \frac{WL + RK}{L}. \tag{3.6.11}$$

Equivalently, the value of gross saving is equal to a fraction s of GNP:

$$\frac{P_I(\dot{K} + \delta K)}{L} = s \left(\frac{WL + RK}{L} \right), \qquad 0 < s < 1. \tag{3.6.12}$$

Dividing (3.6.12) by R and using (3.6.5), we obtain

$$\frac{P_I}{R} [\dot{k} + (g + \delta)k] = s(\omega + k). \tag{3.6.13}$$

However, from (3.6.8) with $i = I$, we see that

$$\frac{R}{P_I} = \frac{\partial F_I(K_I, L_I)}{\partial K_I} = f_I'(k_I),$$

and therefore the saving–consumption assumption expressed by (3.6.12) and (3.6.13) may be written as

$$\dot{k} + (g + \delta)k = sf_I'(k_I)(\omega + k). \tag{3.6.14}$$

This simple but messy model of a two-sector economy is now completed; the six equations (3.6.2), (3.6.5), (3.6.7), (3.6.10) for $i = I$ and c, and (3.6.14) involve the seven variables c, k_c, $\dot{k}$, k_I, β, ω, and k. What is its dynamic behavior? Suppose that we take as given an arbitrary positive value of the overall capital–labor ratio, $k(0) = k^0 > 0$. There are two immediate questions to answer:

(1) Do there *exist* economically meaningful values c^0, k_c^0, $\dot{k}^0$, k_I^0, β^0, and ω^0 which satisfy the equations of the model and thus represent a static general equilibrium solution?

(2) Is such a solution always *unique*?

For the particular saving–consumption function that we have postulated, it can be proved that the answers to both (1) and (2) are affirmative. Under our assumed regularity conditions on the production functions, *existence* of a general equilibrium solution at any instant is ensured for all $0 < k^0 < \infty$, and such momentary (static) equilibria are unique [i.e., there exists one and only one vector $(c, k_c, \dot{k}, k_I, \beta, \omega)$ for each given value of k $(0 < k < \infty)$].[23] Under such circumstances the two-sector model is termed *causal* because these general equilibria solutions imply the existence of a function

$$\dot{k}(t) = \Psi[k(t)]. \tag{3.6.15}$$

The dynamic behavior of the model is then straightforward: given an initial $k(0) = k^0$, the future path for $k(t)$ is determined by (3.6.15), where at each instant of time with $k(t)$ taken as fixed, there is a corresponding unique general equilibrium solution. This scenario is sometimes termed *equilibrium dynamics*.

However, even for causal systems – even when the function (3.6.15) exists – three problems remain:

(3) Does there exist a dynamic rest point [i.e., does there exist a steady-state capital–labor ratio $k^* > 0$ such that $0 = \Psi(k^*)$]?

(4) Is such a k^* unique?

(5) What are the stability properties of steady-state equilibria?

Once again the regularity conditions imposed on the production functions imply the existence of *some* $k^* > 0$ such that $0 = \Psi(k^*)$. Nevertheless, even with our stipulated saving-consumption function, multiple steady-state equilibria can occur, as depicted in Figure 3.6 with alternating stable and unstable steady-state equilibria. Various sufficient conditions can be derived for the following properties to hold simultaneously:

(1) An instantaneous general equilibrium solution exists and is unique for all $0 < k < \infty$ so that the function $\dot{k} = \Psi(k)$ exists.

(2) There exists a unique root $0 < k^* < \infty$ such that $0 = \Psi(k^*)$.

(3) This steady-state capital–labor ratio k^* is *globally stable* and, starting from any finite, positive capital–labor ratio $k(0)$, $\lim_{t \to \infty} k(t) = k^*$.

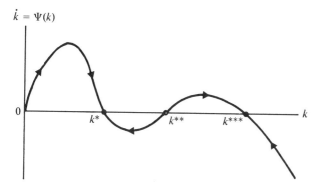

Figure 3.6. Example of multiple steady-state equilibria.

Of course, the various alternative sufficient conditions under which these properties hold depend upon what saving–consumption behavior is assumed. One class of saving–consumption function that has been thoroughly explored is of the form

$$\text{gross investment} = P_I(\dot{K} + \delta K) = \text{gross saving}$$
$$= s_w WL + s_r RK \qquad (3.6.16)$$

where $0 < s_w < 1$, $0 < s_r < 1$. The constants s_w and s_r are the fractions saved out of wage income and gross rental income, respectively. One sufficient condition for properties (1)–(3) is

$$s_r \geq s_w \qquad (3.6.17a)$$

and

$$k_I \leq k_c. \qquad (3.6.17b)$$

Property (3.6.17b) is the *capital-intensity condition* that the capital–labor ratio in the investment-good sector be less than the capital–labor ratio in the consumption-good sector. It is a very strong restriction, as it must hold for *every* value of the economy-wide capital–labor ratio, k.[24] An alternative sufficient condition for properties (*S*) that does not depend upon the relative magnitude of the saving propensities s_w and s_r is

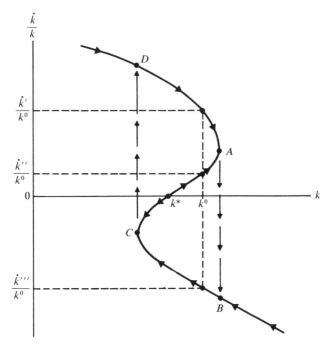

Figure 3.7. Example of cyclic motion around the unstable steady-state point at k^*.

$$\sigma_c \geq 1 \tag{3.6.18}$$

where σ_c denotes the elasticity of substitution between capital and labor in the consumption-good sector. Accordingly, a model in which the consumption good is produced by a Cobb–Douglas production function ($\sigma_c = 1$) exhibits properties (S).[25]

We now turn briefly to the case in which instantaneous general equilibrium is *not unique* for all values of k. Numerical examples show that the situation depicted in Figure 3.7 can exist, and we consider the indicated value k^0 as an initial capital–labor ratio. There are *three* corresponding equilibrium vectors,

$$(c', k'_c, \dot{k}', k'_I, \beta', \omega'),$$
$$(c'', k''_c, \dot{k}'', k''_I, \beta'', \omega''),$$

and

$$(c''', k_c''', \dot{k}''', k_I''', \beta''', \omega'''),$$

all of which satisfy every equation of the two-sector model. The dynamic behavior of the economy under consideration is *non-causal:* given the initial condition $k(0) = k^0$, the system does not even know where to start. That is, given k^0, the initial motion of the system could be $\dot{k}'$, $\dot{k}''$, or $\dot{k}'''$.

To proceed further, some assumptions are required. The following seem reasonable: (1) the capital-labor ratio $k(t)$ is continuous in t; and (2) the motion of the system is such that the continuity of $\dot{k}(t)$ in t is preserved whenever possible. If the full-employment assumption is maintained, property (1) is justified because the quantities of neither machine nor workers can "jump" at an instant in time due to obvious physical considerations. Assumption (2) is more suspect, but it will suffice here to say that on intuitive grounds we may not expect the equilibrium values of variables to change by finite jumps unless there is some "force" acting upon them.

What, then, is the dynamic evolution of this noncausal two-sector economy under our assumptions? The arrows on the curve in Figure 3.7 indicate equilibrium motion, and suppose that we pick $(k^0, \dot{k}'/k^0)$ as an arbitrary starting point. [Given the initial condition $k(0) = k^0$, we could just as well have started at $(k^0, \dot{k}''/k^0)$ or $(k^0, \dot{k}'''/k^0)$.] The motion from our starting point eventually takes the system to the point labeled A. From point A, motion *cannot* proceed along the curve because the arrows indicating equilibrium motion point in the opposite direction. The *only* alternative is for $\dot{k}$ to jump down to the point labeled B. At the instant this jump occurs $\dot{k}(t)$ is discontinuous while $k(t)$ remains continuous, which is consistent with assumptions (1) and (2). From point B the system moves smoothly along the curve, eventually reaching point C. Now, for exactly the same reasons as at point A, a jump to point D must occur. The motion proceeds smoothly along the equilibrium curve from D to A, after which the cyclic motion A-B-C-D repeats itself forever.[26]

In concluding this section we emphasize that there are two important differences between the one-commodity model discussed in Section 3.2 and the two-sector story told here:

First, even when we take the rate of labor force growth, g, as exogenous and assume equal saving propensities out of labor and rental incomes ($s_w = s_r = s$), the two models can exhibit qualitatively different behavior: in the one-commodity world any steady-state equilibrium is necessarily unique and stable, but in the two-sector model there may exist multiple steady-state equilibria with alternating stability properties (compare Figure 3.1b with Figure 3.6).

Second, no issue of causality arises in the one-sector model, and consequently cyclic behavior of $k(t)$ is precluded. On the other hand, in the two-sector model there may exist multiple instantaneous general equilibrium solutions for some values of the capital–labor ratio k, and this fact gives rise to the possible existence of cyclic behavior for $k(t)$ as illustrated in Figure 3.7.

The economic significance of these differences depends upon one's views as to the purpose of such models, aside from their theoretical interest. If one believes that macroeconomic models which allow for the possibilities of unemployment, inflation, and other phenomena of policy interest must take into account changes in capital stocks (rather than focusing only upon the short run with capital stocks fixed), then one lesson we have learned is that in general simple answers should not be expected. The existence of multiple steady-states and cyclic behavior in simple two-sector cases strongly suggests that macroeconomic models with an "aggregate production function," analogous to the one-sector model, may perhaps be misleading – even dangerously so – as to the types of dynamic behavior that may occur in actual economies of the type we are attempting to model.

3.7. A simple two-asset model: introduction to monetary growth models

We have stressed that a crucial economic feature of the models considered thus far in this chapter is that they contain only one asset, the single type of capital good, and hence total wealth in the economy is identically equal to the total capital stock. We now introduce a second asset, called *money,* but retain the one-commodity technology developed in Section 3.2. Money serves as our *numéraire* and we define

> p = price of the one commodity (''output'') in terms of money[27].

The previous link between net capital formation and net saving now is broken. In our one-asset models it was necessarily true that net saving, net capital formation, and the change in wealth are all equal. However, suppose that economic agents in our two-asset model make a decision to save S units of the commodity. A *second* decision is also required: How should S be allocated between new money holdings on the one hand and net capital formation on the other? This decision is a simple example of the general *portfolio-choice problem* facing economic agents living in a multiasset economy who must decide in what forms – in which assets – they wish to hold their wealth.

For our monetary growth model, the value of wealth in terms of output or *real wealth* is equal to the capital stock plus the value of the stock of money in terms of output:

$$W \equiv K + \frac{M}{p}. \tag{3.7.1}$$

Whatever form it may take, aggregate saving in real terms is equal to the change in real wealth, $\dot{W}$, and this equality is expressed by the fundamental *flow equilibrium condition,*

> change in real wealth = real saving

or

$$\dot{W} = S. \tag{3.7.2}$$

Moreover, since we shall want to define

> *real disposable income* = $Y_D \equiv S + C$ $\qquad$ (3.7.3)

where C is consumption of the single commodity, it follows immediately that

$$Y_D = \dot{W} + C. \tag{3.7.4}$$

Many misunderstandings about the proper concept of disposable income can be avoided by using the foregoing chain of reasoning; the flow equilibrium condition (3.7.2) together with the definition (3.7.3) enables one to *derive* expressions for disposable income such as (3.7.4) and (3.7.6).

Differentiating (3.7.1) with respect to time yields

$$\begin{aligned}
\dot{W} &= \dot{K} + \frac{M}{p}\left(\frac{\dot{M}}{M} - \frac{\dot{p}}{p}\right) \\
&= \dot{K} + \frac{\dot{M}}{p} - \frac{\dot{p}}{p}\frac{M}{p}.
\end{aligned} \tag{3.7.5}$$

We then substitute (3.7.5) into (3.7.4) to obtain

$$Y_D = C + \dot{K} + \frac{\dot{M}}{p} - \frac{\dot{p}}{p}\frac{M}{p}. \tag{3.7.6}$$

Equation (3.7.6) has a simple interpretation in terms of macroeconomic principles:

> Real disposable income (Y_D) is equal to consumption (C) plus net capital formation ($\dot{K}$) plus the real value of money transfer payments ($\dot{M}/p$) *minus* the rate of inflation times the real value of the money stock.

The last term, $-(\dot{p}/p)(M/p)$, is the return on real money balances. Sometimes $+(\dot{p}/p)(M/p)$ is identified as *the inflation tax*, but there are other concepts of inflation taxes, and we shall not pursue the issue here, as it is not relevant to the questions at hand. Note, however, that we have omitted taxes and government spending. If real *net* taxes and real government spending (i.e., *net* taxes and government spending measured in terms of the single produced commodity) are denoted by T and G, respectively, then (3.7.6) is modified to

$$Y_D = C + \dot{K} + G - T - \frac{\dot{p}}{p}\frac{M}{p}, \tag{3.7.6a}$$

while the real government deficit is

$$G - T = \frac{\dot{M}}{p}. \tag{3.7.7}$$

Equation (3.7.7) represents a very simple form of the *government budget constraint*. The government's deficit always must be financed somehow, and in this case the only way it can do so is by printing money and issuing it at the flow rate $\dot{M}/p$. However, real *net* taxes equal real tax revenues minus real transfer payments. We *assume* that money is introduced into the economy by making transfer payments to economic agents at the flow rate $\dot{M}/p$, so that defining

Z = real value of tax revenues,

we have net taxes of $T = Z - \dot{M}/p$, and hence (3.7.7) becomes

$$G - T = G - \left(Z - \frac{\dot{M}}{p} \right) = \frac{\dot{M}}{p} \tag{3.7.8}$$

or

$$G - Z = 0. \tag{3.7.9}$$

We simplify our exposition by setting $G = Z = 0$. However, the economic principles enunciated above will allow an interested reader to modify the model below in a variety of ways: for example, government bonds could be introduced, thereby modifying the government budget constraint because issuing bonds provides an alternative means (besides issuing money) of financing the deficit.

The portfolio-choice problem mentioned at the beginning of this section is simplified drastically because of the unrealistic assumption that there is no uncertainty. In fact, however, there need not be perfect foresight into the infinite future; it will suffice to assume that economic agents always know with certainty the current values of every economic variable plus the current rate of change in the price level, $\dot{p}$. The assumption that every current price rate of change is known with certainty is called *perfect myopic foresight*.[28]

Once again two alternative forms of economic organization, as well as any mixture of the two, are possible. Consider first the case in which firms rent the capital goods that are used to produce the single type of commodity as the output. Per capita money profits measured in current dollars $[\pi]$ equal the value of per capita net output $[pf(k) - \delta pk]$ minus the per capita cost of capital and labor inputs. Let

q = money net rental rate for 1 unit of capital stock,
w = money wage rate.

The per capita cost of inputs is then

$qk + w$,

and per capita net money profits are

$$\pi = p[f(k) - \delta k] - qk - w. \tag{3.7.10}$$

Competitive firms maximize π, taking p, q, and w as fixed, thereby implying the necessary condition

$$\frac{d\pi}{dk} = p[f'(k) - \delta] - q = 0 \tag{3.7.11}$$

which may be written as the familiar marginal condition

$$\text{net marginal product of capital} = f'(k) - \delta = \frac{q}{p}$$

$$= \text{real rental rate for capital.} \tag{3.7.12}$$

But what about the owners of the capital who rent to firms? For these owners to be in portfolio equilibrium, in the absence of risk they must be indifferent between holding their wealth in the form of capital and in the form of the alternative asset, money. Accordingly, the net money yields from these two alternative assets must be equalized if portfolio equilibrium prevails. The net money rental income from 1 unit of the capital stock is equal to q, so that the income per unit of money is q/p. However, 1 unit of capital is changing value (in terms of money) at the rate $\dot{p}$, so that the owners of capital also realize capital gains (or losses) per unit of money equal to $\dot{p}/p$. The sum of the latter two returns is the total yield to an owner of capital per unit of money, and in portfolio equilibrium this sum must equal the money rate of interest, r_0:

$$\frac{q}{p} + \frac{\dot{p}}{p} = r_0. \tag{3.7.13}$$

Equation (3.7.13) is of exactly the same form as the discrete-time conditions stated in equation (2.3.7); indeed, they are derived from identical economic principles.

Let us now suppose that firms own their own capital. Upon reflection it should be evident that this alternative form of economic organization can make no difference, for profit-maximizing firms owning capital must take into account the returns on the capital stock they own.[29] However, because the economic principles discussed here are so fundamental to important issues arising in subsequent chapters, we shall analyze in detail the case in which firms own their own capital.

Current per capita money profits $[\pi]$ are now equal to the value of net output $[pf(k) - \delta pk]$ plus the change in the value of the capital stock $[\dot{p}k]$ *minus* the opportunity cost incurred by having the capital stock used for production $[r_0pk]$ minus the wage rate:

$$\pi = p[f(k) - \delta k] + \dot{p}k - r_0pk - w. \tag{3.7.14}$$

Competitive firms maximize π by selecting the optimal value of k for given p, $\dot{p}$, r_0, and w, thereby implying the necessary condition

$$\frac{d\pi}{dk} = p[f'(k) - \delta] + \dot{p} - r_0p = 0. \tag{3.7.15}$$

But (3.7.15) may be written as

$$f'(k) - \delta + \frac{\dot{p}}{p} = r_0, \tag{3.7.16}$$

and clearly (3.7.16) is *equivalent* to (3.7.12) and (3.7.13) taken together. The economic reason for this equivalence, of course, is that we have properly taken into account the opportunity cost entailed by a firm operating with a capital stock valued at pk; this opportunity cost is equal to the money rate of interest times the value of tied-up capital.

How is the competitive wage rate w determined? A zero-profit equilibrium condition imposed on (3.7.14) yields

$$\pi = p[f(k) - \delta k] + \dot{p}k - r_0 pk - w = 0 \qquad (3.7.17)$$

or

$$\text{real wage rate} \equiv \frac{w}{p} = f(k) - \delta k + \left(\frac{\dot{p}}{p} - r_0\right) k. \quad (3.7.18)$$

However, from (3.7.16) [or from (3.7.10) with $\pi = 0$, (3.7.12), and (3.7.13)],

$$\frac{\dot{p}}{p} - r_0 = -f'(k) + \delta,$$

and substituting the latter into (3.7.18) gives

$$\frac{w}{p} = f(k) - kf'(k). \qquad (3.7.19)$$

When $f(k)$ is interpreted as the per capita version of a constant-returns-to-scale function in K and L, that is, when

$$f(k) \equiv F\left(\frac{K}{L}, 1\right) = \frac{F(K, L)}{L}, \qquad (3.7.20)$$

we have the familiar marginal conditions

$$\frac{w}{p} = f(k) - kf'(k) = \frac{\partial F}{\partial L} \qquad (3.7.21)$$

$$= \text{marginal product of labor}$$

and

$$\frac{q}{p} = f'(k) - \delta = \frac{\partial F}{\partial K} - \delta \qquad (3.7.22)$$

$$= \text{net marginal product of capital.}$$

The development of the remainder of our monetary growth

model is straightforward. We already have derived the following building blocks:

Production function and national income identity:

$$\dot{k} = f(k) - c - (g + \delta)k. \tag{3.7.23a}$$

Profit maximization and portfolio equilibrium:

$$f'(k) - \delta + \frac{\dot{p}}{p} = r_0. \tag{3.7.23b}$$

Flow equilibrium condition:

$$\dot{W} = S. \tag{3.7.23c}$$

Per capita real disposable income (see Exercise 3.6):

$$y_D \equiv c + \dot{k} + g\left(k + \frac{m}{p}\right) + \frac{\dot{m}}{p} - \frac{\dot{p}}{p}\frac{m}{p}. \tag{3.7.23d}$$

Three ingredients remain to close the model and write it as a system of two differential equations in two variables having the form

$$\dot{k} = \dot{k}(k, x) \qquad \dot{x} = \dot{x}(k, x) \tag{3.7.24}$$

where

$$x \equiv \frac{M/L}{p} \equiv \frac{m}{p} = \text{per capita real money balances.}$$

We shall require (1) a consumption function, (2) a money demand function, and (3) an assumption about how $\dot{m}$ is determined.

We postulate a consumption function of the simple linear form

$$c = \beta y_D, \quad 0 < \beta < 1, \qquad s \equiv 1 - \beta, \tag{3.7.25}$$

and a demand for money function

$$\frac{m}{p} \equiv x = \phi(k, r_0) \tag{3.7.26}$$

where

$$\frac{\partial \phi}{\partial k} > 0, \qquad \frac{\partial \phi}{\partial r_0} < 0.$$

We shall not discuss the specification for the money demand function, but rather here only note that *any* specification that implies the existence of a function

$$r_0 = \Psi(k, x) \qquad \text{with } \frac{\partial \Psi}{\partial k} > 0, \quad \frac{\partial \Psi}{\partial x} < 0, \tag{3.7.27}$$

will suffice for our purposes; the particular functional form (3.7.26) is but one example that meets this requirement. However, observe that equation (3.7.27) is intuitively plausible. It asserts that the money rate of interest falls with increases in the real per capita money stock, and rises with increases in the capital–labor ratio. These effects are consistent with portfolio equilibrium combined with a transactions demand for money that rises with the capital–labor ratio.

Finally, we complete the model by setting

$$\frac{\dot{M}}{M} \equiv \theta = \text{exogenous policy parameter.} \tag{3.7.28}$$

It then follows that

$$\dot{m} = (\theta - g)m \tag{3.7.29}$$

and

$$\dot{x} = \left(\theta - g - \frac{\dot{p}}{p} \right) x. \tag{3.7.30}$$

Algebraic manipulation of (3.7.23a), (3.7.23d), (3.7.25), and the definitions of x and θ, left as Exercise 3.7 for the reader, results in

$$\dot{k} = sf(k) - (1 - s) \left(\theta - \frac{\dot{p}}{p} \right) x - (g + s\delta)k. \tag{3.7.31}$$

Thus it remains only to express $\dot{p}/p$ as a function of k and x, for then substitution of this function into (3.7.30) and (3.7.31) will enable us to express both $\dot{k}$ and $\dot{x}$ as functions of only k and x.

Profit-maximization and portfolio equilibrium conditions implicit in (3.7.23b) along with (3.7.27) (which is implied by the money demand function) immediately yield

$$-\frac{\dot{p}}{p} = f'(k) - \delta - \Psi(k, x). \tag{3.7.32}$$

Thus we finally have the following two-dimensional differential equation system:

$$
\begin{aligned}
\dot{k} &= \dot{k}(k, x) \\
&= sf(k) - (1 - s)[f'(k) - \delta - \Psi(k, x) + \theta]x \\
&\quad - (g + s\delta)k \\
\dot{x} &= \dot{x}(k, x) = [f'(k) - \delta - \Psi(k, x) + \theta - g]x.
\end{aligned} \tag{3.7.33}
$$

Note first that $(\bar{x}, \bar{k}) = (0, \bar{k})$, where $\bar{k}$ satisfies

$$sf(\bar{k}) - (g + s\delta)\bar{k} = 0,$$

is a rest point of the system (3.7.33) for which $\dot{k} = \dot{x} = 0 = \dot{k}(\bar{k}, 0) = \dot{x}(\bar{k}, 0)$. This rest point, of course, is one where real per capita money balances, $x \equiv m/p$, are zero, so we are back in a world for which there is no money.

However, by imposing suitable regularity conditions upon $f(k)$ and $\Psi(k, x)$, the existence of a unique rest point $(k^*, x^*) > (0, 0)$ can be established. One may then perform a number of "comparative dynamics" exercises asking how the dynamic equilibrium point (k^*, x^*) changes with respect to changes in our one policy parameter, namely the rate of growth in nominal money stock, θ. The following conclusions emerge:

(1) An increase in θ will increase the equilibrium capital–labor ratio (i.e., $dk^*/d\theta > 0$). In this sense, "money matters."

(2) The equilibrium rate of inflation is

$$\left(\frac{\dot{p}}{p}\right)^* = \theta - g,$$

and thus

$$\frac{d(\dot{p}/p)^*}{d\theta} = 1 > 0.$$

(3) $\bar{k} > k^*$; that is, the rest point "without money" is featured by a higher capital–labor ratio than the one with positive real money balances. However, if $\bar{k}$ should happen to lie above the Golden Rule value, a reduction in the capital–

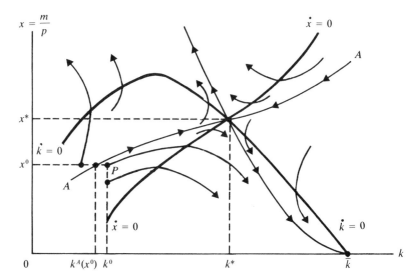

Figure 3.8. The steady-state equilibrium at (k^*, x^*) is a saddle-point. Only the path labeled AA converges to this saddlepoint.

labor ratio from $\bar{k}$ to k^* may be desirable, since $\bar{k}$ is a consumption-inefficient steady-state equilibrium.

The dynamic behavior of the model is illustrated by Figure 3.8, and obviously it is considerably more complex than anything yet encountered. The ''no money'' equilibrium point $(\bar{k}, 0)$ is *stable* in the sense that $\lim_{t\to\infty} k(t) = \bar{k}$ for all initial starting points (k^0, x^0) lying below the curve labeled AA. The equilibrium $(k^*, x^*) > (0, 0)$ is a *saddlepoint,* and the stability property

$$\lim_{t\to\infty} k(t) = k^*, \qquad \lim_{t\to\infty} x(t) = x^*$$

prevails *if and only if* the initial starting point (k^0, x^0) lies *exactly* on the AA curve. This curve is called the *stable arm of the saddlepoint* or, more generally, the *convergent manifold* of the dynamic system (3.7.33).

Suppose, for example, that we select an arbitrary initial value for per capita real balances, some $x^0 > 0$. Let us consider the evolution of $\{k(t), x(t)\}$ over time when the initial capital–labor ratio, k^0, lies just to the right of the capital–labor associated with x^0 on the AA curve (e.g., a point such as that labeled P in Figure 3.8). Because from (3.7.32) we have

$$\frac{\partial(\dot{p}/p)}{\partial k} = \frac{\partial \Psi}{\partial k} - f''(k) > 0, \qquad (3.7.34)$$

at $x = x^0$ we know that the corresponding inflation rate is "too high" in the sense that it is larger than it would have been if k^0 had been the "*correct*" value on AA, namely $k^A(x^0)$. The yield on holding capital includes capital gains, and loosely speaking, economic agents would be willing to hold larger real balances if only the yield on the capital asset were not so high because of "excessive inflation," a $\dot{p}/p$ that is "too large." Under these circumstances inspection of the $\dot{k}$ equation reveals that k will continue to grow, and portfolio managers are willing to hold this growing capital stock only because the rate of inflation continues to grow and there are capital gains. This process counteracts the tendency for the yield on capital to fall because of accumulation [since $f''(k) < 0$].

The process continues, and the system is driven toward the "no-money" equilibrium $(\bar{k}, 0)$.[30] Analogous stories can be told starting from any other initial point (k^0, x^0) not lying on the stable AA arm of the saddlepoint equilibrium.

Is there any reason to suspect the existence of some underlying economic mechanism which assures that an economy *always* starts on the stable AA arm? First, note that at an initial time $t = 0$ it is reasonable to take the capital–labor ratio $k(0) = k^0$ and per capita cash balances $m(0) = M(0)/L(0) = m^0$ as exogenously given. Thus, given k^0 and m^0, selecting the "correct" value of x^0 lying on the AA curve, say $x^0 = A(k^0)$, is *equivalent* to selecting the "correct" value of p^0, namely

$$p^0 = \frac{m^0}{A(k^0)} \qquad (3.7.35)$$

where $A(k^0)$ is the value of x^0 on the AA curve for given k^0.

We thus may ask: Is there any reason to suppose that the initial

price level is determined by some mechanism which implies that
(3.7.35) always holds? In a world of perfect *myopic* foresight –
one in which economic agents base current decisions only upon
the levels of current variables and the known inflation rate
$\dot{p}/p$ – the answer is clearly *no*. *Any* initial (positive) value of the
price level is perfectly consistent with all the static equilibrium
conditions in the model. On the other hand, suppose that economic agents look ahead to some finite time $t = \tau$. Again there is
no uncertainty, so the equilibrium paths of all variables are
known from every initial starting point. Now it may be true that
there exists *some* finite time $t = \tau$ such that either

$$p(\tau) = 0$$

or

$$\frac{1}{p(\tau)} = 0$$

for all initial starting points not lying on the stable AA curve.[31]
Since both a zero and an infinite price for commodities at some
finite time τ [when $k(\tau)$ is necessarily positive and finite] is inconsistent with equilibrium in the markets for commodities and
money, all such paths could be rejected as being inconsistent with
market equilibrium for all $t \in [0, \tau]$. However, presumably the
only mechanism by which such paths could be rejected entails the
existence, at time $t = 0$, of future markets for commodities to be
delivered at every future date up to and including $t = \tau$. Thus this
approach for selecting the "correct" p^0 is of dubious relevance,
especially if τ is large.

Another possibility entails a modification of the model to include intertemporal utility maximization on the part of infinitely
lived economic agents. With some rather special assumptions, it
turns out that the condition

$$\lim_{t \to \infty} p(t) \text{ is finite}$$

becomes *necessary* for intertemporal utility maximization, in
which case at least some of the pathological paths can be ruled

out. However, there are sound reasons for skepticism about the relevance of results that crucially depend upon planning for the *infinite* future. For example, it will only take a finite time for our sun to burn out, a fact that vividly illustrates why no one can possibly believe that the model specification will remain appropriate for infinite time.[32]

A third approach is simply to *assume* the result: if p^0 does not lie on the stable AA curve, assume that there must be a discontinuous jump in $p(0)$ to the "correct" value. We will have more to say about this idea in the context of "rational expectations" models with an explicit stochastic process as the source of uncertainty. The "correct" initial price level is then determined by an *assumption* that economic agents believe the path of their *expected* prices is convergent. However, expected and actual price paths coincide with perfect foresight, and the assumption of "convergent expectations" is equivalent to assuming the answer to the question at hand!

Finally, since the government controls the rate of nominal money growth – $\theta \equiv \dot{M}/M$ is a policy parameter – it is possible to derive various "stabilization policies" such that $\lim_{t \to \infty} \{k(t), x(t)\} = (k^*, x^*)$ starting from all initial points $(k^0, x^0) > (0, 0)$. For example, feedback rules of the form

$$\theta = H\left(k, \frac{\dot{p}}{p}\right) \tag{3.7.36}$$

with

$$\frac{\partial H}{\partial k} < 0, \qquad \frac{\partial H}{\partial(\dot{p}/p)} > 1$$

will often suffice. When $\dot{p}/p$ is "too high" the rate of monetary expansion is *increased;* but, for given k, larger real money balances will be held only if r_0 *falls,* and r_0 can fall (again for fixed k) only by *reducing* $\dot{p}/p$. Such counterintuitive stabilization rules should not be taken as serious policy advice; our perfectly competitive model with full employment is not appropriate for addressing traditional macroeconomic policy questions. However, examination of stabilization rules such as (3.7.36) does serve to illustrate the general nature of saddlepoint instability phenomena. The economic cause of such instability can be traced to the portfolio equilibrium equations in multiasset models with perfect myopic foresight. Because the demand for assets depends upon relative price changes, a price *increase* for a particular asset makes it relatively more attractive due to capital gains, thereby increasing demand for that asset and causing its price to rise even further. What is called for is some plausible economic explanation as to why and how such "speculative booms," once started, eventually come to an end.[33] We shall find this unanswered question recurring in subsequent chapters.

We conclude this section by noting that the role of money in this model is somewhat artificial, and we have not at all dealt with some of the crucial features of a monetary economy: for example, why do monetary economies exist; what is the role of money in the context of liquidity and bankruptcy questions; how do utility-maximizing economic agents derive their money demand functions? Despite the obvious shortcomings through our neglect of such important issues, one conclusion stands out: the introduction of a second asset as an alternative form to hold wealth drastically complicates the dynamic behavior of the model. This feature reappears in subsequent chapters, where we will discuss the dynamic behavior of multiasset models with heterogeneous capital goods, for once again we shall find that the dynamic rest points of conventional economic models often are *saddlepoints*. The results of this section serve to demonstrate that such saddlepoint equilibria also arise in one-commodity models, provided that economic agents can hold wealth in more than one form, there is perfect myopic foresight, and portfolio equilibrium prevails.[34]

3.8. Concluding remarks

The life-cycle model studied in Section 3.4c provides a dramatic example of the fact that an intertemporal competitive economy need not be Pareto optimal. Even though consumers maximize their utility functions, firms maximize profits, and perfect competition prevails, there still exist technologically feasible alternative paths along which every consumer can be made better off in the sense of having more consumption in every time period.

This result, it was seen, simply illustrates the general possibility of capital overaccumulation. The Golden Rule point is that steady-state equilibrium at which the rate of interest is equal to the rate of growth ($r = g$), and it serves as a benchmark to distinguish those steady-state equilibria having ''too much'' capital from those that do not. If the exogenously given growth rate exceeds the steady-state interest rate (if $r < g$), that steady-state equilibrium has capital accumulation, and per capita steady-state consumption could be increased by reducing the steady-state capital stock.

More generally, the concept of consumption inefficiency was introduced in Section 3.5b and we saw that the set of consumption efficient paths, E, is a subset of the dynamically efficient paths, D, which in turn is a subset of the technologically feasible paths, F (i.e., $E \subseteq D \subseteq F$). Moreover, Theorem 3.1 provides a necessary and sufficient condition for consumption efficiency. The transversality condition that the value of capital approach zero as the time horizon becomes infinite is only sufficient for consumption efficiency.

Another basic theme running throughout Chapter 3 involves the question of dynamic stability: Starting from an arbitrary initial capital stock, will the economy evolve over time along a time path for which the capital stock converges to some steady-state value? And is this value necessarily the same for all starting points? Standard one-sector models, either with technological change (Section 3.3) or without (Section 3.2), generally are dynamically stable and have unique steady-state equilibria. However, this simple result is not true for either the standard two-sector model (Section 3.6) or the monetary growth model (Section 3.7). Although with special assumptions a two-sector model may converge, starting from an arbitrary initial capital stock, to a unique steady-state equilibrium, in general it is possible that (1) the ultimate steady state depends on the starting point, and

(2) the capital stock might not converge at all, but rather might oscillate around a dynamically unstable steady-state equilibrium.

Stability problems are even more serious in the monetary-growth model, for there we have seen that the steady-state equilibrium point is a saddlepoint; thus, given any initial value of the stocks of capital and money, there corresponds one and only one value of the initial price level for which the economy converges to a steady-state equilibrium having positive real money balances. This type of ''saddlepoint instability'' often occurs in models for which there is a portfolio problem (i.e., in models for which wealth may be held in various different assets). The problem will arise again in Chapter 6 in the context of heterogeneous capital good models, and there we will discuss various mechanisms by which an economy might select the ''right initial conditions'' (i.e., initial conditions that assure convergence to a steady-state equilibrium).

However, before studying the dynamic behavior of economic models with many different types of capital goods (Chapters 5 and 6), we turn in Chapter 4 to a survey of their steady-state properties; these properties constitute much of the so-called ''Cambridge capital theory controversies.''

Exercises

3.1 Derive equation (3.4.4).

3.2 Derive equation (3.5.10).

3.3 Consider a continuous-time model with

$$\dot{k}^t = f(k^t) - c^t - (1 + g)k^t,$$

and let the consumption function be

$$c^t = (1 - s_w)w^t + (1 - s_r)(1 + r^t)k^t$$

where the real wage rate is

$$w^t = f(k^t) - k^t f'(k^t),$$

and the net marginal product of capital is

$$r^t = f'(k^t) - 1.$$

Prove that if $s_w = 0$ and $s_r = 1$, the economy converges to the Golden Rule point with

$$\lim_{t \to \infty} k^t = k^*$$

where k^* denotes the Golden Rule capital–labor ratio.

3.4 Solve the intertemporal utility maximization problem (3.5.12) to derive (3.5.13).

3.5 Prove the equivalence of (3.5.23) and (3.5.24a)–(3.5.24c) by using (3.5.25).

3.6 Derive equation (3.7.23d) from (3.7.6), where, as always, $\dot{L}/L = g$.

3.7 Derive equation (3.7.31) from (3.7.23a), (3.7.23d), (3.7.25), and the definitions of x and θ.

4

Cambridge controversies in capital theory

4.1. Introduction to the controversies: reswitching, paradoxical behavior, aggregate production functions, the labor theory of value, Sraffa's "Standard Commodity," and the neo-Austrian approach and indexes of "roundaboutness"

The Cambridge capital theory controversies, which have flourished since Joan Robinson's 1953 paper, arise when we generalize the one-capital-good models of Chapter 3 and explicitly recognize the existence of heterogeneous capital goods. The issue, of course, is not whether models allowing for heterogeneous capital goods are more realistic than those with one capital good – obviously they are in that we live in a world with many different types of machines (e.g., hammers, tractors, lathes, etc.). Rather, it is to what extent economic insights and significant conclusions rely on the assumption that there is only one type of capital good. That is, given that we live in a world with heterogeneous capital goods, we wish to identify those economic features of one-capital-good models which are dangerously misleading in being either (1) false or (2) true only under unrealistically restrictive circumstances.

Once such features have been identified, and once we understand the behavior of generalized heterogeneous capital-good models, the issue of which model to use hinges upon the fact that

100

all models are simplifications of reality. We can evaluate whether any particular specification is appropriate only if we also carefully delineate the economic questions to be answered by the model. For example, if we wish to examine the relative price of hammers to wrenches, obviously a heterogeneous capital model is necessary. However, as we see in Chapter 5, many results derived for one-capital-good models – the Golden Rule, for example – remain valid despite the existence of heterogeneous capital goods.

Unfortunately, one can never be certain whether the conclusions derived from any particular set of assumptions will be robust when those assumptions are relaxed unless one actually constructs and analyzes the more general model. Since this is a never-ending process, ultimately theoretical models must be rejected or tentatively accepted on the basis of empirical evidence.

In this chapter we limit our attention to steady-state equilibria. Such a limitation is dangerously restrictive, but will serve to introduce both economically relevant as well as the unfortunately misdirected questions that constitute the Cambridge capital theory controversies. In Section 4.2 we study the *choice of technique* (i.e., how particular methods of production are chosen in a steady-state equilibrium with an exogenously given interest rate). In Sections 4.3 and 4.4 we show that "reswitching of techniques" can occur, and the economic implications of such reswitching are examined. Sections 4.5 through 4.7 deal with "regular economies" for which the real Wicksell effect, as defined in Section 4.5, is always negative. Such economies exhibit behavior that in some important qualitative respects is similar to that of the standard one-sector model. Section 4.8 contains a critique of the labor theory of value, and Section 4.9 is a discussion of Sraffa's unsuccessful attempt to rescue certain results which hold only under the extraordinarily restrictive conditions that render valid a labor theory of value. Attempts to "solve" capital theoretic problems by defining certain neo-Austrian indexes which measure the "roundaboutness of production techniques" (e.g., some measure of the "length" of production processes) are discussed in Section

4.10, and it is seen that no "well-behaved" index of "round-aboutness" exists. Exercise 4.4 is designed to illustrate these important results.

All the issues discussed in Chapter 4 are predicated upon the completely unrealistic assumption that some steady-state equilibrium always prevails; this assumption precludes an analysis of the economically feasible options, namely the set of dynamic paths that are technologically feasible from specified initial conditions. As already noted in Chapter 1, many misguided economic questions have preoccupied much of the literature; Chapter 4 is intended to acquaint students with some of these mistaken approaches so that they might avoid unproductive research topics.

4.2. **Leontief–Sraffa models and the choice of technique**

One crucial aspect of the Cambridge controversy concerns the "reswitching of techniques," or simply "reswitching." To define "reswitching" and to illustrate the economic issues involved, we shall develop the simplest Leontief–Sraffa model. However, the results of this section do not depend upon this particular formulation of the model and are valid generally.

In the economy there are n different types of commodities produced, which, together with homogeneous labor, are used as productive inputs in their own production. For simplicity we suppose that only commodity 1 is also consumed. Thus for commodity 1 we have

$$Y_1^{t+1} = C^{t+1} + K_1^{t+1} \tag{4.2.1}$$

where Y_1^{t+1} = quantity of commodity 1 produced during period t and available for use at the beginning of period $t + 1$;

C^{t+1} = quantity of commodity 1 consumed at the beginning (or perhaps during) period $t + 1$;

K_1^{t+1} = quantity of commodity 1 used as a capital input for the production of other commodities during period $t + 1$.

None of the other commodities are ever consumed, so that we have

$$Y_i^{t+1} = K_i^{t+1}, \qquad i = 2, \ldots, n. \tag{4.2.2}$$

Only positions that exhibit dynamic equilibrium will be considered, and as we take the homogeneous labor supply as fixed at the quantity L, such steady-state equilibria necessitate that

$$C^{t+1} = C^t \equiv C \qquad \text{for all } t \tag{4.2.3a}$$

and

$$K_i^{t+1} = K_i^t \equiv K_i \qquad \text{for all } t \text{ and for all } i = 1, \ldots, n. \tag{4.2.3b}$$

Of course, when (4.2.3a) and (4.2.3b) hold, per capita quantities are also constant over time at the levels

$$c \equiv \frac{C}{L} \tag{4.2.4a}$$

and

$$k_i \equiv \frac{K_i}{L}, \qquad i = 1, \ldots, n. \tag{4.2.4b}$$

The *technology* consists of alternative techniques of production which are all of the Leontief–Sraffa fixed-coefficient type. For example, when the economy is producing by using technique a, the numbers a_{ij} are taken to be fixed, nonnegative parameters with

a_{0j} = quantity of labor directly required to produce 1 unit of output of the jth-type commodity ($j = 1, \ldots, n$);

a_{ij} = quantity of the ith-type capital input ($i = 1, \ldots, n$) directly required to produce 1 unit of output of the jth-type commodity ($j = 1, \ldots, n$).

For any alternative method of production (say technique b), different fixed coefficients (say b_{ij}'s) are defined analogously.

No matter what technique of production is used, full employment of labor and capital goods is presumed. For example, letting K_i^a denote the steady-state quantity of the ith-type capital good when technique a is used, we have the full-employment conditions for capital goods

$$K_i^a = \sum_{j=1}^n a_{ij} Y_j, \qquad i = 1, \ldots, n, \qquad (4.2.5a)$$

and for labor

$$L = \sum_{j=1}^n a_{0j} Y_j. \qquad (4.2.5b)$$

Finally, as is traditional in all the literature dealing with this problem, we take the interest rate as an exogenously given nonnegative number, denoted by r. For alternative values of r, the economy may employ different techniques of production and hence find itself in different steady-state equilibria. It is important to note that the formulation does *not* constitute a general equilibrium model, since the interest rate is not determined endogenously. The model described is partial equilibrium in nature, with the interest rate (denoted by r) serving as a parameter.

Given some value of r, what determines equilibrium prices? First consider technique a, remembering that we are confining our attention to steady-state equilibria in which current prices must satisfy

$$P_i^{t+1} = P_i^t \equiv P_i, \qquad i = 1, \ldots, n. \qquad (4.2.6)$$

The price of the jth commodity, in competitive equilibrium, equals the unit cost of production, this cost consisting of the cost of (1) labor, (2) capital inputs, and (3) the opportunity cost incurred because capital inputs must be purchased at the beginning of a period although output is not available until the end of that production period.

Let W denote the nominal wage rate, and assume that workers are paid at the end of the production period. The cost of labor required to produce 1 unit of commodity j is simply

$$Wa_{0j}, \tag{4.2.7a}$$

a result that obviously follows from the definition of a_{0j}. Analogously, from the definition of the a_{ij}'s, we have that the average total cost of the capital inputs used to produce commodity j is

$$\sum_{i=1}^{n} P_i a_{ij}. \tag{4.2.7b}$$

However, since these capital inputs must be purchased at the beginning of the production period, a competitive firm producing the jth commodity incurs an opportunity cost per unit produced of

$$r \sum_{i=1}^{n} P_i a_{ij} \tag{4.2.7c}$$

where r denotes the steady-state interest rate.[1] Adding these three costs – (4.2.7a), (4.2.7b), and (4.2.7c) – gives prices for all j:

$$P_j = Wa_{0j} + (1 + r) \sum_{i=1}^{n} P_i a_{ij}, \qquad j = 1, \ldots, n. \tag{4.2.8}$$

The n price equations represented by (4.2.8) involve the $n + 2$ variables $P_1, \ldots, P_n$, W, and r. We can divide each equation in (4.2.8) by W to express prices in terms of the nominal wage rate as *numéraire;* that is, when we define

$$p_j \equiv \frac{P_j}{W}, \qquad j = 1, \ldots, n, \tag{4.2.9}$$

from (4.2.8) we have that

$$p_j = a_{0j} + (1 + r) \sum_{i=1}^{n} p_i a_{ij}, \qquad j = 1, \ldots, n. \tag{4.2.10}$$

The system (4.2.10) has n equations in the $n + 1$ variables $p_1, \ldots, p_n$, and r. Provided that the a_{ij}'s meet certain conditions which need not bother us, there exists a number $r_a^* > 0$ such that there exist functions $\psi_j^a(r)$ with

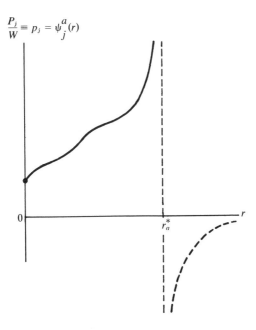

Figure 4.1. Equilibrium steady-state prices for commodity j when production technique a is used.

$$p_j = \psi_j^a(r) > 0 \qquad \text{for all } r \text{ satisfying } 0 \leq r < r_a^*,$$
(4.2.11)

as illustrated in Figure 4.1. The superscript a on the function $\psi_j^a(r)$ indicates that these are the equilibrium prices (normalized in terms of the wage rate) when technique a is used.[2]

Referring to Figure 4.1, we see that at $r = 0$, $p_j = \psi_j^a(0) > 0$; then p_j rises monotonically with r, because higher values of r involve larger opportunity costs reflected in price. As r approaches r_a^* from below, p_j approaches $+\infty$. Mathematically, equations (4.2.10) have solutions for $r > r_a^*$, but these entail *negative* prices (the dashed curve in Figure 4.1) and hence are economically meaningless.[3]

The reciprocals of the $\psi_j^a(r)$ functions define the *factor-price curves for technique a*:

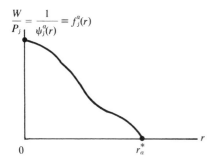

Figure 4.2. Factor-price curve for commodity j using technique a.

$$\frac{W}{P_j} = \frac{1}{\psi_j^a(r)} \equiv f_j^a(r), \qquad 0 \leqslant r < r_a^*, \qquad j = 1, \ldots, n.$$

$$(4.2.12)$$

The factor-price curve for commodity j, as illustrated in Figure 4.2, gives the real wage in terms of the jth commodity as a function of r. At $r = 0$ this real wage is at its maximum value, and it falls monotonically with increases in r, approaching zero as r approaches r_a^*.

We now turn to the question of the *choice of technique*. Thus far we have seen how equilibrium prices are determined when the production coefficients are $(a_{0j}, a_{1j}, \ldots, a_{nj}), j = 1, \ldots, n$, a set of production activities that defines technique a. Suppose that the nth commodity can also be produced with different fixed coefficients $(b_{0n}, b_{1n}, \ldots, b_{nn})$. Even though the method of production (or *activity*) for only the nth commodity has changed, the set of coefficients

$$a_{01}, a_{11}, \ldots, a_{n1}$$
$$\cdot$$
$$\cdot$$
$$\cdot$$
$$a_{0,n-1}, a_{1,n-1}, \ldots, a_{n,n-1}$$
$$b_{0n}, b_{1n}, \ldots, b_{nn}$$

defines a new technique for the economy which we shall call technique b.[4]

Equilibrium prices using technique b are derived exactly as before, and we have

$$p_j = \psi_j^b(r), \qquad 0 \leq r < r_b^*, \quad j = 1, \ldots, n. \qquad (4.2.13)$$

Given some value of r, say $r = \bar{r} > 0$, which is less than both r_a^* and r_b^*, will an economy in competitive equilibrium use technique a or technique b? Clearly, it will produce using that technique which gives the *lower* prices. For suppose initially that technique a is employed. If the activity $(b_{0n}, b_{1n}, \ldots, b_{nn})$ were used to produce the nth commodity, its unit cost of production evaluated at technique a prices is

$$c_n \equiv b_{0n} + (1 + \bar{r}) \sum_{i=1}^{n} \psi_i^a(\bar{r}) b_{in}. \qquad (4.2.14)$$

Now if $c_n > \psi_n^a(\bar{r})$, the alternative activity for producing the nth commodity will not be introduced, and technique a will be used at $r = \bar{r}$. If, on the other hand, $c_n < \psi_n^a(\bar{r})$, clearly the alternative activity will be introduced because there exist "excess profits"

$$\psi_n^a(\bar{r}) - c_n > 0. \qquad (4.2.15)$$

Such excess profits cannot persist in a competitive equilibrium, so all prices must equal the $\psi_i^b(\bar{r})$ values appropriate for technique b. We thus see that at $r = \bar{r}$ we have

$$p_n = \psi_n^b(\bar{r}) = b_{0n} + (1 + \bar{r}) \sum_{i=1}^{n} \psi_i^b(\bar{r}) b_{in}$$

$$c_n \equiv b_{0n} + (1 + \bar{r}) \sum_{i=1}^{n} \psi_i^a(\bar{r}) b_{in}$$

$$\psi_n^a(\bar{r}) = a_{0n} + (1 + \bar{r}) \sum_{i=1}^{n} \psi_i^a(\bar{r}) a_{in}. \qquad (4.2.16)$$

The foregoing discussion is an elementary example of a much more general result stated here:[5]

THEOREM 4.1. SAMUELSON'S NONSUBSTITUTION
THEOREM

Consider any economy with one primary factor, labor, which is free of joint production and exhibits constant returns to scale in the production of every commodity. Given an exogenous (and economically viable) value of the interest rate, in a competitive steady-state equilibrium the price of every commodity in terms of the wage rate is *minimized*. These steady-state equilibrium prices depend on the value of the interest rate alone and are independent of the quantities produced. Equivalently, in equilibrium the real wage rate in terms of any commodity as *numéraire* – that is, W/P_j for any j – is *maximized* by the "invisible hand" of perfect competition.

This theorem, which represents an essentially trivial generalization of the original theorem and proof given by Samuelson in 1951, does not even necessitate the Leontief–Sraffa fixed-coefficient representation of the technology in this chapter. Most important for our purposes, it enables us to answer the choice of technique question in complete generality. Consider the choice between techniques a and b. Possible factor-price curves in terms of commodity j for these two techniques are illustrated in Figure 4.3a and b. In the case illustrated by Figure 4.3a, technique b dominates technique a in the sense that it generates a higher real wage (a lower price $p_j \equiv P_j/W$) at *every* value of r less than r_b^*. Thus for economic purposes, technique a is irrelevant, at least if we restrict ourselves to steady-state equilibria.

A case of economic interest is depicted in Figure 4.3b. For low values of the interest rate $(0 \leqslant r < r_1)$, the economy is in steady-state equilibrium with technique a since it generates the highest real wage in terms of commodity j (the lowest price $p_j \equiv P_j/W$). However, for higher interest rates $(r_1 < r < r_b^*)$, technique b is used for the same reason. The interest rate $r = r_1$ is termed a *switch point* between techniques a and b. When $r = r_1$,

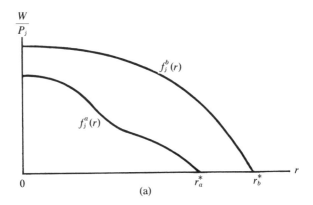

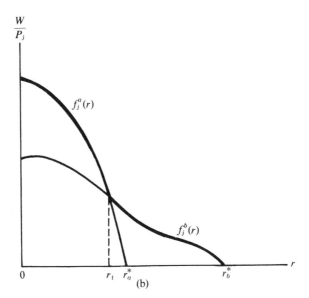

Figure 4.3. (a) Case in which technique a is economically irrelevant because technique b gives a higher real wage (lower price $p_j \equiv P_j/W$) at every feasible value of r. (b) Only technique a is employed for all r such that $0 \leqslant r < r_1$; only technique b is used when $r_1 < r < r_b^*$. The interest rate $r = r_1$ is a *switch point* at which both techniques may coexist in equilibrium. The heavy line represents the economy's *factor-price frontier* and is the outer envelope of the factor-price curves.

both techniques *a* and *b* may be used in equilibrium because both generate *identical* prices.

We see, therefore, that at a switch point prices are identical, or, equivalently the real wages in terms of commodity *j* are identical with

$$f_j^a(r) - f_j^b(r) = 0 \qquad \text{at the switch point } r = r_1. \quad (4.2.17)$$

An immediate consequence of Samuelson's Nonsubstitution Theorem is that the roots of (2.17) *are independent of j*; that is, if (4.2.17) holds for some $r = r_1$, then

$$f_i^a(r_1) - f_i^b(r_1) = 0 \qquad \text{for all } i = 1, \ldots, n. \quad (4.2.18)$$

This crucial conclusion follows immediately from the fact, stated in the theorem, that *all* prices, $p_j \equiv P_j/W$, are *simultaneously* minimized in a competitive steady-state equilibrium at a given (feasible) value of the interest rate, *r*.

4.3. The reswitching of techniques

To illustrate the reswitching of techniques, consider a technology, consisting of techniques *a* and *b*, which has factor-price curves as illustrated in Figure 4.4. For interest rates satisfying $0 \leq r < r_1$, technique *a* is employed; for $r_1 < r < r_2$, technique *b* is employed; but technique *a* is employed again for still higher interest rates satisfying $r_2 < r < r_a^*$. The interest rates $r = r_1$ and $r = r_2$ are both *switch points* between techniques *a* and *b*. Technique *a* is said to *recur*, and the economy exhibits the *reswitching of techniques*. In general, there is nothing to preclude reswitching. Our assumptions thus far do imply that every factor-price curve is downward-sloping with

$$\frac{d(W/P_i)}{dr} < 0, \qquad i = 1, \ldots, n, \quad (4.3.1)$$

(see Exercise 4.1), but there is no reason why two downward-sloping factor-price curves cannot intersect several times.[6] Indeed, that such a result is possible should have been clear from Irving Fisher's classic 1907 work, *The Rate of Interest;*[7] it is a

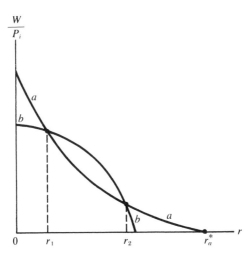

Figure 4.4. Reswitching between techniques a and b with switch points at $r = r_1$ and $r = r_2$.

straightforward generalization of "multiple internal rates of return" which are known to exist for intertemporal investment options.

Why, then, did the 1965 "discovery" of reswitching attract such attention?[8] The reason is that reswitching implies the existence of certain types of "paradoxical behavior." The "paradox" is that reswitching contradicts traditional neoclassical intuition stemming from economic models with a single type of capital good. To illustrate how widespread this intuition once was, one need only refer to the sixth edition of Samuelson's famous elementary textbook (1964, pp. 595–7), from which the following neoclassical parable is summarized.

For simplicity ignore technological change and the growth of any primary factors so that an economy in steady-state equilibrium enjoys a constant per capita level of consumption. Initially, at time $t = 0$, suppose this economy has a steady-state consumption level c', but that consumption is lowered to $c' - \epsilon$ for the time interval from $t = 0$ to $t = \Delta t$; see Figure 4.5a. The foregone

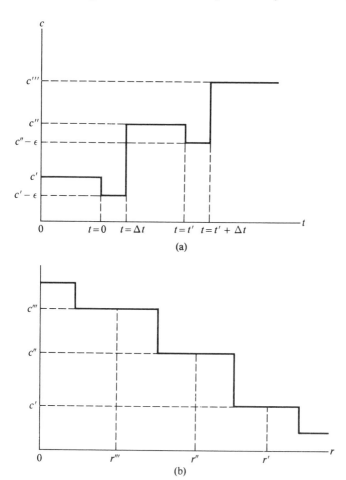

Figure 4.5. Transitions between steady-state equilibria.

consumption over this time interval frees resources that are used to produce more capital goods. Because there has been an act of "saving" with consumption lowered from c' to $c' - \epsilon$, at time $t = \Delta t$, the economy has larger stocks of capital goods than it would have had if consumption had been kept at the higher constant level c'.

With these larger stocks of capital goods at time $t = \Delta t$, the economy can enter a new steady-state equilibrium having per capita consumption $c'' > c'$. Moreover, as shown in Figure 4.5b, the steady-state interest rate falls from $r = r'$ to $r = r''$, reflecting that the steady-state with $c = c''$ has "more capital" than the steady-state with $c = c'$.

The economy can remain in this new steady-state equilibrium with per capita consumption c'' and an interest rate r''. Suppose, however, that at time $t = t'$ the previous act of reducing consumption is replicated: consumption is lowered to $c'' - \epsilon$ from time $t = t'$ to time $t = t' + \Delta t$. Once again this lower consumption level frees resources which are used to increase capital stocks. At time $t = t' + \Delta t$ the stocks of capital goods are larger than they would have been if consumption had been held constant at c'' and these larger capital stocks enable the economy to attain yet another steady-state equilibrium with $c''' > c''$. However, because of diminishing returns,

$$c'' - c' > c''' - c'',$$

i.e., the first time consumption is reduced by ϵ for a length of time Δt, the increase in steady-state consumption $(c'' - c')$ is greater than the increase in consumption the second time consumption is so reduced $(c''' - c'')$. And because the steady state with $c = c'''$ has a still larger stock of "capital," the associated steady-state interest rate is again lower with $r''' < r'' < r'$.

This neoclassical parable – which is valid for economies having no joint production and a single type of capital good – is not generally valid in a world with many capital goods. It is false because the relationship between steady-state consumption and the steady-state interest rate is not always as depicted in Figure 4.5b; as we shall see, sometimes a *lower* interest rate may be associated with a *lower* level of per capita consumption. However, the behavior illustrated in Figure 4.5a *is* generally valid, a fact that will become clear from our detailed analysis in Chapter 5.

Many authors can agree that the existence of reswitching is economically unimportant, because, ironically, reswitching *is not necessary* for the conclusion that the neoclassical parable is false.[9] Nevertheless, the existence of reswitching provides a clear and immediate contradiction to the behavior illustrated by Figure 4.5b, and therefore reswitching plays a significant role in *revealing* the possibility of "paradoxical behavior" that contradicts the neoclassical parable. We now turn to proofs of these assertions.

4.4. The implications of reswitching and paradoxical behavior

That the existence of reswitching contradicts the neoclassical parable follows immediately from the fundamental result described below.

THEOREM 4.2

For any technique of production, the height at $r = 0$ of the associated factor-price curve in terms of commodity 1 is equal to the steady-state level of per capita consumption when that technique is employed. That is, denoting per capita consumption when technique α is employed by c^α,

$$c^\alpha = f_1^\alpha(0) \tag{4.4.1}$$

where $f_1^\alpha(r)$ is the factor-price curve in terms of commodity 1 for technique α.

Proof. In general, in a closed economy

net national product = value of consumption + the value of net capital formation;
= total wages + interest on the value of capital.

Since we are restricting our attention to steady states in which the value of net capital formation is zero, we have that

$$\text{net national product} = P_1 C^\alpha + 0 = WL + rV^\alpha \tag{4.4.2}$$

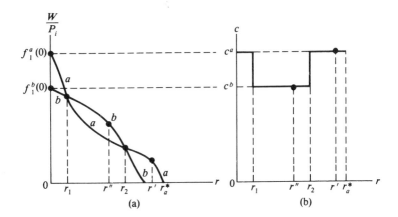

Figure 4.6. The existence of reswitching reveals "paradoxical consumption behavior" which contradicts the neoclassical parable as illustrated in 4.5b.

where V^α is the value of capital in a steady-state equilibrium using technique α. Substituting $r = 0$ into (4.4.2) yields

$$P_1 C^\alpha = WL$$

or

$$\frac{C^\alpha}{L} \equiv c^\alpha = \frac{W}{P_1} = f_1^\alpha(0),$$

as stated in the theorem.

$$Q.E.D.$$

Consider an economy with techniques a and b exhibiting reswitching as illustrated in Figure 4.6a. Suppose that initially there is a steady-state equilibrium at the interest rate r'. We see from Figure 4.6a that in this case technique a is employed. Using Theorem 4.2, we also see that the level of per capita consumption is c^a in Figure 4.6b.

Now assume that this economy, *for whatever reasons,* achieves a new steady-state equilibrium at the *lower* interest rate

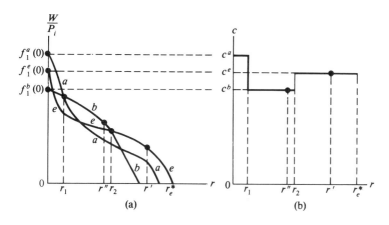

Figure 4.7. For the economy illustrated in (a) and (b), "paradoxical consumption behavior" occurs *without* any reswitching.

$r = r''$. Referring to Figure 4.6a, technique b is then employed and the steady-state level of per capita consumption is also *lower* with $c = c^b < c^a$. *Thus reswitching reveals that lower steady-state interest rates are not always associated with higher levels of steady-state consumption.*

However, reswitching *is not necessary* for this "paradoxical" result. To see this fact, assume that in addition to techniques a and b, an economy has available a third technique, technique e. Assuming that the factor-price curves are as illustrated in Figure 4.7a, *there is no reswitching* in this economy with these three techniques of production. Techniques a, b, and e are employed for interest rates satisfying $0 \leq r < r_1$, $r_1 < r < r_2$, and $r_2 < r < r_e^*$, respectively, while both techniques a and b may be employed at the switch point $r = r_1$ and both techniques b and e may be employed at the switch point $r = r_2$.

Despite the fact that there is no reswitching, "paradoxical consumption behavior" still exists, as is clear from Figure 4.7b. At $r = r'$ technique e is employed and consumption is c^e; but at the *lower* interest rate $r = r''$, technique b is employed and consumption is also *lower*, with $c = c^b < c^e$.

What are we to conclude about the economic significance of these results?

(1) Reswitching itself is interesting only in that its existence clearly reveals that the neoclassical parable is false. However, as we have just seen, the neoclassical parable can be false even when there is no reswitching. Accordingly, any economic restrictions that only preclude the possibility of reswitching are not important.

(2) Paradoxical consumption behavior has been illustrated, but it is clear that other types of paradoxes can also be considered (e.g., the steady-state value of expressions such as the ratio of the value of capital to the value of output will not change monotonically with the steady-state interest rate).

(3) Most important, whether the term "paradox" is appropriate depends upon one's point of view. As stated, the only paradox is that models with heterogeneous capital goods are capable of generating steady-state behavior that is impossible in simple one-capital-good models. Such models, therefore, are seen to lack robustness with respect to the assumption of homogeneous capital. Moreover, restricting attention only to steady-state comparison is unrealistic by precluding examination of the intertemporal options available to an economy with given initial conditions and a given technology. In Chapter 5 we examine the relevant dynamic options open to an economy.

(4) Paradoxical consumption behavior does not depend upon the Leontief–Sraffa specification of the technology with fixed coefficient production techniques. In Section 4.5, when we analyze an economy with a differentiable technology, we will gain additional economic insights into the complexities caused by the presence of heterogeneous capital goods.

4.5. Real Wicksell effects and regular economies[10]

Why is the paradoxical consumption behavior we have discussed – where steady-state consumption rises across steady-state equilibria with increases in the interest or profit rate – economically significant? The answer lies in that macroeconomists, both in the Keynesian and monetarist traditions, find it convenient to employ an aggregate production function in which net national product depends on an index of "capital" and an index of "labor." Moreover, even if we were to build a theoretically rigorous disaggregated macroeconomic model, data limitations would preclude econometric estimation, which is crucial for policy applications. *Thus some degree of aggregation is essential if macroeconomics is to be relevant for policy decisions.*

But, as we have seen, the analysis of reswitching reveals that certain types of paradoxical behavior exist even without reswitching, and this paradoxical behavior is not consistent with the neoclassical parable based on an aggregate production function. Therefore, the paradoxes are significant not in microeconomic applications, where aggregation is not essential, but in macroeconomic applications, where aggregation is a necessity.

The paradoxes revealed by reswitching are significant for at least two other reasons. First, it would be a convenient simplification in many economic problems (cost–benefit analysis, for example) if steady states with lower interest rates (but above the Golden Rule value) always corresponded to higher levels of social welfare as measured by per capita consumption. In such cases the Solow–Swan one-sector model of Chapter 3 provides at least a *qualitatively* correct picture of alternative steady states. Second, when paradoxical consumption behavior does exist, dynamic considerations which we so far have ignored can lead to both multiple and unstable equilibria.

Before discussing these problems, we will derive a necessary and sufficient condition to preclude paradoxical behavior. It will be convenient to consider a differentiable, constant-returns-to-scale technology summarized by the production-possibilities frontier

$$T(c_1 + \dot{k}_1, \ldots, c_n + \dot{k}_n; k_1, \ldots, k_n) = 0 \qquad (4.5.1)$$

where c_i = per capita consumption of commodity i, $i = 1, \ldots, n$;

$\dot{k}_i$ = net per capita capital formation of type i machines, $i = 1, \ldots, n$;

k_i = per capita stock of type i machines, $i = 1, \ldots, n$.

Across steady states where $\dot{k}_i = 0$, $i = 1, \ldots, n$, total differentiation of (4.5.1) yields[11]

$$\sum_{i=1}^{n} T_i \frac{dc_i}{dr} + \sum_{i=1}^{n} T_{n+i} \frac{dk_i}{dr} = 0. \qquad (4.5.2)$$

But competition or efficiency requires that in a steady-state equilibrium

$$T_i = -P_i, \qquad i = 1, \ldots, n,$$

and

$$T_{n+i} = rP_i, \qquad i = 1, \ldots, n$$

where P_i is the price of commodity i and r is the interest or profit rate. Hence we have

$$\sum_{i=1}^{n} P_i \frac{dc_i}{dr} = r \sum_{i=1}^{n} P_i \frac{dk_i}{dr} \qquad (4.5.3a)$$

across steady-state equilibria. Now if a social utility function $u(c_1, \ldots, c_n)$ is maximized, it can be shown that du/dr is proportional to[12]

$$\sum_{i=1}^{n} P_i \frac{dc_i}{dr}.$$

For the simplest case with $u = c_1$, (4.5.3a) reduces to

$$\frac{dc_1}{dr} = r \sum_{i=1}^{n} \frac{P_i}{P_1} \frac{dk_i}{dr}. \qquad (4.5.3b)$$

Thus we have the following fundamental theorem:

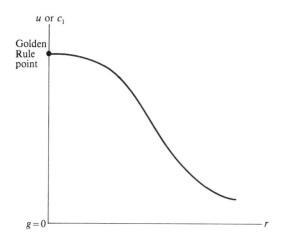

Figure 4.8. A regular economy.

THEOREM 4.3

du/dr (or dc_1/dr) is negative at all values of $r > 0$ if and only if the expression

$$R \equiv \sum_{i=1}^{n} \frac{P_i}{P_1} \frac{dk_i}{dr}$$

is negative at all (feasible) values of $r > 0$.

Following Burmeister and Turnovsky (1972), an economy for which the expression R is negative at all nonnegative values of r is termed *regular*. Regular economies are free of paradoxical consumption behavior. Such a "well-behaved" or regular economy with $R < 0$ is depicted in Figure 4.8; social welfare or c_1 always falls across steady states with increases in r. Figure 4.9 depicts an irregular economy where there exists a paradoxical range for which steady-state social welfare rises with r.

Further, although we have derived our regularity condition for differentiable technologies, an exactly analogous condition

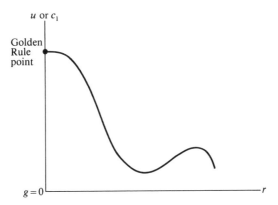

Figure 4.9. An irregular economy exhibiting paradoxical behavior.

occurs in a nondifferentiable Leontief–Sraffa technology. In these cases the expression R is replaced by

$$R^* \equiv \sum_{i=1}^{n} \frac{P_i^j}{P_1^j} \Delta k_i^j, \tag{4.5.4}$$

which must be negative at every switch point j, where P_i^j is the price of commodity i at the switch-point interest rate r_j and Δk_i^j is the increment, as r is *increased* in a small neighborhood of $r = r_j$, to the ith capital stock between the two techniques that are both competitive at the switch point $r = r_j$. These complications have been discussed in detail elsewhere.[13] The important conclusion is that the concept of a regular economy, a necessary and sufficient condition to preclude paradoxical consumption behavior, does not necessitate a differentiable technology.

Luigi Pasinetti has asserted that the "unobtrusive postulate" of neoclassical economics is that the steady-state *value* of the capital stock falls with increases in the steady-state interest or profit rate.[14] This assertion is false, but it relates to our regularity condition and merits elaboration. Let prices be normalized by the rule $P_1 \equiv 1$. The change in the value of capital is

$$\frac{dv}{dr} = \sum_{i=1}^{n} \frac{dP_i}{dr} k_i + \sum_{i=1}^{n} P_i \frac{dk_i}{dr}$$
$$\equiv \quad P \quad + \quad R \tag{4.5.5}$$

where the value of capital is

$$v \equiv \sum_{i=1}^{n} P_i k_i. \tag{4.5.6}$$

The first term, P, is a *price Wicksell effect* equal to the change in v due to the fact that steady-state prices are functions of r. The second term, R (which we require to be negative for a regular economy), is a *real Wicksell effect* equal to the change in v due to the fact that steady-state capital stocks vary with r. But the sign of the price Wicksell effect P, and hence the sign of dv/dr, depends upon the price normalization. Thus the sign of dv/dr is not invariant to the choice of *numéraire!* Once a normalization rule is selected, the sign of P will depend upon capital intensity conditions, a fact that is obvious from the familiar one-capital-good two-sector model. It is foolish to assert that an ''unobtrusive postulate'' of neoclassical economics is sensitive to the choice of *numéraire!*

There is an element of truth in Pasinetti's proposition if we select the nominal wage rate as *numéraire*. In this case define

$$v^w \equiv \sum_{i=1}^{n} p_i \frac{dk_i}{dr} \tag{4.5.7}$$

where, as before, $p_i \equiv P_i/W$; we then have

$$\frac{dv^w}{dr} = \sum_{i=1}^{n} \frac{dp_i}{dr} k_i + \sum_{i=1}^{n} p_i \frac{dk_i}{dr} \tag{4.5.8}$$
$$\equiv P^w \qquad + R^w. \tag{4.5.9}$$

In a non-joint-production technology with only one primary factor, labor, it is true that $dp_i/dr > 0$ for all i provided that labor is required, either directly or indirectly, to produce every commodity. In this case, regardless of capital-intensity conditions, the price Wicksell effect, P^w, is always positive. Hence it is true that

$$\frac{dv^w}{dr} < 0 \quad \text{implies} \quad R^w < 0.$$

That is, the Pasinetti condition that dv^w/dr be negative is *sufficient* for a negative real Wicksell effect ($R^w < 0$). But in general such a condition is not necessary; dv/dr or dv^w/dr may be positive, even for regular economies in which R or R^w is always negative.[15]

Note, however, that the *sign* of the real Wicksell effect does not depend on the price normalization; it is a *numéraire*-free concept, as any "real" expression must be. Thus we have that $R < 0$ if and only if $R^w < 0$.

4.6. **Regular economies and dynamics**[16]

It was the phenomenon of reswitching that triggered the discovery of paradoxical consumption behavior, which in turn led to the concept of a *regular economy* in which

$$R \equiv \sum_{i=1}^{n} \frac{P_i}{P_1} \frac{dk_i}{dr} < 0 \qquad \text{for all (feasible) } r \geqslant 0. \qquad (4.6.1)$$

If an economy is not regular, then at some feasible interest or profit rates, steady-state per capita utility or consumption will not fall with increases in r.

Regular economies constitute a subset of the set of alternative technologies. One property of this subset is that paradoxical behavior is excluded. Do regular economies have other desirable properties? The answer is, *yes*. Thus, as a prelude to Chapter 6, in this section we briefly turn our attention to some dynamic questions.

First, consider the objective functional of the standard optimal control problem

$$\int_{t=0}^{\infty} u[c_1(t), \ldots, c_n(t)]e^{-\rho t} \, dt \qquad (4.6.2)$$

where $\rho > 0$ is the rate of time discount. Often, even when joint production is excluded, the dynamic solutions to the constrained maximization of (4.6.2) can have more than one rest-point equilibrium. In such instances of multiple rest points, the point toward which the optimizing economy converges depends crucially upon the initial capital-stock conditions. Therefore, the dynamics of the problem become very complex, since every rest point cannot be stable in a saddlepoint sense, except in the trivial case when the rest-point equilibrium to (4.6.2) is unique.

Such difficulties do not arise in regular economies; condition (4.6.1) is sufficient for the uniqueness of the rest-point solution to the optimization of (4.6.2).[17] Moreover, in recent work Brock and Scheinkman (1976) have derived a sufficient condition for the global stability of the optimal trajectories which maximize (4.6.2), and this sufficient condition implies that the economy is regular.[18] The latter is really only one example of the close connection between dynamic stability and points that exhibit paradoxical consumption behavior. We now turn to this issue.

In many models steady states that are paradoxical – that is, steady states where the expression R given by (4.6.1) is not negative – are also steady states that are dynamically unstable.[19] Of course, the precise nature of the instability depends upon the particular dynamic rules, but one case is of special interest and will serve as an example of Samuelson's Correspondence Principle.

Consider a model with two capital goods. Per capita utility or social welfare at time t is

$$u^t = F(\dot{k}_1^t, \dot{k}_2^t; k_1^t, k_2^t). \tag{4.6.3}$$

At time $t = 0$, initial per capita stocks, k_1^0 and k_2^0, are given. A *feasible* policy is to remain in a steady-state equilibrium with

$$k_i^t = k_i^0, \qquad i = 1, 2, \tag{4.6.4}$$

with constant per capita utility

$$u^t = u^0 = F(0, 0; k_1^0, k_2^0). \tag{4.6.5}$$

However, as pointed out in another context by Samuelson in 1960, it is usually inefficient to follow the policy (4.6.4)–(4.6.5). When there is more than one capital good, unless the arbitrary initial conditions k_1^0, k_2^0 happen to satisfy Samuelson's dynamic efficiency condition

$$\frac{F_3(0, 0; k_1^0, k_2^0)}{F_1(0, 0; k_1^0, k_2^0)} = \frac{F_4(0, 0; k_1^0, k_2^0)}{F_2(0, 0; k_1^0, k_2^0)}, \tag{4.6.6}$$

a policy other than (4.6.4) can be found which will make everyone better off.

But how should we select among the alternative policies which are "better" than (4.6.4)–(4.6.5)? One rule is the "New York City policy" of never sacrificing *any* present utility for the future, a rule which is consistent with political considerations that would prevent any current sacrifices. Accordingly, we shall hypothesize the following constraints:

For times $\tau \geqslant 0$, a feasible policy is to set utility constant at

$$u^\tau = F(0, 0; k_1^\tau, k_2^\tau).$$

Any path the economy follows must satisfy the "New York City political constraint" that

$$u^t \geqslant u^\tau \qquad \text{for all } t \geqslant \tau \text{ and all } \tau \geqslant 0. \tag{4.6.7}$$

With a little reflection the constraint (4.6.7) leads us to a maximin criterion:

$$\max_t \inf (u^t). \tag{4.6.8}$$

Optimal capital accumulation paths satisfying (4.6.8) obey a Correspondence Principle; regular points are stable, while irregular ones are unstable,[20] as Figures 4.10 and 4.11 illustrate. The economy is irregular, and the steady-state utility level $u = u^*$ corresponds to three distinct interest or profit rates ($r = r_1$, $r = r_2$, $r = r_3$), as in Figure 4.10. Figure 4.11 depicts the k_1–k_2 capital-stock space. The curve EE is the efficiency locus for which k_1^0 and k_2^0 satisfy (4.6.6) with $\dot{k}_1 = \dot{k}_2 = 0$. The stretch la-

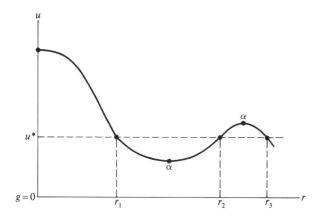

Figure 4.10. Points (r_1, u^*) and (r_2, u^*) are regular because at those points du/dr is negative, with (r_2, u^*) an irregular point. The economy is irregular because of the curve segment $\alpha\alpha$ where u rises with increases in r.

beled $\alpha\alpha$ in Figure 4.10 gives rise to $\alpha\alpha$ in Figure 4.11, and vice versa.

If initial capital stocks k_1^0, k_2^0 happen to fall on the *EE* efficiency locus in Figure 3.11, the highest possible constant utility path is simply[21]

$$u^0 = F(0, 0; k_1^0, k_2^0). \tag{4.6.9}$$

It should be noted that in any model with only one type of capital good, the highest possible constant utility path is always $u^0 = F(0; k^0)$ *for all* initial values of the homogeneous capital stock, k^0, below the Golden Rule value. Thus the problem we are now considering, like the reswitching question, simply does not arise unless there are heterogeneous capital goods.

Generally, however, arbitrary initial capital stocks will not fall on the *EE* locus, and hence we can do better than (4.6.9): we can find a maximin path with constant utility

$$u^t = u^* > u^0 \qquad \text{for all } t \geqslant 0. \tag{4.6.10}$$

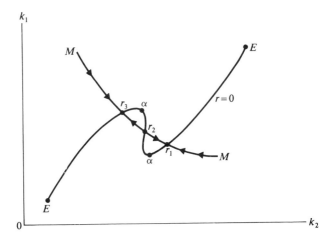

Figure 4.11. The optimal maximin path with $u^t = u^*$ is labeled *MM*, and the set of efficient capital stocks is the *EE* locus.

Such a path in capital space is labeled *MM* in Figure 4.11. Note that this path satisfies our constraint (4.6.7).

The important conclusion is that the point of "paradoxical behavior" at the steady state with $r = r_2$ is *unstable*, while the two "regular" steady states with $r = r_1$ or $r = r_3$ are both *stable*. The arrows on the maximin path MM in Figure 4.11 illustrate this Correspondence Principle between stability of maximin paths and the paradoxical behavior revealed to exist by reswitching.

4.7. Regular economies and the existence of a well-behaved aggregate production function

There have been serious misunderstandings about the correct economic conclusions implied by the existence of "paradoxical behavior." For example, Pasinetti has written:

> Yet, the marginal productivity theory of income distribution depends crucially on the "unobtrusive postulate of neoclassical economics," as I argued at length in the article to which Burmeister refers. And if such postu-

late falls, *the marginal productivity distribution theory
cannot stand* [italics added]. (1977, pp. 2–3)

Pasinetti's italicized conclusion is either false or involves a
serious misunderstanding about what is usually meant by the
marginal productivity theory of income distribution. Consider a
heterogeneous-capital world in which the *j*th firm faces a neoclassical production function (F^j) giving the output of commodity *j*
(Y_j) as a function of the inputs of *n* different types of capital goods
$(K_{1j}, K_{2j}, \ldots, K_{nj})$ and labor (L_j):

$$Y_j = F^j(K_{1j}, \ldots, K_{nj}, L_j). \tag{4.7.1}$$

Taking the price of output (P_j), the factor prices or gross rental
rates for the *n* capital goods $(Q_1, Q_2, \ldots, Q_n)$, and the nominal
wage rate (W) as given, the competitive firm maximizes profits,

$$\pi_j = P_j Y_j - (Q_1 K_{1j} + Q_2 K_{2j} + \cdots + Q_n K_{nj} + WL_j), \tag{4.7.2}$$

subject to (4.7.1). The solution to this maximization problem, or
to a mathematically equivalent cost minimization problem for
producing a given output level $Y_j = \bar{Y}_j$, entails the well-known
necessary conditions

$$P_j \frac{\partial F^j}{\partial K_{1j}} = Q_1$$

$$\begin{array}{cc} \cdot & \cdot \\ \cdot & \cdot \\ \cdot & \cdot \end{array} \tag{4.7.3}$$

$$P_j \frac{\partial F^j}{\partial K_{nj}} = Q_n$$

$$P_j \frac{\partial F^j}{\partial L_j} = W.$$

The equation system (4.7.3) constitutes an essential ingredient of
any neoclassical theory of income distribution in an economy
with heterogeneous capital goods. The marginal products

$$\frac{\partial F^j}{\partial K_{1j}}, \cdots, \frac{\partial F^j}{\partial K_{nj}}, \frac{\partial F^j}{\partial L_j}$$

do exist by virtue of the assumption that the production functions – the F^j's – are neoclassical. The point is simple: one can criticize marginal productivity theories of income distribution on a variety of grounds, one of them being the assertion that the marginal products in (4.7.3) do not exist as an empirical fact about the technology. However, such properties of the technologically feasible set of input–output vectors have nothing to do with paradoxical behavior.[22]

Apparently, Pasinetti has in mind an entirely *different* concept of "the marginal productivity theory of income distribution." It seems clear that he believes the rate of profit must equal "the marginal product of something." In a one-commodity neoclassical world for which

$$per\ capita\ net\ output\ =\ c\ +\ \dot{k}\ =\ f(k), \qquad (4.7.4)$$

it is true that (at steady-state equilibria points with $\dot{k} = 0$),

$$net\ marginal\ product\ of\ capital\ =\ f'(k)$$
$$=\ r\ =\ steady\text{-}state\ profit\ rate. \quad (4.7.5)$$

Pasinetti quite correctly claims that a result such as (4.7.5) does not generally hold in a heterogeneous capital world where, e.g., the technology is described by n different production functions such as (4.7.1). Yet, this fact only means that an *aggregate production function,* defined across steady-state equilibria, need not exist. However, the possibility of reswitching only alerts us to the fact that in general such an aggregate production function need not exist; reswitching is sufficient but it is *not* necessary for such nonexistence of an aggregate production function.

What are we to conclude in cases for which an aggregate production function does not exist? It *does not* follow that marginal productivity theories are invalid, for equations such as (4.7.3) may still exist,[23] allowing a perfectly legitimate *microeconomic* theory of income distribution.

There can be no quarrel with Pasinetti's position that the non-existence of an aggregate production function *does* have significant consequences for economic science. Further, the condition that an economy be regular is of *fundamental* importance, not the "unobtrusive postulate" that $dv/dr < 0$. This fact is underscored by the following theorem.

THEOREM 4.4

Consider a neoclassical technology with one pure consumption good and n heterogeneous capital goods having an underlying per capita production possibility frontier

$$c = G(\dot{k}_1, \ldots, \dot{k}_n; k_1, \ldots, k_n).$$

Assume that the economy is regular with

$$R(r) \equiv \sum_{i=1}^{n} \frac{P_i}{P_1} \frac{dk_i}{dr} < 0 \qquad \text{for all feasible } r \geqslant 0.$$

There then exists an index K and a function $F(K)$ such that, across steady-state equilibria for which

$$c = G(0, \ldots, 0; k_1, \ldots, k_n),$$

the function $F(K)$ has *all* the properties of a well-behaved neoclassical production function, namely:

(a) $F(K) = c$ [the function $F(K)$ gives per capita net output].

(b) $F'(K) = r$ (the "marginal product" of the index K is equal to the rate of profit).

(c) $F''(K) < 0$ [the function $F(K)$ exhibits "diminishing returns"].

Proof. For all viable values of r, define the index of "capital" by

$$K = K_0 + \int_{\theta=0}^{r} R(\theta) \, d\theta = \psi(r). \tag{4.7.6}$$

Differentiation of (4.7.6) yields

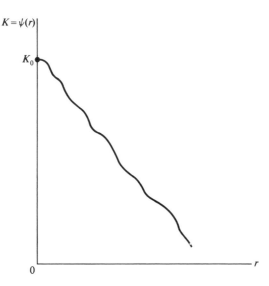

Figure 4.12. The index $K = \psi(r)$ decreases monotonically with increases in r.

$$\frac{dK}{dr} = R(r) = \psi'(r). \tag{4.7.7}$$

But, from equation (4.5.3b) we see that

$$\frac{dc}{dr} = rR(r) = r\frac{dK}{dr}. \tag{4.7.8}$$

Since $R(r)$ is negative by assumption, the function $\psi(r)$ is monotonically decreasing, as illustrated in Figure 4.12. Hence $\psi(r)$ may be inverted; that is,

$$r = \psi^{-1}(K) \qquad \text{with } \psi^{-1}(K_0) = 0. \tag{4.7.9}$$

Accordingly, there must exist some function $H(K)$ with the properties

$$r = H'(K) \equiv \psi^{-1}(K) \qquad \text{with } H'(K_0) = 0. \tag{4.7.10}$$

Combining (4.7.8) and (4.7.10) yields

$$\frac{dc}{dr} = rR(r) = H'[K(r)]\frac{dK}{dr}, \tag{4.7.11}$$

and therefore we can define a "pseudo aggregate production function" across steady-state equilibria by

$$\begin{aligned}
c(r) = F[K(r)] &\equiv C_0 + \int_{\theta=0}^{r} \frac{dc(\theta)}{d\theta}\, d\theta \\
&= C_0 + \int_{\theta=0}^{r} \theta R(\theta)\, d\theta \\
&= C_0 + \int_{\theta=0}^{r} H'[K(\theta)]\frac{dK}{d\theta}\, d\theta \\
&= C_0 + H[K(r)] \tag{4.7.12}
\end{aligned}$$

where $H[K(0)] = H(K_0) = 0$. In addition, we have that

$$\frac{dc}{dK} = F'(K) = H'(K) = r \tag{4.7.13}$$

measures the "marginal product of capital." Thus parts (a) and (b) of the theorem are proved.

Finally, differentiating (4.7.13) gives

$$\begin{aligned}
\frac{d^2c}{dK^2} = F''(K) = \frac{dr}{dK} &= \frac{dr}{dc} \cdot \frac{dc}{dK} \\
&= \frac{r}{rR(r)} \qquad [\text{using } (4.7.8)] \\
&= R(r).
\end{aligned}$$

Thus the assumption $R(r) < 0$ implies that

$$F''(K) < 0,$$

as was to be proved in (c).

Q.E.D.

We conclude this section with a generalization of the previous results to include nondifferentiable technologies. In such cases the definition of a regular economy is modified by requiring that the expression R^* defined by (4.5.4) above be negative at every switch point; that is, *regular economies* have the property that the changes in the value of capital (measured at switch point prices) as the steady-state rate of profit increases *are negative for every switch point*. Given this modified definition of a regular economy, Theorem 4.4 can be extended to include *all* cases:[24]

THEOREM 4.5
An aggregate steady-state production function $F(K)$ exists if and only if the economy is regular, with $F(K)$ having the following properties:

(a) $F(K) = c.$

(b) $F'(K^-) \equiv \lim_{\Delta K \to 0^-} \dfrac{F(K + \Delta K) - F(K)}{\Delta K} \geq r$

$\qquad \geq \lim_{\Delta K \to 0^+} \dfrac{F(K + \Delta K) - F(K)}{\Delta K} \equiv F'(K^+).$

(c) $F(K)$ is a concave function.

Note that the condition of a regular economy is not only sufficient, it is *necessary;* with an irregular economy one *cannot* construct a well-behaved neoclassical production function having properties (a)–(c).

We conclude this section by noting that even if we restrict our attention to regular economies, the aggregate production function $F(K)$ might not be very useful in many important applications because it is restricted to steady-state comparisons. And, more important, the construction of an appropriate "index of aggregate capital" such as K may be impossible because the index involves unobservable economic variables.

4.8. The labor theory of value
When labor is the *only* primary factor – that is, if *all* other inputs in the economy are produced – then one can define the "total embodied labor" contents of commodities and ask how these magnitudes compare with "values" as measured by competitive commodity prices. One might further hope that the

problems associated with heterogeneous capital might somehow be clarified or even resolved if we analyze a system in which the "values" of commodities are measured by their "total embodied labor" contents. The purpose of this section is to demonstrate that any such attempts are futile.

Unfortunately, only by introducing a vector-matrix notation can we keep the exposition brief.[25] Thus consider a technology consisting of a single Leontief–Sraffa technique, technique a. We introduce the notation

$$
\begin{bmatrix} a_0 \\ \hline a \end{bmatrix} = \begin{bmatrix} a_{01} \cdots a_{0n} \\ \hline a_{11} \cdots a_{1n} \\ \cdot \qquad \cdot \\ \cdot \qquad \cdot \\ \cdot \qquad \cdot \\ a_{n1} \cdots a_{nn} \end{bmatrix}
$$

where, as before, the a_{ij}'s are fixed input coefficients indicating the quantity of factor i required to produce 1 unit of commodity j, and where the subscript 0 designates a labor input.

The *direct* labor required to produce commodities $1, \ldots, n$ is given by the row vector of labor coefficients, $a_0 = (a_{01}, \ldots, a_{0n})$. However, the other labor inputs (produced last period) required labor to produce them, and thus *first-round indirect labor inputs* are given by $a_0 a$. But, of course, the commodities used as inputs last period were themselves produced using commodities that had direct labor inputs another period earlier, and so the *second-round indirect labor inputs* are $a_0 a^2$. Evidently, the *total embodied labor contents* are equal to the sum of direct labor + first-round indirect labor + second-round indirect labor + $\cdots$, an infinite sum reflecting all the indirect labor inputs from production in every previous period.[26] In our vector-matrix notation we have

$$
a_0 + a_0 a + a_0 a^2 + a_0 a^3 + \cdots = (\ell_1, \ldots, \ell_n) = \ell \tag{4.8.1}
$$

where

ℓ_i = total embodied labor content of commodity i

$i = 1, \ldots, n$.

It is a theorem in linear algebra that if $r_a^* > 0$ (r_a^* is defined in note 2), as we shall assume, then

$$I + a + a^2 + a^3 + \cdots = [I - a]^{-1} \qquad (4.8.2)$$

where I is an n-by-n identity matrix. Thus for (4.8.1) and (4.8.2) we see that

$$\ell = a_0[I - a]^{-1}. \qquad (4.8.3)$$

Moreover, as shown in note 2, prices in terms of labor as *numéraire* are $a_0[I - (1 + r)a]^{-1}$, or, using the notation $p(r)$ to emphasize that prices depend upon the interest rate as a parameter,

$$p(r) = a_0[I - (1 + r)a]^{-1} \atop \text{for all } r \text{ such that } 0 \le r < r_a^*. \qquad (4.8.4)$$

Comparing (4.8.3) and (4.8.4), we see immediately that

$$\ell = p(0). \qquad (4.8.5)$$

That is, *the total embodied labor vector is equal to the competitive price vector* (in terms of the nominal wage rate) *when the rate of interest is zero.*

We already know that

$$\frac{dp(r)}{dr} > 0,$$

and consequently

$$\ell < p(r) \qquad \text{for } r > 0.$$

However, it still may be true that *relative prices* reflect total embodied labor requirements in the sense that

$$\frac{p_i(r)}{p_j(r)} = \frac{\ell_i}{\ell_j}, \qquad 0 \le r < r^*. \qquad (4.8.6)$$

To put the matter another way, if relative prices are independent of the profit rate, they must equal relative prices at the particular profit rate $r = 0$, and hence they must equal relative total embodied labor requirements. *If relative prices are independent of r, we have*

$$\frac{p_i(r)}{p_j(r)} = \frac{p_i(0)}{p_j(0)} = \frac{\ell_i}{\ell_j}. \tag{4.8.7}$$

Conversely, (4.8.6) and (4.8.7) cannot hold whenever relative prices change with the profit rate.

Thus if, and only if, relative prices do not change with the interest or profit rate r, price ratios equal the ratios of total embodied labor inputs, as asserted by equations (4.8.6) and (4.8.7). When equations (4.8.6) and (4.8.7) hold, we shall say that the *pure labor theory of value* is valid.

Under what circumstances does such a pure labor theory of value prevail? Several equivalent necessary and sufficient conditions might be set forth, but we shall state only two that have straightforward economic interpretations.

First, (4.8.6) and (4.8.7) hold if, and only if, there exists a *scalar* function $\alpha(r)$ [with $\alpha(0) > 1$] such that

$$p(r) = \alpha(r)a_0. \tag{4.8.8}$$

We may interpret $\alpha(r)$ as a markup function; every price p_i is equal to the *same* markup function times direct labor [i.e., $p_i(r) = \alpha(r)a_{0i}$ for all $i = 1, \ldots, n$, as stated by (4.8.8)].

Second, (4.8.7) and (4.8.8) are valid if and only if the ratio of the value of direct labor input to the value of capital is the same for every industry, a case in which the economy is said to have *equal organic composition of capital* with

$$\frac{WL_j}{\sum\limits_{i=1}^{n} P_i K_{ij}} = \frac{a_{0j}}{\sum\limits_{i=1}^{n} p_i a_{ij}} \tag{4.8.9}$$

$$= r_a^* - r \qquad \text{for all } j = 1, \ldots, n.$$

The proofs of (4.8.8) and (4.8.9), although straightforward, involve algebraic details that are relegated to the appendix of this chapter. The economic conclusion which emerges is that the pure labor theory of value is false because (4.8.8) and (4.8.9) will not hold except in empirically freak circumstances. Generally, one would rarely observe technologies in which direct labor and other production inputs are used in the exact proportions necessary to validate (4.8.8) and (4.8.9).[27]

We have already discussed paradoxical consumption behavior that results from the existence of heterogeneous capital goods. Recall that such behavior cannot occur in one-capital-good models where there is, by assumption, no problem of aggregating bolts and hammers into a single index of "capital" and where a lower steady-state interest rate always implies a larger steady-state stock of homogeneous machines (Swan's mechano sets or Joan Robinson's LEETS, "steel" spelled backward). But suppose that the pure labor theory of value did hold so that all relative prices are independent of the interest rate. Under these circumstances one may apply the Hicks composite commodity theorem (1946, pp. 312–13) to aggregate the heterogeneous capital goods into one well-behaved capital index.[28] It follows, therefore, that in economies for which the pure labor theory of value is valid, *none* of the problems associated with heterogeneous capital can arise.

In summary, it is obvious that one must question the theoretical relevance of the pure labor theory of value.[29] Of course, the word "value" itself is misleading because, in fact, it is a *labor cost of production theory;* and "value" is at best dubious terminology since consumer preferences have been neglected completely!

Once one realizes that it is the cost of production that is at issue, it is evident that all problems of joint production, such as wool–mutton examples, must be excluded if the labor theory is to hold.[30] Joint production issues aside, one must also question the choice of *labor* as the unique factor of production used to measure "value." In general, the vector of labor input coefficients

$$(a_{01}, \ldots, a_{0n})$$

must be replaced by the matrix

$$\begin{bmatrix} b_{11} \cdots b_{1n} \\ \cdot \\ \cdot \\ \cdot \\ b_{m1} \cdots b_{mn} \end{bmatrix}$$

where b_{ij} designates the quantity of the ith primary factor ($i = 1, \ldots, m$) required to produce 1 unit of commodity j ($j = 1, \ldots, n$). If

$$w = (w_1, \ldots, w_m)$$

is a vector of primary factor prices, in place of (4.8.4) we will have

$$p(w, r) = wb[I - (1 + r)a]^{-1}, \qquad 0 \le r < r_a^*. \qquad (4.8.10)$$

In particular, note that this criticism includes the obviously realistic case in which there are many types of heterogeneous labor inputs because these different types of labor inputs may be included in the b matrix and their corresponding wage rate in the vector w. A complete analysis of such a model with many primary factors is given by Burmeister (1975c), but here we make one important observation: *even at $r = 0$, at best one could have a valid "primary factor theory of cost," and even that would require knowledge of relative primary factor prices.* Since these primary factor prices are determined in general equilibrium and are *not* independent of demand, such a "primary factor theory of cost" must be rejected. This observation is absolutely fatal for all attempts to construct a theory of "value" based on labor alone, or a theory of "value" that is independent of the demands and preferences of economic agents. That realistic economies are simultaneous general equilibrium systems is a complication we cannot ignore.

Finally, in addition to all the objections discussed above, a "labor" or "primary factor" theory of "value" (or cost) is a statement *only* about steady-state equilibria positions. Out of steady-state equilibria prices will not be constants and commodity price changes will be reflected in factor prices, so that factor prices, q_i, will equal $(1 + r)p_i$ only in steady-state equilibria. Thus rates of price change do influence costs of production, and these changes destroy any labor theory of value out of steady states.

In closing, we warn the reader about what has *not* been said. It does not necessarily follow from our critique of the pure labor theory of value that all Marxian conclusions about the capitalistic system are erroneous. Purely as a matter of logic, a theorem is not proved false because a step in its proof is shown to be wrong. However, when that step is apparently a cornerstone of the general argument, one cannot help but become suspicious.

4.9. The labor theory of value and Sraffa's "Standard Commodity"

As we have seen, the pure labor theory of value is valid only under very restrictive conditions, and for such special cases some very strong results can be established. In particular, consider any feasible vector of per capita consumption levels

$$c = \begin{bmatrix} c_1 \\ \cdot \\ \cdot \\ \cdot \\ c_n \end{bmatrix}$$

satisfying the steady-state condition

$$y = c + ay \tag{4.9.1}$$

$$\text{(where } y = \begin{bmatrix} y_1 \\ \cdot \\ \cdot \\ \cdot \\ y_n \end{bmatrix} = \text{the output vector)}$$

and the labor constraint

$$a_0 y = 1. \tag{4.9.2}$$

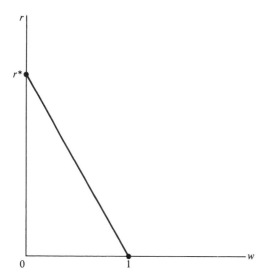

Figure 4.13. Linear relationship between the profit rate, r, and the real wage rate, w, for *any* consumption basket weights when the pure labor theory of value is valid.

We define the *real wage* in terms of any such consumption vector by

$$\text{real wage} = w \equiv \frac{W}{Pc} = \frac{1}{pc}. \tag{4.9.3}$$

It is proved in the appendix to this chapter that when the pure labor theory of value is valid, the interest rate, r, is related to this real wage, w, by the simple linear function

$$r = r_a^*(1 - w), \tag{4.9.4}$$

as illustrated in Figure 4.13. Thus the maximum real wage, $w = 1$, is associated with a zero interest rate; then $W = Pc$ or $WL = PC$ and the wage bill is equal to the value of total consumption. At the opposite extreme, the real wage tends to zero when the interest rate approaches its maximum value, r_a^*.

As already stated, (4.9.4) holds no matter which consumption vector is selected, provided that the pure labor theory of value is valid. Sraffa (1960) discovered a *particular* choice of the consumption vector such that this linear relationship is preserved even when the pure labor theory of value does not hold. It is proved in Theorem 4A.5 of the appendix to this chapter that there exists a unique consumption vector c^* such that

$$pc^* = \frac{r_a^*}{r_a^* - r}.$$ (4.9.5)

Thus, defining

$$\text{Sraffa's real wage} = w^s \equiv \frac{W}{Pc^*} = \frac{1}{pc^*},$$ (4.9.6)

we have from (4.9.5) and (4.9.6) that

$$r = r_a^*(1 - w^s).$$ (4.9.7)

The latter is precisely the relationship asserted by Sraffa,[31] and there is no quarrel with its validity. Equation (4.9.7) is a logical conclusion that must hold under the stated assumptions.[32] But how does this fact in any way imply a "generalized labor theory of value"? The following passage from Meek illustrates one futile attempt at justification:

> What both economists [Marx and Sraffa] are trying to show, in effect, is that (*when wages are given*) [italics added] the average rate of profits, and therefore the deviations of price ratios from embodied labour ratios, are governed by the ratio of direct to indirect labour in the industry whose conditions of production represent a sort of "average" of those prevailing over the economy as a whole. Marx reached this result by postulating as his "average" industry one whose "organic composition of capital" was equal to the "social average." But his result could only be a provisional and approximate one, since in reaching it he had ab-

stracted from the effect which a change in the wage would have on the prices of the means of production employed in the "average" industry. Sraffa shows that the same result can be achieved, without abstracting from this effect at all, if we substitute his "standard" industry for Marx's industry of "average organic composition of capital." Sraffa's "standard" industry, seen from this point of view, is essentially an attempt to *define* "average conditions of production" in such a way as to achieve the identical result which Marx was seeking. (1967, pp. 177–8)

This argument contains a fatal flaw. The phrase "when wages are given" must be understood to mean "when *given* wages are measured in terms of the very special weights defined by Sraffa's Standard Commodity." But this "real" wage, w^s, is not related in any way to human needs or preferences. *Sraffa's unique consumption basket weights are determined from the technology alone; they are the weights derived from the right-hand characteristic vector associated with the Frobenius root of the production technique matrix a.*[33] *There is absolutely no economic reason why these weights should be relevant for defining any "real" wage.*

For example, Sraffa's Standard Commodity might require that we assign a relatively large weight in his consumption basket to a commodity such as pig iron which is *never* consumed by human beings! To argue that "the deviations of price from embodied labor ratios"[34] are "determined" when wages, assumed given, are calculated using these special weights is an absurd proposition because, except in completely freak cases, any consumption basket for an actual economy will bear no resemblance to Sraffa's weights which define his "real" wage w^s.[35] Moreover, once the economic *insignificance* of Sraffa's Standard Commodity is realized, any attempt to base a notion of "worker exploitation" on this foundation, such as that by Eatwell (1975), is doomed to fail.[36]

4.10. **The neo-Austrian approach and indexes of "roundaboutness"**

The neo-Austrian approach to capital theory, based on the Austrian tradition associated with such economists as Böhm-Bawerk, Wicksell, and Hayek, is a generalization of the basic idea that a *time flow* of inputs produces current output.[37] For simplicity of exposition, we shall here make the simplifying assumption, common in the economic literature, that a single type of homogeneous input (labor) is employed over time to produce a homogeneous final output (consumption good). Using this final output as the standard of value or *numéraire* commodity, we let b^t denote both the physical quantity and value of output available at the end of period t (which, as always, for economic purposes coincides with the beginning of period $t + 1$). The quantity of labor input during period t is designated by a^t, and we define w^t as the wage rate in terms of the consumption good (i.e., w^t is the real wage rate paid to workers at the end of period t).

A *production process* is a time sequence of input–output pairs

$$\{(a^1, b^1), (a^2, b^2), \ldots, (a^T, b^T)\} \equiv \{(a^t, b^t)\}_{t=1}^T \tag{4.10.1}$$

yielding a net output stream, measured in terms of the consumption good, of

$$\{(b^1 - w^1 a^1), (b^2 - w^2 a^2), \ldots, (b^T - w^T a^T)\}$$
$$\equiv \{(b^t - w^t a^t)\}_{t=1}^T \equiv \{q^t\}_{t=1}^T . \tag{4.10.2}$$

A *neo-Austrian technology* consists of a set of such production processes, and following the Austrian tradition, it is usually postulated that every process has the property that

$$a^t > 0 \quad \text{and} \quad b^t = 0 \qquad \text{for } t = 1, \ldots, m < T. \tag{4.10.3}$$

Thus for the first m production periods, positive labor inputs do not result in any output of final goods; Hicks terms this time duration the *construction period*.[38]

This description of the feasible technology is incomplete because, as the word "construction" implies, workers presumably are producing *something* during the first m periods, but that "something" is never specified.[39] It is as if the economy were contained in a black box; we observe only a time flow of labor inputs and a time flow of final outputs, without ever observing the intermediate goods or capital equipment which may have been produced and utilized inside the black box. Clearly, such a description is incomplete—fatally so if one of our primary concerns is capital theory and we cannot observe any capital goods in the economy!

One can provide a trivial interpretation that does admit the existence of capital goods. Suppose that a^1 workers produce one "machine of type 1"; a^2 workers plus one "machine of type 1" produce one "machine of type 2"; . . . ; and a^m workers plus one "machine of type $m - 1$" produce one "machine of type m." Then for $t \geq m$, suppose that a^t workers plus one "machine of type $t - 1$" produce b^t units of final consumption goods plus one "machine of type t."

Later we use precisely this scheme to demonstrate that the neo-Austrian model in fact is a very special case of the von Neumann approach.[40] For now, however, note that the technology just described has a triangular structure in which the production of new capital goods requires only older machines. For example, during the first period, the production of a machine of type 1 requires *only* labor (and no capital goods of any type). Surely this is unreasonably restrictive. Does the technology not contain *some* process through which labor working with a hammer, for example, can produce a machine of type 1?

It is sometimes argued that if history could be traced far enough back in time, the production of every capital good must be explained by labor inputs alone. This argument, which is reminiscent of a labor theory of value, is entirely useless to this issue. Although one might admit that there exists a process by which a hammer *could* be produced by labor alone, this fact may be irrelevant. Thus once labor working with one hammer produces a machine of type 1, *it might never again be efficient to produce hammers by the process that uses labor alone.* All that is required is the existence of a (sufficiently productive) alternative process for producing hammers using labor *and* a machine of type 1. When such realistic simultaneity is admitted, the neo-Austrian description of the feasible technology becomes inadequate.

Stated in another way, the issue is whether the stock of capital goods available in period 1 allows an unrestricted choice of production processes. If such an unrestricted choice is not possible, the most efficient processes may become available to the economy only after the stocks of various capital goods (various types of machines) have been built using other processes that can be operated from the given initial conditions. The assumption that there are *no* capital goods available at the beginning of the first production period is very special.

These serious objections can be circumvented by allowing a^t and b^t to represent vectors of heterogeneous inputs and outputs, a modification that would again lead us to adopt a von Neumann approach. However, let us proceed by asking how the economic lifetime of a project, a time $N \le T$, is determined. Let r^t denote the own rate of interest prevailing over period t so that

$$V \equiv \sum_{t=1}^{T} \frac{q^t}{(1 + r^t)^{t-1}} \equiv \sum_{t=1}^{T} \frac{b^t - w^t a^t}{(1 + r^t)^{t-1}} \tag{4.10.4}$$

is the present discounted value of a production process if it is operated for the longest feasible duration (through time period T). We now introduce the absolutely crucial neo-Austrian assumption that production processes may be *truncated;* that is, if the process

$$\{(a^t, b^t)\}_{t=1}^{T} \tag{4.10.5a}$$

is feasible, then so is the *truncated process*

$$\{(\bar{a}^t, \bar{b}^t)\}_{t=1}^{T}$$
$$\equiv \{(a^1, b^1), (a^2, b^2), \ldots, (a^n, b^n), \underbrace{(0, 0), \ldots, (0, 0)}_{T - n \text{ periods}}\} \tag{4.10.5b}$$

for all nonnegative values of $n < T$.[41]

Provided truncation is assumed, and attention is restricted to steady-state equilibria for which $w^t = w$ and $r^t = r$, the optimal length of a project is found simply by selecting the maximum of

$$V_0 \equiv 0$$
$$V_1 \equiv b^1 - wa^1$$
$$V_2 \equiv (b^1 - wa^1) + \frac{b^2 - wa^2}{1 + r}$$
$$V_3 \equiv (b^1 - wa^1) + \frac{b^2 - wa^2}{1 + r} + \frac{b^3 - wa^3}{(1 + r)^2} \qquad (4.10.6)$$

$$\cdot$$
$$\cdot$$
$$\cdot$$

$$V_T \equiv \sum_{t=1}^{T} \frac{b^t - wa^t}{(1 + r)^{t-1}} \cdot$$

Denoting this maximum present discounted value by V_N, we call N the *optimal length of a production process*. Note that we allow for the possibility that $N = 0$, in which case the process is never even started. A process is termed *viable* at a given wage rate, w, if $N > 0$ for a zero interest rate $(r = 0)$.

If a process is viable at the prevailing wage rate, it is a theorem that the equation

$$V_N = 0 \qquad (4.10.7)$$

has a *unique* positive root $r = r*$.[42] The number $r*$ is the *internal rate of return* for the project.

Since the uniqueness of this internal rate of return is an essential result which depends crucially upon the assumption that truncation is possible, truncation merits further discussion. There are two obvious instances in which this assumption is not reasonable.

(1) Even though a process is terminated, certain consequences that the firm cannot avoid may occur after the truncation time. Damage lawsuits are one example.[43] However, if such consequences are unknown at the beginning of period zero, as seems likely with examples such as lawsuits, the *existence of uncertainty* becomes a separate issue as important as truncation.

(2) Truncation is not an appropriate assumption if important externalities continue after the operation of a process has stopped. The permanent effects of strip mining provide an example. However, externalities are an issue with or without the truncation assumption. We have ignored that certain effects (pollution, for example) are *produced jointly* with the final output of goods; such simplifications are justified if the produced effects are costless to the firm (i.e., if polluting is a free activity).[44] If such jointly produced effects are not costless, the description of the technology must reflect this fact.

If one assumes the absence of both uncertainty and externalities, the possibility of costless truncation becomes more reasonable. However, we may capture some of the effects of externalities by assuming that every process has associated "cleanup costs" which are known with certainty. For example, we may presume that by law a firm incurs nonnegative cleanup costs (measured in terms of final goods)

$$\{e^t\}_{t=1}^T$$

which must be paid at the end of every production period during which a process is operated (a "pay-as-you-go" antipollution scheme). With $w^t = w$ and $r^t = r$, the problem the firm faces at the beginning of period 1 is to select an optimal truncation time; that is, the feasible project lifetimes are $t = 0, t = 1, \ldots,$ or $t = T$, and the optimal duration is that value $t = N$ which solves the problem

$$\max_{t=0,1,\ldots,T} \begin{cases} V_t = 0 & \text{for } t = 0 \\ V_t = \sum_{i=1}^{t} \dfrac{b^i - e^i - wa^i}{(1 + r)^{i-1}} & \text{for } t = 1, \ldots, T. \end{cases} \tag{4.10.8}$$

Clearly, the maximized present discounted value depends on the rate of interest, and as in the case without cleanup costs (where $e^t = 0$ for all t), it is a decreasing monotonic function of r.[45] Thus any solution of $V_N(r) = 0$ (i.e., the internal rate of return r^*) is unique even in the presence of these cleanup costs. When only e^0

is positive, we can interpret that single cost as the price of a license to operate a particular process. Of course, if the e^t are sufficiently large, the process will not be operated at all ($N = 0$).

It is important to note that this formulation of cleanup costs is different from the alternative assumption that costs are incurred only *after* truncation. For example, one might formulate a model in which there is a penalty imposed at the end of the truncation period; such a penalty may be a once-and-for-all shutdown cost (which in general would vary with the choice of N). However, such a shutdown cost is logically identical to a *negative* scrap value for the firm, in which case the internal rate of return for the process need not be unique.[46]

For every fixed value of the wage rate, the internal rate of return, r^*, is unique under the stated assumptions. Accordingly, these pairs define a function

$$r = f(w), \tag{4.10.9}$$

where the asterisk on r^* has been dropped for simplicity. Moreover, it is obvious that $f(w)$ is simply the *factor-price frontier for a neo-Austrian process,* and it is downward sloping with[47]

$$\frac{dr}{dw} \equiv f'(w) < 0. \tag{4.10.10}$$

When there are many alternative neo-Austrian processes, the one employed in competitive equilibrium is that which renders the highest value of r for a given value of w. Obviously, given (4.10.10), we can invert (4.10.9) to obtain

$$w = f^{-1}(r). \tag{4.10.11}$$

The economic interpretation is then identical to the "choice of technique" question discussed in Section 4.2 for Leontief–Sraffa models.

Indeed, this equivalence points out that, without additional restrictions, *all* of the reswitching and "paradoxical behavior" phenomena can also occur in neo-Austrian models. This observation makes it obvious that all attempts to define a well-behaved index of "roundaboutness" will fail, except under restrictive conditions.[48] To see this most clearly, consider any index τ measuring the roundaboutness of a neo-Austrian production process. For τ to be a well-behaved index, it must exhibit the following two properties:

$$\frac{dc}{d\tau} > 0 \qquad\qquad (4.10.12a)$$

and

$$\frac{d\tau}{dr} < 0, \qquad\qquad (4.10.12b)$$

where c is per capita steady-state consumption and r is the steady-state interest rate. Condition (4.10.12a) is consistent with the intuition[49] that "time is productive," which means that an economy using more "time-intensive methods of production" must enjoy a higher level of per capita consumption in steady-state equilibrium. Condition (4.10.12b) states the property that a rise in the steady-state interest rate will result in the use of a "less time intensive" or "less roundabout" production process.

But, of course, if both (4.10.12a) and (4.10.12b) hold, then

$$\frac{dc}{dr} = \frac{dc}{d\tau} \cdot \frac{d\tau}{dr} < 0, \qquad\qquad (4.10.13)$$

which precludes the existence of "paradoxical consumption behavior" known to exist. Accordingly, an index of roundaboutness that is well behaved – that is, which satisfies both (4.10.12a) and (4.10.12b) – *does not exist.*[50]

As we shall see in Chapter 5, the economic intuition leading to a belief in conditions (4.10.12a) and (4.10.12b) is not entirely misguided, but one is led astray by examining only comparisons of steady-state equilibria. The more realistic and relevant economic question concerns the properties of feasible transition paths leading from one steady-state equilibrium to another, a subject to which we will return in Chapter 5.[51]

Finally, we shall show that the neo-Austrian approach to capital theory is in fact but a special case of conventional methods based upon the von Neumann model.[52] Thus consider the neo-Austrian process

$$\{(a^1, 0), (a^2, b^2), (a^3, 1)\} . \tag{4.10.14}$$

The present discounted value of this process, at given real wages and interest rates, must equal zero if there is free entry and if capital markets are to be in equilibrium. Hence

$$V = \frac{0 - wa^1}{1 + r} + \frac{b^2 - wa^2}{(1 + r)^2} + \frac{1 - wa^3}{(1 + r)^3} = 0 \tag{4.10.15}$$

is an equilibrium condition. Now, however, we shall derive the same equilibrium condition by using the von Neumann method in which "goods in process" are treated as *different* commodities.

Thus define:

Activity 1: a^1 workers produce one machine of type 1.

Activity 2: b^2 units of consumption are produced jointly with a "1-period-old machine" (a machine of type 2) by employing a^2 workers and one new machine (a machine of type 1).

Activity 3: a^3 workers plus 1 1-period-old machine (a machine of type 2) produce 1 unit of the final consumption goods.

These three activities may be represented by the column vectors

$$\begin{bmatrix} a^1 \\ 0 \\ 0 \\ 0 \end{bmatrix}, \quad \begin{bmatrix} a^2 \\ 1 \\ 0 \\ 0 \end{bmatrix}, \quad \text{and} \quad \begin{bmatrix} a^3 \\ 0 \\ 1 \\ 0 \end{bmatrix}, \tag{4.10.16}$$

respectively, where the rows (reading from top to bottom) correspond to inputs of labor, machines of type 1, machines of type 2, and the consumption good. These three activity vectors define the *input matrix*

$$\left[\frac{A_0}{A} \right] = \begin{bmatrix} a^1 & a^2 & a^3 \\ 0 & 1 & 0 \\ 0 & 0 & 1 \\ 0 & 0 & 0 \end{bmatrix} . \tag{4.10.17}$$

The corresponding *output matrix* is

$$B = \begin{bmatrix} 1 & 0 & 0 \\ 0 & 1 & 0 \\ 0 & b_2 & 1 \end{bmatrix}. \tag{4.10.18}$$

An element b_{ij} of B represents the output of commodity i from the jth activity operated at the unit intensity level.[53] Note that activity 2 involves joint production; 1-year-old machines and consumption goods are produced together.

Let the row vector

$$p = (p_1, p_2, 1)$$

designate the prices of commodity 1, commodity 2, and the consumption good which we select as *numéraire*. In a steady-state equilibrium, commodities 1, 2, and 3 are produced in positive quantities. If all three activities are operated at positive intensity levels, the von Neumann inequalities

$$wA_0 + p(1 + r)A \geqslant pB \text{ (with } p \geqslant 0, \, p \neq 0) \tag{4.10.19}$$

are replaced by equalities, and the condition

$$wA_0 = p[B - (1 + r)A] \qquad \text{(with } p > 0) \tag{4.10.20}$$

must be satisfied. Provided that $[B - (1 + r)A]^{-1}$ exists, we may calculate the equilibrium price vector

$$p = wA_0[B - (1 + r)A]^{-1}. \tag{4.10.21}$$

For this example,

$$[B - (1 + r)A]^{-1} = \begin{bmatrix} 1 & \dfrac{1 + r}{1 + b^2(1 + r)} & \dfrac{(1 + r)^2}{1 + b^2(1 + r)} \\ 0 & \dfrac{1}{1 + b^2(1 + r)} & \dfrac{1 + r}{1 + b^2(1 + r)} \\ 0 & \dfrac{- b^2}{1 + b^2(1 + r)} & \dfrac{1}{1 + b^2(1 + r)} \end{bmatrix},$$

$$\tag{4.10.22}$$

and we find, from (4.10.21), that

$$p_1 = wa^1, \tag{4.10.23a}$$

$$p_2 = \frac{wa^1(1 + r)}{1 + b^2(1 + r)} + \frac{wa^2}{1 + b^2(1 + r)} - \frac{wb^2a^3}{1 + b^2(1 + r)}, \tag{4.10.23b}$$

$$p_3 \equiv 1 = \frac{wa^1(1 + r)^2}{1 + b^2(1 + r)} + \frac{wa^2(1 + r)}{1 + b^2(1 + r)} + \frac{wa^3}{1 + b^2(1 + r)}. \tag{4.10.23c}$$

Equations (4.10.23a) through (4.10.23c) give the steady-state equilibrium prices for commodities 1, 2, and 3. In particular, multiplying equation (4.10.23c) by $1 + b^2(1 + r)$, rearranging terms, and dividing by $(1 + r)^3$ yields precisely the previous equilibrium condition given by equation (4.10.15), thus demonstrating the equivalence of the two approaches.[54]

We conclude this section with several observations:

(1) The neo-Austrian model is a very special case of a general von Neumann approach.[55]

(2) The "new machine" produced by activity 1, as well as the "1-year-old machine" produced by activity 2, might be purely contrived.[56]

(3) Even if machines do exist physically, there need not be any market for them. Nevertheless, a firm operating the process described by equation (4.10.14) must impute shadow prices equal to the p_1 and p_2 we have calculated; otherwise, the process would not have a zero present discounted value in steady-state equilibrium.

(4) Once the appropriate economic translation has been completed, one is in a position to apply all the mathematical results that have been proved for the von Neumann case to the neo-Austrian model. This feature becomes especially important if one attempts a generalization of the neo-Austrian model to include many heterogeneous inputs and outputs.[57]

(5) In conclusion, the neo-Austrian approach to capital theory offers no significant advantages in terms of economic theory. With a proper economic interpretation of "goods in process" as

different commodities, conventional approaches encompass the neo-Austrian method as one special case.

4.11. Concluding remarks

The particular aspects of the "Cambridge capital theory controversy" discussed in this chapter represent only a few issues judged to be of most interest and economic significance. Two conclusions emerge:

(1) It is evident that theoretically rigorous aggregation of heterogeneous machines into a single, well-behaved index of "capital" is possible only under extraordinarily restrictive assumptions. Therefore, we must question the conclusions derived from the one-capital-good models in Chapter 3 and determine which of the results are robust with respect to the assumption of homogeneous capital, and which are misleading. Chapter 5 provides some important answers to this question.

(2) The relevant dynamic choices open to an economy – that is, those paths which are feasible from given initial stocks with a given technology – *cannot* be analyzed using the models discussed in this chapter, because the latter are all constructed assuming steady-state equilibria. This unrealistic and restrictive assumption is the basis for misunderstandings about certain "paradoxical" results which, as we see in Chapter 5, are no longer so surprising when we begin by asking the appropriate economic questions.

How, then, can the "Cambridge controversies" have generated so much heat when there is so little fire? The answer, best left to historians of economic thought or even sociologists, obviously involves issues of ideology and political economy which should play no role in scientific inquiry. G. C. Harcourt, readily identified with the anti-neoclassical Cambridge group by his published works,[58] wrote a paper to which Frank Hahn responded.[59] Hahn, labeling the anti-neoclassical group "neo-Ricardians," summarizes the issues of "the Cambridge controversy":[60]

> Everyone agrees that the modelling of institutions by neoclassical economics is too sparse. No one considers

that we have a satisfactory account of expectation formations. No one believes that any actual economy can be studied free of initial conditions ("history"). Now think of a single contribution of Harcourt's group to a single one of these issues. Or put it the other way round: think of a question you would like to ask of an actual economy which can be answered by means of Sraffa prices? Or if that is too much to ask: what is the operational content of neo-Ricardian theory? What observation will falsify it or at least make it doubtful? Is it enough to say that "the profit rate" is not observed and that there is almost universal joint production and absence of constant returns? And if not, what issue intellectual or otherwise is solved by what must then be taken as accounting identities?

The really extraordinary thing is this. The arid exercises of the neo-Ricardians are by Harcourt taken to denote a more humane and wider intellectual sympathy than is customary among neoclassicals. Somehow, because the "classical" economists lived a long time ago, concern with them denotes not only the scholar but the man who asks the real questions. For instance, it is endlessly repeated that Ricardo is to be praised for being concerned with the distribution of income between social classes and perhaps growth. But in 1975 we can recognize that these are not well-formulated questions – not every grand-sounding question is: Is the share of miners to be explained in the same way as the share of nurses? Why do people balk only at the aggregation of machines and not of people? Or take "the laws of motion of capitalism."[61] Does one understand this splendid phrase? The motion of what exactly? Or take the quoted remarks by Joan Robinson.[62] What *exactly* do they portend? What precise programme of thought do they entail? In short, Harcourt shares with many people a habit of thinking elevating and grand-sounding questions or sentences as constituting humane and penetrating thought. The "technician" is the man who merely does the thinking. But if there is anything to be said for the Ricardians at all, it is not that they conform to Harcourt's vision of the grand social scientist but that they carried a purely technical and abstract problem (capital aggregation) to a logical conclusion. If then there is a real issue it is not the observation that economic theory has many lacunae; that is uncontroversial. The real issue is whether future progress will come as a natural development of what we have or whether a radical Kuhn-like change is required. I do not know. But I do know that, for instance, the observation that Marx was concerned with history and sociology and their interaction with economics is not one to lead one to conclude that *therefore* his approach is to be preferred to the orthodox one which is agnostic on most of these issues. One actually has to look at what Marx achieved or even just at what is achievable in this way. To this the neo-Ricardians have contributed precisely nothing. Where is the class-struggle in their theory of "the rate of profit," where power, where history?

I conclude with another non-issue – the relation of ideology and theory. This is an interesting question in its own right for the historian of thought (although of course his treatment in turn presumably is not independent of his ideology). But the matter is beside the point when we discuss economic theories *qua* theorists, since it cannot be the case that a theory should be rejected or accepted by an appeal to the motives, conscious or otherwise, of proponents. This is really all that needs to be said in this matter.

Harcourt refers to "The Great Debate" – an endearing but false *New Yorker*-kind characterization of what went on. "The Great Charade" would be more appropriate.

Appendix

THEOREM 4A.1

The pure labor theory of value is valid if, and only if, equation (4.8.8) holds, and equation (4.8.8) is equivalent to equation (4.8.9).

Proof. If (4.8.8) holds, then

$$\frac{p_i(r)}{p_j(r)} = \frac{\alpha(r)a_{0i}}{\alpha(r) a_{0j}} = \frac{a_{0i}}{a_{0j}} \tag{4A.1}$$

for all $0 \leqslant r < r_a^*$; hence, substituting $r = 0$ and using (4.8.5), we conclude that

$$\frac{p_i(r)}{p_j(r)} = \frac{\ell_i}{\ell_j} \qquad \text{for all } 0 \leqslant r < r_a^* , \tag{4A.2}$$

which is the pure labor theory of value. The proof that (4.8.8) is also necessary is more complex, and the interested reader is referred to Burmeister (1976a).

Next, observe that (4.8.9) may be written as

$$(1 + r)p(r)a = \gamma(r)a_0 \tag{4A.3}$$

where $\gamma(r)$ is a scalar function of r to be determined. To prove that (4.8.8) holds if and only if (4A.3) holds, simply write (4.8.8) as

$$p(r) = \alpha(r)a_0 = a_0 + (1 + r)p(r)a \tag{4A.4}$$

or

$$(1 + r)p(r)a = [\alpha(r) - 1]a_0 = \gamma(r)a_0$$

with

$$\gamma(r) \equiv \alpha(r) - 1 .$$

From Theorem 4A.2 we have

$$\alpha(r) = \frac{(1 + r_a^*)/r_a^*}{1 - r/r_a^*} ,$$

so that

$$\gamma(r) \equiv \alpha(r) - 1 = \frac{1 + r}{r_a^* - r}.$$ (4A.5)

Finally, writing (4A.3) as

$$a_0 = \frac{1 + r}{\gamma(r)} p(r)a,$$

and substituting (4A.5), we have

$$a_0 = (r_a^* - r)p(r)a,$$ (4A.6)

which is equivalent to (4.8.9).

Q.E.D.

THEOREM 4A.2

$\frac{1}{\alpha(r)}$ is a linear function of r with

$$\frac{1}{\alpha(r)} = \frac{1 - r/r_a^*}{(1 + r_a^*)/r_a^*},$$

$$\alpha(0) = \frac{1 + r_a^*}{r_a^*} > 1 \quad \text{and} \quad \lim_{r \to r_a^*} \alpha(r) = \infty.$$ (4A.7)

Proof. Substituting (4.8.8) into (4A.5) gives

$$\alpha(r)a_0 = a_0 + (1 + r)\alpha(r)a_0 a$$ (4A.8)

or

$$a_0[\lambda(r)I - a] = 0$$ (4A.9)

where

$$\lambda(r) \equiv \frac{\alpha(r) - 1}{\alpha(r)(1 + r)}.$$

It is well known that (4A.9) has a solution with $a_0 > 0$ if and only if $\lambda(r) = \lambda^*$, where λ^* is the Frobenius root of a. Thus, a_0 is a left-hand eigenvector associated with the Frobenius root, λ^*, of a.[63] But it also is well known that λ^* is related to the maximal interest or profit rate r^* by[64]

$$r^* = \frac{1}{\lambda^*} - 1,$$

and thus

$$\frac{\alpha(r) - 1}{\alpha(r)(1 + r)} \equiv \lambda(r) = \lambda^* = \frac{1}{1 + r^*}$$

or

$$\alpha(r) = \frac{(1 + r^*)/r^*}{1 - r/r^*},$$

as was to be proved.

Q.E.D.

THEOREM 4A.3[65]
Assume that the matrix a is indecomposable, and let y^* be the (right-hand) characteristic vector associated with the Frobenius root λ^*, normalized by the labor constraint $a_0 y^* = L \equiv 1$. Then

$$py^* = \frac{(1 + r_a^*)/r_a^*}{1 - r/r_a^*} \tag{4A.10}$$

where $p = P/W$.

Proof

$$p = a_0 + (1 + r)pa,$$

and postmultiplying by y^* gives

$$py^* = a_0 y^* + (1 + r)pay^*. \tag{4A.11}$$

But y^* satisfies

$$ay^* = \lambda^* y^* = \frac{y^*}{1 + r^*}$$

and

$$a_0 y^* = 1.$$

Substituting the latter into (4A.11) yields (4A.10).

Q.E.D.

THEOREM 4A.4

Equation (4.9.4) holds when the pure labor theory of value is valid.

Proof. Using $y = c + ay$ or $pc = py - pay$, we may calculate

$$1 - w \equiv 1 - \frac{1}{pc} = 1 - \frac{1}{py - pay}$$

$$= 1 - \frac{1}{[a_0 + (1 + r)pa]y - pay}$$

$$= 1 - \frac{1}{a_0 y + rpay} \cdot \tag{4A.12}$$

Using the labor constraint $a_0 y = 1$, (4A.12) may be written as

$$1 - w = \frac{rpay}{1 + rpay} \cdot \tag{4A.13}$$

But since the labor theory of value is valid by assumption, equation (4A.13) holds, and postmultiplying it by the vector y and again using $a_0 y = 1$ yields

$$pay = \frac{1}{r_a^* - r} \cdot \tag{4A.14}$$

Finally, substituting (4A.14) into (4A.13) gives

$$1 - w = \frac{r_a^*}{r}$$

or

$$r = r_a^*(1 - w),$$

as was to be proved.

Q.E.D.

THEOREM 4A.5

Equation (4.9.7) holds; that is,

$$r = r_a^*(1 - w^s)$$

where

$$w^* \equiv \frac{1}{pc^*},$$
$$c^* = y^* - ay^*,$$

and y^*, as defined in Theorem 4A.3, is Sraffa's Standard Commodity.

Proof. Since

$$ay^* = \frac{y^*}{1 + r_a^*}$$

(see the proof of Theorem 4A.3) and the labor constraint must be satisfied with $a_0 y^* = 1$, we have

$$
\begin{aligned}
pc^* &= py^* - pay^* \\
&= py^* - \frac{py^*}{1 + r_a^*} \\
&= py^* \left(\frac{r_a^*}{1 + r_a^*} \right).
\end{aligned}
\tag{4A.15}
$$

Substitution of (4A.10) into (4A.15) gives

$$pc^* = \frac{1}{1 - r/r_a^*}$$

or

$$w^s \equiv \frac{1}{pc^*} = 1 - \frac{r}{r_a^*}$$

or

$$r = r_a^* (1 - w).$$

$$\text{Q.E.D.}$$

Exercises

4.1 Referring to note 6, the price equation for technique a may be written as

$$p = a_0 [I - (1 + r)a]^{-1}.$$

Prove that $dp/dr > 0$ to establish equation (4.3.1) in the text (i.e., to conclude that a factor-price curve is always downward-sloping). [*Hint:* Let $A \equiv [A_{ij}(\theta)]$ be a matrix whose elements are differentiable functions of the parameter θ. Use the fact that

$$\frac{dA^{-1}}{d\theta} = -A^{-1}\left(\frac{dA}{d\theta}\right)A^{-1}\Big].$$

4.2 Generalize Theorem 4.1 to the case in which labor grows at the rate $g > 0$ by proving that

$$c^{\alpha} = f_1^{\alpha}(g).$$

(*Hint:* The value of net capital formation must equal gV^{α} if the per capita stocks of every capital good are to remain constant.)

4.3 Prove that the factor-price frontier for a neo-Austrian process is negatively sloped with $f'(w) < 0$.

4.4 Consider the two neo-Austrian production processes

$$\text{process } \alpha = \{(0, a^1), (0, a^2), \ldots, (0, a^{N-1}), (1, 0)\}$$

and

$$\text{process } \beta = \{(0, \bar{a}^1), (0, \bar{a}^2), \ldots, (0, \bar{a}^{N-1}), (1, 0)\},$$

both of which yield a point output of 1 unit of the consumption good at the end of period N. (Note that truncation is not an issue because both processes must be operated for all N periods to yield *any* output.)

(a) Assuming steady-state equilibria with $r^t = r$ and $W^t = W$, derive the factor-price curves for these two processes:

$$\left(\frac{W}{P}\right)^{\alpha} = \frac{1}{\displaystyle\sum_{i=1}^{N-1} a^i/(1 + r)^{i-N}} \equiv f_{\alpha}(r)$$

and

$$\left(\frac{W}{P}\right)^{\beta} = \frac{1}{\displaystyle\sum_{i=1}^{N-1} \bar{a}^i/(1 + r)^{i-N}} \equiv f_{\beta}(r).$$

(b) Prove that per capita consumption is given by

$$c^{\alpha} = f_{\alpha}(0)$$

and

$$c^{\beta} = f_{\beta}(0).$$

(c) Prove by numerical example that reswitching and hence paradoxical behavior can exist.

(d) Consider the index of roundaboutness[66]

$$
\tau_\alpha \equiv \frac{NP - \sum_{i=1}^{N-1} iW(1 + r)^{N-i}a^i}{P}
$$

with an analogous definition to τ_β. Show that

$$
\tau_\alpha \equiv \frac{\sum_{i=1}^{N-1} (N - i)i(1 + r)^{N-i}a^i}{P/W} .
$$

(e) Derive

$$
\frac{d(P/W)^\alpha}{d(1 + r)} = \sum_{i=1}^{N-1} (N - i)(1 + r)^{N-i-1}a^i
$$

to show that

$$
\frac{1 + r}{P/W} \cdot \frac{d(P/W)}{d(1 + r)} = \tau_\alpha .
$$

(f) Suppose that r' is a switch point between processes α and β with

$$
f_\alpha(r') = f_\beta(r') .
$$

Now if we switch from α to β as r is increased near r', then show that

$$
f_\alpha'(r') < f_\beta'(r') ,
$$

implying that

$$
\frac{d(P/W)^\alpha}{d(1 + r)} > \frac{d(P/W)^\beta}{d(1 + r)} .
$$

(g) Conclude that

$$
\tau^\beta < \tau^\alpha
$$

so that the property

$$
\frac{\Delta\tau}{\Delta r} < 0
$$

holds at $r = \bar{r}$. (See note 49.)

(h) In light of (c), what may be true of

$$\frac{\Delta c}{\Delta r} \text{ at } r = \bar{r}?$$

(i) Show that no paradoxes arise when

$$a^i = a \qquad \text{for all } i = 1, 2, \ldots, N - 1$$

and

$$\bar{a}^i = \bar{a} \qquad \text{for all } i = 1, 2, \ldots, N - 1.$$

4.5 Use equations (4.10.23b) and (4.10.23c) to derive

$$p_2 = \frac{1}{1 + r} - \frac{wa^3}{1 + r} \,,$$

and interpret the latter in terms of the fundamental economic proposition that the equilibrium price of a machine is equal to the present discounted value of its future net earnings stream.

5

Properties of dynamic paths

5.1. Introduction to dynamic paths

Although the "comparative dynamics" questions analyzed in Chapter 4 may be beneficial in providing certain economic insights, they do *not* accurately reflect the set of feasible alternatives open to an economy that happens to find itself in some particular steady-state equilibrium. "Comparative dynamics" does tell us how the original steady state compares with alternative steady states, but the set of technologically feasible steady states does not constitute the relevant choices open to an economy. Rather, starting from a steady state, the set of *technologically feasible dynamic paths* (all having the same initial steady-state conditions) constitutes the choices open to an economy. Some of these feasible paths may converge to other steady states either in finite or infinite time, but in actuality such paths constitute only a proper subset of the feasible options. In any event, an economy cannot move instantaneously from an initial steady-state equilibrium to another steady-state equilibrium, except perhaps in freak cases; a movement from one steady state to another involves a transition path with a duration of at least one time period. Accordingly, in this chapter we free ourselves of the steady-state straitjacket and examine some economic properties of the relevant dynamic choices open to an economy.

First, however, in Section 5.2 we introduce many primary (i.e.,

165

nonproduced) factors of production and compare alternative steady-state equilibria. This example again stresses the distinction between comparisons of genuinely feasible options, and comparisons of alternative steady-state equilibria which may not be technologically feasible and which, therefore, may lead to erroneous conclusions.

In Section 5.3 we specify a general technology with certain standard properties and define the subset of technologically feasible paths that are *competitive*. The properties of these competitive paths are studied in Section 5.4; in particular, we see from Theorem 5.2 that, under fairly weak conditions, a competitive path also maximizes the present value of consumption.

The concept of the *intertemporal rate of transformation* is introduced in Section 5.5, and Section 5.6 contains a simple but comprehensive numerical example to illustrate the economic principles involved. In Section 5.7 the results are generalized to allow for many heterogeneous capital goods and primary factors, and we see that the previous conclusions derived for simple cases remain valid: There is a fundamental inequality that relates the marginal rates of transformation to the dynamic equilibrium consumption-good prices associated with a competitive path, and this result holds under very general conditions.

In Section 5.8 we turn to Solow's concept of the *rate of return,* and we identify conditions under which it can be used to make welfare inferences. In Section 5.9 we see that Theorem 3.1, which characterizes consumption-efficient paths in one-capital-good models, generalizes in a very natural way to models with heterogeneous capital goods, as stated in Theorem 5.4. Section 5.10 contains some concluding remarks.

5.2. Many primary factors and feasible steady-state equilibria

To illustrate more clearly the fact that restricting one's attention to steady-state equilibria can possibly lead to mistaken inferences, we briefly will consider a model with n produced commodities and m primary (nonproduced) factors of production.

First, note that the rate of growth in any steady-state equilibrium is limited by the slowest growing primary factor. Having made this observation, it is convenient to assume fixed supplies of primary factors and to ignore technological change by restricting our attention to steady states with zero growth ($g = 0$).

The gross output of the ith produced commodity (y_i) is split into consumption (c_i), net capital formation ($\dot{k}_i$), and depreciation:

$$y_i = c_i + \dot{k}_i + \delta_i k_i, \qquad i = 1, \ldots, n. \tag{5.2.1}$$

Given fixed capital stocks $k_1, \ldots, k_n$ and fixed stocks of primary factors $\ell_1, \ldots, \ell_m$, the technologically feasible set of outputs $y_1, \ldots, y_n$ is summarized by a *production-possibilities frontier*

$$y_1 = F(y_2, \ldots, y_n; k_1, \ldots, k_n, \ell_1, \ldots, \ell_m) \tag{5.2.2}$$

which is analogous to equation (2.2.1). Assuming that $F(\cdot)$ has the usual neoclassical properties, in a competitive equilibrium we have that

$$\frac{\partial F}{\partial y_i} = -\frac{p_i}{p_1}, \qquad i = 2, \ldots, n, \tag{5.2.3a}$$

$$\frac{\partial F}{\partial k_i} = \frac{q_i}{p_1}, \qquad i = 1, \ldots, n, \tag{5.2.3b}$$

and

$$\frac{\partial F}{\partial \ell_i} = \frac{w_i}{p_1}, \qquad i = 1, \ldots, m, \tag{5.2.3c}$$

where p_i = price of commodity i ($i = 1, \ldots, n$)

q_i = rental rate for 1 unit of the ith capital stock ($i = 1, \ldots, n$)

w_i = rental rate for 1 unit of the ith primary factor ($i = 1, \ldots, m$).

We shall restrict our attention to steady states with $\dot{k}_i = 0$, all i, so that (5.2.2) may be written as

$$c_1 + \delta_1 k_1 = F(c_2 + \delta_2 k_2, \ldots, c_n \\ + \delta_n k_n; k_1, \ldots, k_n, \ell_1, \ldots, \ell_m). \tag{5.2.4}$$

Consider the maximization problem

$$\max_{\{k_i\}} c_1 \qquad \text{subject to (5.2.4),} \ c_2 \geq \bar{c}_2, \ldots, c_n \geq \bar{c}_n \text{ for prescribed (feasible) } \bar{c}_2, \ldots, \bar{c}_n \text{ and fixed } \ell_1, \ldots, \ell_m. \qquad (5.2.5)$$

Assume that the maximization problem (5.2.5) has a "regular interior solution" and that we therefore may ignore inequalities. The first-order necessary conditions for a maximum are

$$\frac{\partial c_1}{\partial k_1} = \frac{\partial F}{\partial k_1} - \delta_1 = 0 \qquad (5.2.6a)$$

$$\frac{\partial c_1}{\delta k_i} = \frac{\partial F}{\partial k_i} + \frac{\partial F}{\partial y_i} \delta_i = 0, \qquad i = 2, \ldots, n. \qquad (5.2.6b)$$

And from (5.2.3a)–(5.2.3b) and (5.2.6a)–(5.2.6b), we have that

$$\frac{q_i}{p_1} - \frac{p_i}{p_1} \delta_i = 0, \qquad i = 1, \ldots, n. \qquad (5.2.7)$$

However, we are considering only competitive steady states for which we know

$$q_i = p_i(r + \delta_i), \qquad i = 1, \ldots, n \qquad (5.2.8)$$

where r is the steady-state profit rate. Accordingly, we see that (5.2.7) implies that $r = 0$.

The set of n equations (5.2.6a)–(5.2.6b) or, equivalently, (5.2.7) involves the $2n - 1 + m$ variables ($c_2, \ldots c_n, k_1, \ldots, k_n, \ell_1, \ldots, \ell_m$), but with fixed ℓ_i's and $c_i = \bar{c}_i$, $i = 2, \ldots, n$, we are left with n remaining k_i's as unknowns. If the underlying technology does not involve joint production, as we shall assume, the maximization problem (5.2.5) implies a solution for the capital stocks, say $k_1^*, \ldots, k_n^*$, which is unique up to a constant factor of proportionality.[1] Accordingly, under our assumptions, the n equations (5.2.7) define the function

$$c_1 = T(c_2, \ldots, c_n; \ell_1, \ldots, \ell_m). \qquad (5.2.9)$$

Moreover, it easily may be proved that

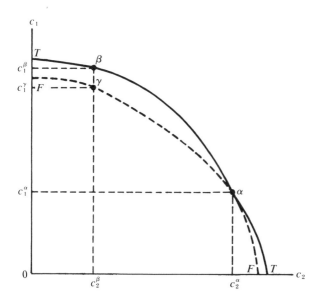

Figure 5.1. In this example it is not technologically feasible to move from α to β without changing the capital stocks.

$$\frac{\partial T}{\partial c_i} = -\frac{p_i}{p_1}, \qquad i = 2, \ldots, n, \qquad (5.2.10a)$$

and

$$\frac{\partial T}{\partial \ell_i} = +\frac{w_i}{p_1}, \qquad i = 1, \ldots, m. \qquad (5.2.10b)$$

Although at first glance it may appear as if (5.2.9) is a *consumption possibilities frontier*, it definitely is not. Suppose, for example, that we consider a simple $n = 2$, $m = 1$ case as illustrated in Figure 5.1 for fixed $\ell_1 = 1$. The frontier marked TT is the solution to the maximization problem (5.2.5) with $\ell_1 = 1$ and varying c_2. Suppose that the economy initially is in the steady-state equilibrium at the point labeled α with $c_1 = c_1^\alpha$, $c_2 = c_2^\alpha$. *It is not feasible for the economy to move to point β, where $c_1 = c_1^\beta$, $c_2 = c_2^\beta$.* The reason such a move is not feasible is that the capital stocks appropriate for point α, say k_1^α, k_2^α, are derived from the maximization problem (5.2.5). Indeed, it is because capital stocks are *selected* that the solution to (5.2.5) implies, via (5.2.7), the Golden Rule condition $r = 0$ ($= g$). If the initial conditions at the steady state α are taken as given, namely $k_1 = k_1^\alpha$, $k_2 = k_2^\alpha$, and $\ell_1 = 1$, and if we set $c_2 = c_2^\beta$, the maximum technologically feasible c_1 we can attain must be $c_1^\gamma < c_1^\beta$. The steady-state point β can be attained with $\ell_1 = 1$ if and only if the capital stocks are the solution to the maximization problem (5.2.5) with $c_2 = c_2^\beta$ prescribed and $\ell_1 = 1$ given.

On the other hand, the frontier labeled *FF* is simply (5.2.4) with $\ell_1 = 1$, $k_1 = k_1^\alpha$, and $k_2 = k_2^\alpha$. Any point on it is attainable, including the original steady-state equilibrium at α and the point γ with $c_2 = c_2^\beta$, $c_1 = c_1^\gamma < c_1^\beta$. Therefore, we see that feasibility certainly does not imply intertemporal or consumption efficiency.

To pursue this observation, suppose that we take as exogenously given a steady-state profit rate $r > 0$. In a steady-state equilibrium with $\dot{p}_i = 0$, intertemporal efficiency as defined in Chapter 2 necessitates that

$$(r + \delta_1) - \frac{\partial F(\cdot)}{\partial k_1} = 0 \tag{5.2.11a}$$

$$(r + \delta_i) + \frac{\partial F(\cdot)/\partial k_i}{\partial F(\cdot)/\partial y_i} = 0, \qquad i = 2, \ldots, n, \quad \text{(5.2.11b)}$$

where $y_i = c_i + 0 + \delta_i k_i$ and $(\cdot) \equiv (y_2, \ldots, y_n; \, k_1, \ldots, k_n;$ $\ell_1, \ldots, \ell_m)$. For fixed $\ell_1, \ldots, \ell_m$ and prescribed $c_2, \ldots, c_n$, equations (5.2.11a)–(5.2.11b) are n equations in the variables $k_1, \ldots, k_n$. However, with $r > 0$ there is nothing to assure that (5.2.11a)–(5.2.11b) have a unique solution (up to a factor of proportionality) in the k_i's. Thus for fixed $\ell_1, \ldots, \ell_m$ and prescribed $c_2, \ldots, c_m$, there may exist more than one value of c_1 consistent with a steady-state equilibrium. Such a situation is depicted for the $n = 2$, $m = 1$ case by the *EE* locus in Figure 5.2. Moreover, as the reader is asked to prove in Exercise 5.2, the slope of this *EE* locus is not equal to $-p_2/p_1$.

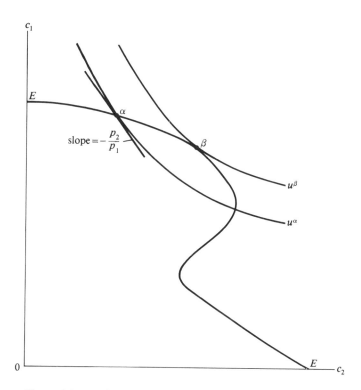

Figure 5.2. In this example, with a positive steady-state interest rate, it is not necessarily true that point β is preferred to point α on welfare grounds.

Suppose that an economy consists of individuals with identical homothetic preferences represented by the utility function $u(c_1c_2)$. Would it be undesirable for this economy to remain at the steady-state equilibrium point α in Figure 5.2? If the relative price at α is tangent to the $u = u^\alpha$ indifference curve as indicated, one might *wrongly* infer that the economy would be better off at point β, where the EE locus is tangent to the higher $u = u^\beta$ indifference curve.[2] However, starting from the initial conditions appropriate to point α, the economy cannot instantaneously move to point β. Given the initial conditions k_1^α, k_2^α, point β is not feasible because usually the k_1^β, k_2^β capital stocks are different.

Indeed, if the exogenously given value of r is equal to the social rate of time preference, and if we seek to maximize the intertemporal welfare function

$$W = \int_{t=0}^{\infty} u(c_1, c_2)e^{-rt} \, dt, \tag{5.2.12}$$

it would be *optimal,* in the sense of maximizing the welfare function (5.2.12), to remain at α *even though* $-p_2/p_1$ *is not equal to the slope of the EE locus.*

In general, then, one must be careful to avoid restricting attention entirely to steady states. Given any initial conditions, including those appropriate to some steady-state equilibrium, the relevant choices open to an economy consist of the technologically feasible dynamic paths. We now turn to some results concerning the properties of this relevant set.

5.3. **Dynamic equilibrium prices**

Most of the relevant literature dealing with consumption efficiency and infinite-time dynamic paths is in discrete time, and we shall follow this tradition. As in Chapter 2, there are m primary (nonproduced) factors of production and n produced commodities which serve both as consumption and capital goods. The net output of the ith-type commodity at the end of period t (and hence available for use during period $t + 1$) is denoted by y_i^{t+1}, and since this output may either be consumed or used as a capital-good input during period $t + 1$, as before we have

$$y_i^{t+1} \geq c_i^{t+1} + k_i^{t+1}, \qquad i = 1, \ldots, n. \tag{5.3.1}$$

The inequality in (5.3.1) allows for the possibility that some of the ith-type output produced in period t is not used during period $t + 1$. The primary factors used during period t are denoted by $\ell_1^t, \ldots, \ell_m^t$. It is clear that $0 \leq \ell_i^t \leq L_i^t$ for all t and $i = 1, \ldots, m$, where L_i^t denotes the quantity of the ith primary factor available for use during period t.

To simplify notation we define the column vectors

$$y^t = \begin{bmatrix} y_1^t \\ \cdot \\ \cdot \\ \cdot \\ y_n^t \end{bmatrix}, \quad c^t = \begin{bmatrix} c_1^t \\ \cdot \\ \cdot \\ \cdot \\ c_n^t \end{bmatrix}, \quad k^t = \begin{bmatrix} k_1^t \\ \cdot \\ \cdot \\ \cdot \\ k_n^t \end{bmatrix}, \quad \text{and } \ell^t = \begin{bmatrix} \ell_1^t \\ \cdot \\ \cdot \\ \cdot \\ \ell_m^t \end{bmatrix}.$$

The *technology* consists of the set of vectors

$$S^t = \{(y^{t+1}, k^t, \ell^t)\} \tag{5.3.2}$$

which are feasible, and S^t is called the *production set;* it designates the outputs, y^{t+1}, which can be produced by the beginning of period $t + 1$ given the capital goods, k^t, and the primary factors, ℓ^t, actually used during period t. For example, the neoclassical production-possibilities frontier expressed as equation (2.2.1) yields the special production set

$$S^t = \{y^{t+1}, k^t, \ell^t | y_1^{t+1} \\ \leq F^t(y_2^{t+1}, \ldots, y_n^{t+1}; k_1^t, \ldots, k_n^t; \ell_1^t, \ldots, \ell_m^t), y^{t+1} \\ \geq 0, k^t \geq 0, \ell^t \geq 0\}.$$

We are concerned only with nonnegative quantities and thus restrict our attention to column vectors satisfying

$$(y^{t+1}, k^t, \ell^t) \geq (0, 0, 0) \quad \text{and} \quad (y^{t+1}, k^t, \ell^t) \neq (0, 0, 0).$$

Assumptions about the properties of the production set S^t are required, and the following list is typical:

ASSUMPTION 5.1
There exists some $(y^{t+1}, k^t, \ell^t) \in S^t$ with $y^{t+1} > 0$ (positive production is possible), and if $(y^{t+1}, 0, 0) \in S^t$, then $y^{t+1} = 0$ (no positive output with zero inputs).

ASSUMPTION 5.2
S^t is a closed, convex set containing the origin [no increasing returns and $(0, 0, 0) \in S^t$].

ASSUMPTION 5.3

If $(y^{t+1}, k^t, \ell^t) \in S^t$, $\bar{k}^t > k^t$, and $\bar{\ell}^t > \ell^t$, then there exists some $(\bar{y}^{t+1}, \bar{k}^t, \overline{\ell^t}) \in S^t$ such that $\bar{y}^{t+1} > y^{t+1}$ (capital and primary factors are productive).[3]

ASSUMPTION 5.4

If $(y^{t+1}, k^t, \ell^t) \in S^t$, then for any $\lambda > 0$ we also have $(\lambda y^{t+1}, \lambda k^t, \lambda \ell^t) \in S^t$ (constant returns to scale).

ASSUMPTION 5.5

If $(y^{t+1}, k^t, \ell^t) \in S^t$, $\bar{k}^t \geq k^t$, $\overline{\ell}^t \geq \ell^t$, and $y^{t+1} \geq \bar{y}^{t+1} \geq 0$, then $(\bar{y}^{t+1}, \bar{k}^t, \overline{\ell^t}) \in S^t$ (free disposal).

This list of assumptions, adapted from Cass (1972a), plays a crucial role in proving the existence of the equilibrium prices to be defined below. Our concern, however, is not with the technical details of such existence proofs.[4]

A *dynamic path* is a sequence of vectors

$$P = \{(c^{t+1}, k^{t+1}, k^t, \ell^t)\}_{t=1}^{T}, \qquad T \leq \infty,$$

such that

$$y^{t+1} \geq c^{t+1} + k^{t+1}$$

and

$$(y^{t+1}, k^t, \ell^t) \in S^t \qquad \text{for all } t \geq 1.$$

In addition, a path P is *feasible* if, for every t, the nonproduced factors $\ell_1^t, \ldots, \ell_m^t$ actually used are less than or equal to the exogenously specified supplies we have denoted by $L_1^t, \ldots, L_m^t$, and if the initial vector of capital goods actually used in the first time period, k^1, is less than or equal to some specified initial vector of capital goods. Thus feasibility entails $\ell^t \leq L^t$ for all $t \geq 1$ *and* $k^1 \leq K^1$, where we take K^1 as an initial condition satisfying $K^1 \geq 0$, $K^1 \neq 0$ (so that at least one component of the n-dimensional vector K^1 is positive).

As in Chapter 2, we denote present value prices by p_i^t (for the produced commodities $i = 1, \ldots, n$) and w_i^t (for the primary factors $i = 1, \ldots, m$). Thus the condition for (discounted) profit maximization in period t is simply that the present value of outputs minus the present value of inputs be maximized at given (p^{t+1}, p^t, w^t); that is,[5]

$$\max p^{t+1} \cdot y^{t+1} - p^t \cdot k^t - w^t \cdot \ell^t.$$

A feasible path $\bar{P}$ is termed *competitive* if there exist prices (p^{t+1}, p^t, w^t), for all t, such that:

(1) $p^t \geq 0$ and $p^t \neq 0$ for all t (nonnegative commodity prices and not all free goods).
(2) $w^t \geq 0$ and $w^t \neq 0$ for all t (nonnegative primary factor prices and not all free primary factors).
(3) If any primary factor in some time period is not fully utilized, its price in that period is zero, implying that all units of a primary factor receive the same payment and $w^t \cdot (\ell^t - L^t) = 0$.
(4) Along the path $\bar{P}$ the associated vectors $(\bar{y}^{t+1}, \bar{k}^t, \bar{\ell}^t)$ are profit maximizing at these prices; that is, *for all* t and *for all vectors* $(y^{t+1}, k^t, \ell^t) \in S^t$, we have

$$p^{t+1} \cdot \bar{c}^{t+1} + p^{t+1} \cdot \bar{k}^{t+1} - p^t \cdot \bar{k}^t - w^t \cdot \bar{\ell}^t \\ \geq p^{t+1} \cdot y^{t+1} - p^t \cdot k^t - w^t \cdot \ell^t. \quad (5.3.3)$$

Note that k^t and ℓ^t on the right-hand side of (5.3.3) are not constrained by feasibility considerations, as is the case for an atomistic firm facing horizontal factor supply schedules.

Competitive paths have the following familiar properties for all t:

(1) If $\bar{\ell}_i^t < L_i^t$, then $w_i^t = 0$. In other words, if the quantity of the ith primary factor actually used is less than the exogenous supply, then its factor price is zero.
(2) $p^{t+1} \cdot \bar{c}^{t+1} + p^{t+1} \cdot \bar{k}^{t+1} - p^t \cdot \bar{k}^t - w^t \cdot \ell^t \leq 0.$ (5.3.4)

That is, along a competitive path, the present value of profits is nonpositive.
(3) If $\bar{y}_i^{t+1} > \bar{c}_i^{t+1} + \bar{k}_i^{t+1}$, then $\bar{p}_i^{t+1} = 0$. Thus if the production of the ith commodity exceeds its actual usage as a consumption good and a capital input, there is excess supply and its price is zero. The proofs of these three propositions rely upon the assumptions of free disposal and constant returns, and they are left as Exercise 5.3.

5.4. **Properties of competitive paths**

Competitive paths as defined in Section 5.3 are, of course, nothing but dynamic paths along which the economy is always in general equilibrium, exactly as was the case for the dynamic paths we studied previously in Chapters 2 and 3. One should be cautious, however, to avoid the false inference that such paths are consistent only with "free competition." Competitive paths *are* consistent with the ordinary notion of free competition, but other institutional forms (e.g., central planning) are also consistent with the purely technical definition of a competitive path.[6]

We now will focus upon competitive paths, freeing us from the unrealistic straightjacket imposed by restricting attention to steady-state equilibria. In general, what economic properties are exhibited by competitive paths? Without further technological assumptions, two features may be asserted. First, short-run efficient dynamic paths (in a sense to be defined precisely) are also competitive. Second, under certain conditions (to be stated) competitive paths maximize the present value of consumption with the equilibrium prices as discount factors. These are important properties; indeed, the first is simply a generalization of the "dynamic invisible hand" principle discussed in Chapter 2. However, we have already been alerted in Chapter 3 to the possibility of consumption inefficiency through capital overaccumulation, and the task before us is to identify these difficult issues in the context of our general model allowing for the heterogeneity of commodities. By allowing for many different types of commodities, the conclusions we will now reach are free of all "aggregation problems" and, accordingly, may be termed genuine principles for dynamic economics.

We must make the concept of short-run efficiency precise.

DEFINITION 5.1

A feasible path $\bar{P}$ is called *short-run efficient* over the time horizon $t = 1, \ldots, T$ if there does not exist any alternative feasible path over the same time horizon along which (a) consumption of every commodity, for all t, and terminal capital stocks are at least as great, and (b) in some time period consumption of at least one commodity is greater, or some terminal capital stock is greater. Thus if $\bar{P}$ is short-run efficient, there is no feasible path P for which:

(a) $c^t \geq \bar{c}^t$ for all $t = 1, \ldots, T$ and $k^T \geq \bar{k}^T$.

(b) For some time period τ ($1 \leq \tau \leq T$) either $c_i^\tau > \bar{c}_i^\tau$ for the ith consumption good, or $k_i^T > \bar{k}_i^T$ for some terminal capital stock of type i.

This concept of short-run efficiency should be contrasted with our previous notion of consumption efficiency for an infinite time horizon, which we now generalize formally.

DEFINITION 5.2
A feasible dynamic path $\bar{P}$ is called *consumption efficient* (over the infinite time horizon for periods $t = 1, 2, \ldots$) if there does not exist any alternative feasible dynamic path P along which:

(a) $c^t \geq \bar{c}^t$ for all $t = 1, 2, \ldots$.

(b) For some time period $\tau \geq 1$ and for some consumption good, say the ith, $c_i^\tau > \bar{c}_i^\tau$.

The obvious distinction is that short-run efficiency requires consideration of what happens to terminal capital stocks, whereas consumption efficiency involves no such consideration because, of course, there *is* no "terminal" time period for an infinite-horizon path. To clarify this issue, consider two feasible paths $\hat{P}$ and $\check{P}$, both of finite duration with $t = 1, \ldots, T$. Assume that they provide identical consumption streams with

$$\hat{c}^t = \check{c}^t \qquad \text{for } t = 1, \ldots, T,$$

but that the terminal capital stocks differ, with $\hat{k}^T \neq \check{k}^T$. However, suppose that these terminal capital-stock vectors are unequal only because path $\hat{P}$ provides more terminal capital of type 1; that is,

$$\hat{k}_1^T > \bar{k}_1^T, \quad \hat{k}_i^T = \bar{k}_i^T, \qquad i = 2, \ldots, n.$$

Clearly, then, the path $\bar{P}$ is *short-run inefficient* by our definition. What is the economic justification for labeling this situation as "inefficient"? Two considerations must be implicit if "inefficiency" is to be justified on commonsense grounds:

(1) If only consumption matters, obviously one must be thinking of an economic system that survives after period T. If, on the other hand, period T *is* literally the end of the world, it would be unreasonable to call $\bar{P}$ short-run inefficient simply because it provides a smaller quantity of the ith-type capital good at the terminal time ($\hat{k}_1^T > \bar{k}_1^T$). If this capital stock never can be used to produce output for use during period $T + 1$ because there is no world at time $T + 1$, why would one select $\hat{P}$ over $\bar{P}$? After all, both provide identical consumption streams over the relevant time horizon, $t = 1, \ldots, T$, before doomsday!

(2) Even if we (perhaps optimistically) assume that there will be a period $T + 1$, $\hat{k}_1^T > \bar{k}_1^t$ is relevant, again supposing that it is consumption which is of ultimate economic relevance in evaluating performance, only if the larger capital stock of type 1 favorably alters the feasible set of consumption possibilities in future periods ($t \geq T + 1$). Such will be the case if capital of good 1 is used, either directly or indirectly, to produce at least one of the consumption goods. If, on the other hand, type 1 commodity is never used, even indirectly, to produce anything but itself, and if it is *never* consumed (a "pure capital good," perhaps bricks), then having more of this type capital good will not enable greater future consumption of any commodity. The use of the term "short-run inefficient" for path $\bar{P}$ under such circumstances is somewhat misleading from an economic viewpoint.

It is clear that a consumption efficient path must also be short-run efficient for every value of T provided that all pure capital goods (i.e., capital goods that are never consumed) are "productive" in that increases in their stocks also produce increases in the future consumption possibilities. There are various assumptions that make precise the exact sense in which increased capital stocks lead to greater future consumption possibilities. All of these essentially impose conditions on the technology which allow for substitution among the various inputs and outputs, and the following assumption, based upon the work of Cass (1972a), will suffice for our purposes:

ASSUMPTION 5.6

If $(y^{t+1}, k^t, \ell^t) \in S^t$ and $0 \le \bar{c}^{t+1} < c^{t+1}$ (or $0 \le \bar{k}^{t+1} < k^{t+1}$), there exists some $(\tilde{y}^{t+1}, k^t, \ell^t) \in S^t$ with $\hat{k}^{t+1} > k^{t+1}$, $\tilde{y}^{t+1} \ge \bar{c}^{t+1} + \hat{k}^{t+1}$ (or with $\tilde{c}^{t+1} > c^{t+1}$, $\tilde{y}^{t+1} \ge \tilde{c}^{t+1} + \bar{k}^{t+1}$).

Without Assumption (5.6), or a similar alternative, the concept of short-run efficiency loses much (if not all) of its economic relevance. We are interested in the efficiency of capital-good production only when those capital goods can be used directly or indirectly to increase consumption.

Thus let us assume (5.6) and consider a dynamic path P that is both (1) consumption efficient, and (2) short-run inefficient over the finite horizon $t = 1, \ldots, T$. A contradiction arises because, by the definition of short-run efficiency, there must exist some other path $\bar{P}$ over $t = 1, \ldots, T$ which either (a) yields more consumption of at least one commodity in time period τ, $1 \le \tau \le T$, or (b) yields the same consumption, more terminal capital of some type, and at least as much of all other types. If (a) occurs, the original path P cannot be consumption efficient; a new path starting with $\bar{P}$ for the first $t = 1, \ldots, T$ time periods and then following P for $t = T + 1, T + 2, \ldots$ is feasible by virtue of free disposal and the terminal conditions implied by the definition of short-run efficiency. If, on the other hand, (b) applies, by following $\bar{P}$ for $t = 1, \ldots, T$, we will do at least as well in terms of consumption and have a greater terminal capital stock of some type, say $\bar{k}_1^T > k_1^T$, leaving all other terminal capital stocks no worse ($\bar{k}^T \ge k^T$). Then, invoking Assumption (5.6), we see that $\bar{c}^T > c^T$, $\bar{k}^T \ge k^T$ is feasible; it is possible to "substitute" the extra terminal capital of type 1 for more consumption at time T.

But the path so constructed violates the definition of consumption efficiency for the original path P.

This example reveals how Assumption (5.6) can be weakened, for clearly a similar contradiction can be constructed provided the extra terminal capital stock can be converted into more consumption of *some* type at *some* finite time $\tau \geqslant T$, while leaving all other consumption in every other time period no less. Thus Assumption (5.6) can be generalized to "*intertemporal* substitution between capital inputs and future consumption," but we have no need to pursue the details here as the economic message is clear from what already has been said.

Further note that if Assumption (5.6) or a similar restriction on the technology is violated – say, if there exists some pure capital good whose *only* use is to produce itself – then a consumption-efficient path (say $\hat{P}$ over the infinite time horizon $t = 1, 2, \ldots$) may *not* be short-run efficient. The reason, of course, is simply that such a capital good is of no use in producing current or future consumption, and consequently a finite-horizon path that yields as much as possible of this good at a finite time T (while providing the same consumption as on $\hat{P}$ for $t = 1, \ldots, T$) does not allow consumption greater than on $\hat{P}$ for any $t \geqslant T + 1$.

Another insight into the nature of the efficiency question is evident if we observe that even if a dynamic path is short-run efficient for *every* finite value of T, it need not be consumption efficient over an infinite time horizon. Indeed, consider a trivial example with only one type of capital good, all consumption set at zero in every time period, and the terminal capital stock maximized for every finite value of T. Such a path *is* short-run efficient for every T, but it never yields any consumption and clearly is consumption inefficient.

There is, however, an important economic property of short-run efficient paths which we now state:

THEOREM 5.1
If a dynamic path is short-run efficient for every finite time horizon T, then it is also a competitive path.

The proof of this theorem, although straightforward, involves mathematical technicalities beyond the scope of this book, and the interested reader is referred to Cass (1972a) for the general result and to Bliss (1975, chap. 10) for a more restrictive case. In both proofs the essential problem is to demonstrate the existence of the dynamic equilibrium prices as stated in the definition of a competitive path.

An immediate conclusion implied by Theorem 5.1 and the example in the paragraph preceding, sometimes regarded as startling to economists unfamiliar with the subtleties of infinite-time dynamic problems, is that *there exist consumption-efficient paths (over an infinite time horizon) which are not competitive and hence for which dynamic equilibrium prices do not exist.*

What desirable properties do competitive paths exhibit? With one additional assumption stated below, we can prove that competitive paths have the following maximizing property:[7]

Theorem 5.2

Let $\bar{P}$ denote a competitive path, and let P denote any alternative feasible dynamic path, starting from the same initial conditions, which uses the same primary factors as $\bar{P}$ (i.e., any other feasible path for which $\ell^t = \bar{\ell}^t$ for all $t = 1, 2, \ldots$). If, in addition, the price sequence associated with $\bar{P}$, namely $\{\bar{p}^t, \bar{w}^t\}_{t=0}^{\infty}$, has the property that

$$\lim_{T \to \infty} \bar{p}^{T+1} \cdot \bar{k}^{T+1} = 0, \tag{5.4.1}$$

then the competitive path $\bar{P}$ has the property that it *maximizes the present value of consumption* using the dynamic equilibrium prices $\bar{p}^t$ as discount factors in the sense that

$$0 \geqslant \lim_{T \to \infty} \sup \sum_{t=1}^{T} \bar{p}^{t+1} \cdot (c^{t+1} - \bar{c}^{t+1}). \tag{5.4.2}$$

Proof. Using the definition of a competitive path, we have from (5.3.3) that

$$\bar{p}^{t+1} \cdot \bar{c}^{t+1} + \bar{p}^{t+1} \cdot \bar{k}^{t+1} - \bar{p}^t \cdot \bar{k}^t - \bar{w}^t \cdot \bar{\ell}^t$$
$$\geqslant \bar{p}^{t+1} \cdot y^{t+1} - \bar{p}^t \cdot k^t - \bar{w}^t \cdot \ell^t \qquad (5.4.3)$$
$$\text{for all } t = 1, 2, \ldots$$

However, by assumption $\ell^t = \bar{\ell}^t$ for all t, and $y^{t+1} \geqslant c^{t+1} + k^{t+1}$; this and (5.4.3) imply the inequality

$$0 \geqslant \bar{p}^{t+1} \cdot (c^{t+1} - \bar{c}^{t+1}) + \bar{p}^{t+1} \cdot (k^{t+1} - \bar{k}^{t+1})$$
$$- \bar{p}^t \cdot (k^t - \bar{k}^t), \qquad t = 1, 2, \ldots \qquad (5.4.4)$$

Adding (5.4.4) for $t = 1, 2, \ldots, T$ yields

$$0 \geqslant \sum_{t=1}^{T} \bar{p}^{t+1} \cdot (c^{t+1} - \bar{c}^{t+1}) + \bar{p}^{T+1} \cdot (k^{T+1} - \bar{k}^{T+1})$$
$$+ \bar{p}^1 \cdot (k^1 - \bar{k}^1). \qquad (5.4.5)$$

But $k^1 = \bar{k}^1$, because both paths start from the same initial conditions, and thus

$$0 \geqslant \sum_{t=1}^{T} \bar{p}^{t+1} \cdot (c^{t+1} - \bar{c}^{t+1}) + \bar{p}^{T+1} \cdot (k^{T+1} - \bar{k}^{T+1}).$$

$$(5.4.6)$$

From the condition (5.4.1) we know that

$$\lim_{T \to \infty} \bar{p}^{T+1} \cdot (k^{T+1} - \bar{k}^{T+1}) \geqslant 0.$$

Thus even though the term $\sum_{t=1}^{T} \bar{p}^{t+1} \cdot (c^{t+1} - \bar{c}^{t+1})$ may not converge as $T \to \infty$ [it may oscillate or approach $-\infty$, as noted by Bliss (1975, p. 228)], conclusion (5.4.2) follows.

Q.E.D.

Several observations about Theorem 5.2 are in order.

(1) If we assume capital stocks are bounded – that is, if there exists some finite number $B > 0$ such that $\bar{k}_i^t < B$ for all capital goods $i = 1, \ldots, n$ and for all $t = 1, 2, \ldots$ – then the alternative condition

$$\lim_{T \to \infty} \bar{p}^{T+1} = 0 \qquad (5.4.7)$$

implies (5.4.1). Surely boundedness is a reasonable assumption, if for no other fact than the physical limitations imposed by our finite-sized planet. These types of sufficient "transversality conditions" were introduced in the work of Malinvaud (1953) on the efficient allocation of resources.[8]

(2) Under the conditions stated in Theorem 5.2 the competitive path $\bar{P}$ is also consumption efficient. If it were not, the inequality $c_i^\tau > \bar{c}_i^\tau$ would hold for some i and some τ, thus contradicting (5.4.2).

(3) The sufficient condition (5.4.1) is *not* necessary for the conclusion of Theorem 5.2, a fact already evident from the Golden Rule examples discussed in Section 3.5. As with one-capital-good models, the first *necessary and sufficient* conditions for consumption efficiency were discovered by Cass, and we shall state them in Section 5.6.

(4) We conclude this section with the important observations that (a) even given a normalization rule, the dynamic equilibrium prices associated with a competitive path *need not be unique;* and (b) as already noted, without assumption (5.4.6) a consumption-efficient path may not be competitive, and hence the dynamic equilibrium prices asserted in the definition of a competitive path *might not exist* for some consumption-efficient paths.

Regarding observation (a), the reswitching examples of Chapter 4 provide price nonuniqueness examples since the same quantity system is consistent with equilibrium at more than one interest rate, and these interest rates provide different present value price systems that all satisfy the definition of a competitive path at identical steady-state quantities.

Regarding observation (b), we again emphasize that nonexistence problems arise only because there are consumption-efficient paths over infinite-time horizons which are not short-run efficient for every finite value of the terminal time T; otherwise, Theorem 5.1 assures the existence of prices. The question of under exactly what conditions there are dynamic equilibrium prices associated with a consumption-efficient path is a highly technical one which has received a great deal of attention, but the issue is not of central concern to us here.[9]

5.5. Intertemporal rates of transformation

Recall the simple two-period, one-commodity model of production and exchange discussed in Section 2.4. In that model, suppose that 1 unit of current consumption is sacrificed and that this 1 unit is used as a capital input to produce more output and hence make available more future consumption. Let the original consumption pattern be (c^1, c^2) and the new one $(\bar{c}^1, \bar{c}^2)$ with

$$\Delta c^t \equiv c^t - \bar{c}^t, \qquad t = 1, 2.$$

Thus the "consumption sacrifice" of 1 unit of the commodity in period 1 entails

$$\Delta c^1 = c^1 - \bar{c}^1 = +1,$$

while the additional future consumption with $\bar{c}^2 > c^2$ is

$$\Delta c^2 = c^2 - \bar{c}^2 < 0.$$

This additional future consumption equals the product of the extra capital input and the marginal product of capital:

$$- \Delta c^2 = \Delta c^1 \cdot f'(k^1 + \Delta c^1). \tag{5.5.1}$$

For sufficiently small Δc^1 compared with k^1, we have the approximation

$$- \Delta c^2 = \Delta c^1 \cdot f'(k^1). \tag{5.5.2}$$

But in equilibrium

$$f'(k^1) = 1 + r \tag{5.5.3}$$

where r is the own commodity rate of interest from the beginning of period 1 to the beginning of period 2. Accordingly, we have proven, for this special case, the fundamental relationship

$$- \frac{\Delta c^2}{\Delta c^1} - 1 = r. \tag{5.5.4}$$

Thus in equilibrium the interest rate r measures the rate at which current consumption can be "transformed" into future consumption.

We will now generalize the fundamental result (5.5.4) to our model with many heterogeneous commodities. It will be convenient, however, to restrict our attention to cases with a single type of consumption good, and the *scalar* c^t now will denote consumption of this particular commodity at the beginning of period t. In actuality, though, very little is lost by this, for we can interpret c^t either as a particular market basket of n heterogeneous commodities with

$$c^t = \alpha_1 c_1^t + \cdots + \alpha_n c_n^t$$

for basket weights $\alpha_i \geq 0$, or as "utility" where

$$c^t = u(c_1^t, \ldots, c_n^t)$$

and $u(\cdot)$ is a strictly increasing, concave function of the c_i^t's.

The relationship between present and future consumption involves a sacrifice of some consumption in period t ($\Delta c^t > 0$) which allows additional consumption at some future time $\tau \geq t + 1$ ($\Delta c^\tau < 0$) while keeping consumption in every other time period at least as great as it otherwise would have been. Provided such an experiment is technologically feasible, we define

$$-\frac{\Delta c^\tau}{\Delta c^t}, \qquad \tau \geq t + 1, \tag{5.5.5}$$

as the *intertemporal rate of transformation between periods t and τ*.

Upon reflection it is evident that there exist situations for which the stated experiment is impossible and (5.5.5) makes no sense. For example, suppose that the consumption good is corn and time periods are measured in months. If some corn is not consumed in August but instead is planted, clearly no extra consumption is possible in September if it takes more than 1 month to grow corn. Other examples easily can be constructed. However, provided that we assume perfect storage (e.g., if in the example planted corn seed can be costlessly recovered for consumption), it is always true that

$$-\frac{\Delta c^\tau}{\Delta c^t} \geq 1. \tag{5.5.6}$$

The question of when

$$-\frac{\Delta c^\tau}{\Delta c^t} > 1 \tag{5.5.7}$$

is related both to the technology and the length of the time period.

The reader must be careful to remember that we have defined

$$\Delta c^t \equiv c^t - \bar{c}^t$$

where c^t is the consumption on some original path and $\bar{c}^t$ is the consumption on an alternative path. Thus a "consumption sacrifice" in period t in which the new consumption, $\bar{c}^t$, is less than the original c^t, requires that

$$\Delta c^t \equiv c^t - \bar{c}^t > 0.$$

This convention is important because we must distinguish carefully between "consumption sacrifices" (with $\Delta c^t > 0$ and $\Delta c^\tau < 0$ for some future $\tau \geq t + 1$) on the one hand, and "consumption binges" (with $\Delta c^t < 0$ and $\Delta c^\tau > 0$ for some $\tau \geq t + 1$) on the other. Note that "consumption binges" necessitate a *reduction* in future consumption with

$$\bar{c}^\tau < c^\tau$$

or

$$\Delta c^\tau \equiv c^\tau - \bar{c}^\tau > 0 \qquad \text{for some } \tau \geq t + 1.$$

Obviously, there are reasonable technologies for which "consumption binges" are impossible. For example, if the single consumption good is never used as a productive input, and if the original dynamic path is short-run efficient, it is impossible to increase consumption in any time period without first reducing it in an earlier period.

Ignoring such existence questions for the moment, we will introduce notation that clarifies the distinction between "consumption binges" and "consumption sacrifices."

DEFINITION 5.3

Consider a competitive dynamic path and an alternative feasible path with

$$\Delta c^t \equiv c^t - \bar{c}^t \neq 0, \qquad \Delta c^\tau \equiv c^\tau - \bar{c}^\tau = 0$$

for some finite value, $\tau \geq t + 1$. Suppose also that $\Delta c^s \leq 0$ for all $s \neq t, \tau$ and $\bar{k}^\tau \geq k^\tau$. (These requirements ensure that the alternative path provides at least as much consumption as the competitive path except in periods t and τ, i.e., that $\bar{c}^s \geq c^s$ for all $s \neq t$, τ, and that the alternative path ends up at time τ with a capital stock vector at least as large as on the competitive path.) The *left-hand marginal rate of intertemporal transformation between periods t and $\tau \geq t + 1$* is defined as

$$\lim_{\Delta c^t \to 0^+} \left(-\frac{\Delta c^\tau}{\Delta c^t} \right) \equiv \left(-\frac{\Delta c^\tau}{\Delta c^t} \right)^-. \tag{5.5.8}$$

Note that this limit is defined as Δc^t approaches zero through *positive* values, and hence it is our "consumption *sacrifices*" case in which $\bar{c}^t < c^t$.

Similarly, the *right-hand marginal rate of intertemporal transformation between periods t and $\tau \geq t + 1$* is defined as

$$\lim_{\Delta c^t \to 0^-} \left(-\frac{\Delta c^\tau}{\Delta c^t} \right) \equiv \left(-\frac{\Delta c^\tau}{\Delta c^t} \right)^+. \tag{5.5.9}$$

5.6. **A numerical example of the intertemporal rate of transformation**

The economic meaning of the intertemporal rate of transformation is more easily understood by considering a simple example. *For the remainder of this section alone,* we postulate a single type of capital good (whose quantity is denoted by the scalar k^t) and a single primary factor (whose quantity is denoted by ℓ^t).[10]

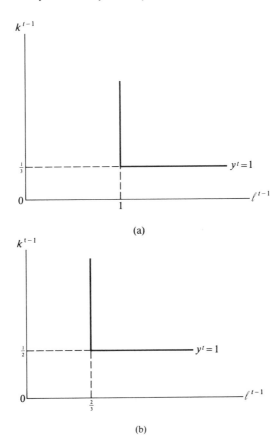

Figure 5.3. (a) Activity α: $y^t = \min(3k^{t-1}, \ell^{t-1})$. (b) Activity β: $y^t = \min(2k^{t-1}, \frac{3}{2}\ell^{t-1})$.

The technology consists of two activities: activity α produces output

$$y^t = \min(3k^{t-1}, \ell^{t-1}), \tag{5.6.1}$$

whereas activity β produces output

$$y^t = \min(2k^{t-1}, \tfrac{3}{2}\ell^{t-1}). \tag{5.6.2}$$

The unit isoquants for these two activities are illustrated in Figure 5.3a and b.

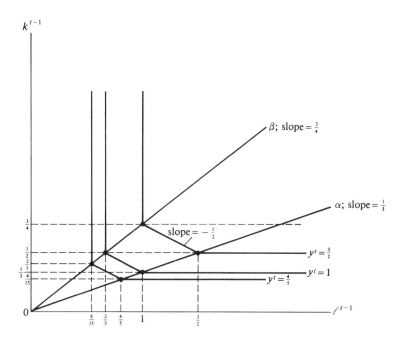

Figure 5.4. Activities α and β together yield the isoquants pictured here and the production function stated in the text as equation (5.6.3).

The technology consists of the feasible $(y^t, k^{t-1}, \ell^{t-1})$ as illustrated by Figure 5.4. Observe that along the line with slope $k^{t-1}/\ell^{t-1} = \frac{3}{4}$, only activity β is used, while only activity α is used along the line with slope $k^{t-1}/\ell^{t-1} = \frac{1}{3}$. When the k^{t-1}/ℓ^{t-1} ratio satisfies $\frac{1}{3} < k^{t-1}/\ell^{t-1} < \frac{3}{4}$ both activities α and β are used to produce the indicated output of y^t. When $k^{t-1}/\ell^{t-1} > \frac{3}{4}$, again only activity β is used, but now capital is redundant in that the same output can be produced with less k^{t-1} input. Similarly, when $k^{t-1}/\ell^{t-1} < \frac{1}{3}$, only activity α is used and ℓ^{t-1}, which we may as well call "labor," is redundant.

It is left as an exercise for the reader to derive the production function for this technology consisting of activities α and β, namely

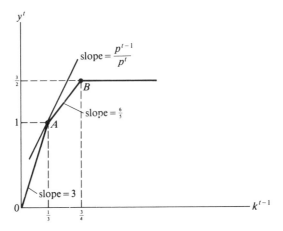

Figure 5.5. The production function for $\ell^t = 1$:

$$y^t = \begin{cases} 3k^{t-1}, & 0 \leq k^{t-1} \leq \frac{1}{3} \\ \frac{6}{5}k^{t-1} + \frac{3}{5}, & \frac{1}{3} \leq k^{t-1} \leq \frac{3}{4} \\ \frac{3}{2}, & k^{t-1} \geq \frac{3}{4} \end{cases}$$

$$y^t = \begin{cases} 3k^{t-1}, & 0 \leq k^{t-1}/\ell^{t-1} \leq \frac{1}{3} \\ \frac{6}{5}k^{t-1} + \frac{3}{5}\ell^{t-1}, & \frac{1}{3} \leq k^{t-1}/\ell^{t-1} \leq \frac{3}{4} \\ \frac{3}{2}\ell^{t-1}, & k^{t-1}/\ell^{t-1} \geq \frac{3}{4} \end{cases} \qquad (5.6.3)$$

In particular, for $\ell^{t-1} = 1$ we have the production function illustrated in Figure 5.5.

Consider now an economy during the time period $t - 1$ which is producing at point A in both Figures 5.4 and 5.5 with $k^{t-1} = \frac{1}{3}$ and $\ell^{t-1} = 1$. Since $k^{t-1}/\ell^{t-1} = \frac{1}{3}$, point A lies on the line labeled α in Figure 5.4 along which only activity α is used, and at A output is $y^t = 1$.

Assume that the exogenous supply of the primary factor ("labor") is constant at $L^{t-1} = L^t = L^{t+1} = \cdots = 1$. The output $y^t = 1$ must be split between consumption, c^t, and capital for use next period, k^t. Clearly, it is feasible to set $c^t = \frac{2}{3}$ and $k^t = \frac{1}{3}$, so that the economy can continue to produce at point A during period t with $k^t = \frac{1}{3}$, $\ell^t = 1$, and $y^{t+1} = 1$. Therefore, point A represents a steady-state equilibrium for which

$$c^t = \tfrac{2}{3}, \quad k^t = \tfrac{1}{3}, \quad \ell^t = 1, \qquad t = 1, 2, \ldots. \qquad (5.6.4)$$

As we have emphasized, remaining in this steady-state equilibrium producing at point A is only one of the dynamic alternatives open to this economy, and not a very interesting alternative. Given that the economy is producing at point A in period $t - 1$ (with $k^{t-1} = \frac{1}{3}$, $\ell^{t-1} = 1$, and $y^t = 1$), what are the feasible pairs of consumption (c^t, c^{t+1}) which are consistent with leaving a terminal capital stock of $k^{t+1} = \frac{1}{3}$? Note that by setting $k^{t+1} = \frac{1}{3}$ as a terminal condition, the economy has the same consumption possibilities open to it after period $t + 1$ as it would have had if it had been in a steady-state equilibrium over periods t, $t + 1$ with $c^t = c^{t+1} = \frac{2}{3}$ and $k^{t-1} = k^t = k^{t+1} = \frac{1}{3}$.

Consider first the "consumption sacrifice" case. Since Figure 5.5 is a description of the production function (with a unit labor input), it holds when k^{t-1} and y^t are replaced by k^t and y^{t+1}, respectively.[11] Clearly there is no benefit from having $k^t > \frac{3}{4}$ because $y^{t+1} = \frac{3}{2}$ is the maximum output that can be achieved under the constraint that $\ell^t = 1$. We start this economy producing at point A in both Figures 5.4 and 5.5 with $k^{t-1} = \frac{1}{3}$, $\ell^{t-1} = 1$, and $y^t = 1$. Thus the *smallest* c^t we should want to select is $c^t = \frac{1}{4}$ which yields the maximum desired capital stock $k^t = \frac{3}{4}$, with $y^t = 1 = c^t + k^t = \frac{1}{4} + \frac{3}{4}$. Now with $k^t = \frac{3}{4}$, $\ell^t = 1$, the output $y^{t+1} = \frac{3}{2}$ is produced. Because we insist that $k^{t+1} = \frac{1}{3}$, we have that $c^{t+1} = y^{t+1} - k^{t+1} = \frac{3}{2} - \frac{1}{3} = \frac{7}{6}$.

Now refer to Figure 5.6. The economy could have remained in the steady-state equilibrium with $(c^t, c^{t+1}) = (\frac{2}{3}, \frac{2}{3})$. However, by reducing consumption to $\frac{1}{4}$, it is possible to achieve $c^{t+1} = \frac{7}{6}$. Moreover, output is linearly related to k^t (with $\ell^t = 1$) for $\frac{1}{3} \le k^t \le \frac{3}{4}$, and thus setting c^t at any value between $\frac{1}{4}$ and $\frac{2}{3}$ produces linear changes in c^{t+1}. Thus in Figure 5.6 a straight line connects the points $(c^t, c^{t+1}) = (\frac{2}{3}, \frac{2}{3})$ and $(c^t, c^{t+1}) = (\frac{1}{4}, \frac{7}{6})$.

However, a value of c^t less than $\frac{1}{4}$ does not make possible $c^{t+1} > \frac{7}{6}$ because, given the labor constraint $\ell^t = 1$, as already

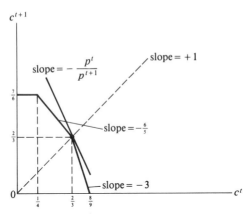

Figure 5.6. The consumption possibilities (c^t, c^{t+1}) feasible with the technology described by equation (5.6.3) when the initial conditions are $k^{t-1} = \frac{1}{3}$, $\ell^{t-1} = \ell^t = 1$.

noted y^t cannot exceed $\frac{3}{2}$. Accordingly, the points $(c^t, c^{t+1}) = (\frac{1}{4}, \frac{7}{6})$ and $(c^t, c^{t+1}) = (0, \frac{7}{6})$ are connected by the horizontal line segment in Figure 5.6.

A "consumption binge" occurs when we pick a value of $c^t > \frac{2}{3}$. Clearly, the maximum value of c^t consistent with the terminal capital-stock condition $k^{t+1} = \frac{1}{3}$ occurs when $y^{t+1} = \frac{1}{3}$ and $c^{t+1} = 0$. To produce this necessary output $y^{t+1} = \frac{1}{3}$, we require inputs of $k^t = \frac{1}{9}$, $\ell^t = 1$, as is evident from both Figures 5.4 and 5.5. But we started with $y^t = 1$, and hence the maximum possible c^t is $c^t = y^t - k^t = 1 - \frac{1}{9} = \frac{8}{9}$. Thus the points $(c^t, c^{t+1}) = (\frac{2}{3}, \frac{2}{3})$ and $(c^t, c^{t+1}) = (\frac{8}{9}, 0)$ are connected by a straight-line segment in Figure 5.6.

To summarize our results so far, Figure 5.6 represents the pairs of (c^t, c^{t+1}) which are consistent with:

(1) The exogenous primary factor supply constraints

$\ell^{t-1} \leq L^{t-1} = 1$ and $\ell^t \leq L^t \leq 1$.

(2) The initial capital-stock condition $k^{t-1} = \frac{1}{3}$.
(3) The terminal capital-stock condition $k^{t+1} = \frac{1}{3}$.
(4) The given technological conditions of production.

Let us now turn to the properties of the price system in this simple numerical example. It is clear that the steady state with

$$c^t = \tfrac{2}{3}, \quad k^t = \tfrac{1}{3}, \quad \ell^t = 1, \qquad t = 1, 2, \ldots \qquad (5.6.4)$$

is short-run efficient and hence, by Theorem 5.1, *competitive*. Indeed, the reader may easily verify that

$$p^t = \left(\frac{1}{1+r}\right)^t \qquad (5.6.5)$$

and

$$w^t = \left(\frac{1}{1+r}\right)^t \left(\frac{1}{1+r} - \frac{1}{3}\right) \qquad (5.6.6)$$

are dynamic equilibrium prices associated with this steady state for all constant values of the interest rate r satisfying $0 < r \leqslant 2$, where $p^t/p^{t+1} = 1 + r$.

Thus consider some dynamic equilibrium prices (p^{t-1}, p^t, p^{t+1}) and (w^{t-1}, w^t) associated with the steady state (5.6.4). Let $(\bar{c}^t, \bar{k}^t, \bar{\ell}^t = 1)$ and $(\bar{c}^{t+1}, \bar{k}^{t+1} = \tfrac{1}{3}, \bar{\ell}^{t+1} = 1)$ represent an alternative feasible path during periods t and $t + 1$; these feasible $(\bar{c}^t, \bar{c}^{t+1})$ pairs are illustrated in Figure 5.6. Because the steady-state point is competitive, production during period $t - 1$ must satisfy equation (5.3.3); that is,

$$\begin{aligned}
&p^t(c^t + k^t) - p^{t-1}k^{t-1} - w^{t-1}\ell^{t-1} \\
&= p^t(\tfrac{2}{3} + \tfrac{1}{3}) - p^{t-1} \cdot \tfrac{1}{3} - w^{t-1} \cdot 1 \\
&\geqslant p^t(\bar{c}^t + \bar{k}^t) - p^{t-1} \cdot \tfrac{1}{3} - w^{t-1} \cdot 1
\end{aligned} \qquad (5.6.7)$$

or

$$p^t(\tfrac{2}{3} - \bar{c}^t) + p^t(\tfrac{1}{3} - \bar{k}^t) \geqslant 0. \qquad (5.6.8)$$

Similarly, during period t we have

$$\begin{aligned}
p^{t+1}(\tfrac{2}{3} + \tfrac{1}{3}) - p^t \cdot \tfrac{1}{3} - w^t \cdot 1 \\
\geqslant p^{t+1}(\bar{c}^{t+1} + \tfrac{1}{3}) - p^t\bar{k}^t - w^t \cdot 1
\end{aligned} \qquad (5.6.9)$$

or

$$p^{t+1}(\tfrac{2}{3} - \bar{c}^{t+1}) - p^t(\tfrac{1}{3} - \bar{k}^t) \geqslant 0. \qquad (5.6.10)$$

Now add the inequalities (5.6.8) and (5.6.10):

$$p^{t+1}(\tfrac{2}{3} - \bar{c}^{t+1}) + p^t(\tfrac{2}{3} - \bar{c}^t) \geqslant 0. \tag{5.6.11}$$

The inequality (5.6.11) is economically significant because it provides bounds on the own interest rates

$$r^t \equiv \frac{p^t}{p^{t+1}} - 1$$

associated with the dynamic equilibrium prices for the steady state (5.6.4). Thus, referring to Figure 5.6, let us set $(\bar{c}^t, \bar{c}^{t+1}) = (\tfrac{8}{9}, 0)$ in (5.6.11); we then have

$$p^{t+1}(\tfrac{2}{3} - 0) + p^t(\tfrac{2}{3} - \tfrac{8}{9}) \geqslant 0$$

or

$$p^{t+1} + p^t(1 - \tfrac{4}{3}) \geqslant 0$$

or

$$\frac{p^t}{p^{t+1}} \leqslant 3. \tag{5.6.12}$$

Likewise setting $(\bar{c}^t, \bar{c}^{t+1}) = (\tfrac{1}{4}, \tfrac{7}{6})$ in (5.6.11) yields

$$p^{t+1}(\tfrac{2}{3} - \tfrac{7}{6}) + p^t(\tfrac{2}{3} - \tfrac{1}{4}) \geqslant 0$$

or

$$p^{t+1}(8 - 14) + p^t(8 - 3) \geqslant 0$$

or

$$-\frac{6}{5} + \frac{p^t}{p^{t+1}} \geqslant 0$$

or[12]

$$\frac{6}{5} \leqslant \frac{p^t}{p^{t+1}}. \tag{5.6.13}$$

Combining (5.6.12) and (5.6.13) provides the desired restriction on r^t:

$$\frac{6}{5} \leqslant \frac{p^t}{p^{t+1}} = r^t + 1 \leqslant 3. \tag{5.6.14}$$

It is, of course, no coincidence that the slopes of the line segments in Figure 5.6 correspond exactly to (the negative of) the slopes of the line segments of the production function in Figure 5.5. Indeed, some additional economic insight can be gained by considering this production function directly. If production at point A is to be consistent with a competitive path, profits must be zero during period t at dynamic equilibrium prices; that is,

$$p^{t+1} \cdot 1 - p^t \cdot \tfrac{1}{3} - w^t \cdot 1 = 0. \tag{5.6.15}$$

But since $w^t \geqslant 0$, (5.6.15) implies (5.6.12).[13] Now refer to Figure 5.4 and observe that $y^{t+1} = \tfrac{4}{5}$ can be produced using inputs $k^t = \tfrac{1}{3}$ and $\ell^t = \tfrac{2}{3}$ during period t. This option cannot be more profitable than producing at A, so that we have

$$p^{t+1} \cdot 1 - p^t \cdot \tfrac{1}{3} - w^t \cdot 1 \geqslant p^{t+1} \cdot \tfrac{4}{5} - p^t \cdot \tfrac{1}{3} - w^t \cdot \tfrac{2}{3} \tag{5.6.16}$$

which implies

$$w^t \leqslant \tfrac{3}{5} p^{t+1}. \tag{5.6.17}$$

But, substituting (5.6.17) into (5.6.15), we derive

$$p^{t+1} - p^t \cdot \tfrac{1}{3} = w^t \leqslant \tfrac{3}{5} p^{t+1}$$

or

$$\frac{6}{5} \leqslant \frac{p^t}{p^{t+1}} ,$$

which is (5.6.13) again.

Our example is completed by referring back to the definitions of left-hand and right-hand marginal rates of intertemporal substitution, (5.5.8) and (5.5.9) in Section 5.5. Setting $\tau = t + 1$ in (5.5.8) and (5.5.9), it is evident from Figure 5.6 and (5.6.14) that

$$\left(- \frac{\Delta c^{t+1}}{\Delta c^t} \right)^- = \tfrac{6}{5} \leqslant \frac{p^t}{p^{t+1}} = r^t + 1 \leqslant 3 = \left(- \frac{\Delta c^{t+1}}{\Delta c^t} \right)^+ . \tag{5.6.18}$$

The limiting operations as $\Delta c^t \equiv c^t - \bar{c}^t \to 0^+$ and $\Delta c^t \equiv c^t - \bar{c}^t \to 0^-$ are not necessary for this linear example, but they are required in the general case when the straight-line segments in Figure 5.6 are replaced by curved-line segments. Also, with more and more alternative linear activities such as α and β, there will be more and more line segments in Figure 5.6, so that (5.6.18) will provide the strongest possible restriction on p^t/p^{t+1} since the limiting values in (5.6.18) will correspond to the absolute values of the slopes of the line segments adjacent to the steady-state point.

How general are the results we have established in this section? We already know from Chapter 4 that a well-behaved "production function" relating "output" to "capital inputs" may not even exist for models with heterogeneous commodities. Therefore, it is impossible in general to find a "production function" such as the one illustrated in Figure 5.5 whose slope is associated with p^t/p^{t+1}. However, Figure 5.6 *does* hold under quite unrestrictive conditions, and thus the inequality (5.6.18) remains valid *even for technologies that admit the reswitching "paradoxes" arising from steady-state comparisons.* Moreover, this type of result does not depend upon any of the special assumptions we have made in this section for simplicity. In particular:

(1) The original path with which alternatives are compared need not be a steady-state equilibrium.
(2) The changes in consumption need not occur in adjacent time periods.

In the next section we state these general results precisely.

5.7. **Marginal rates of intertemporal transformation and prices**

The example in Section 5.6 can now be generalized to a model with n heterogeneous capital goods, m different primary factors, and (for convenience of exposition), a single consumption good. The associated prices for these commodities are denoted by the row vector $p^t = (p_1^t, \ldots, p_n^t)$, the row vector $w^t = (w_1^t, \ldots, w_m^t)$, and the scalar p_c^t. We will achieve some notational simplicity, without loss of generality, by supposing that the capital good of type 1 and the consumption good are identical commodities so that $p_c^t \equiv p_1^t$, and we shall adopt the convention that $c^t + k^t \equiv (c^t + k_1^t, k_2^t, \ldots, k_n^t)$ and $p^t = (p_1^t, p_2^t, \ldots, p_n^t) \equiv (p_c^t, p_2^t, \ldots, p_n^t)$.

The result to be proved is that the marginal rates of intertemporal transformation between periods t and $\tau \geq t + 1$ are related to the dynamic equilibrium consumption-good prices associated with a competitive path by the inequality

$$0 < \left(- \frac{\Delta c^\tau}{\Delta c^t} \right)^- \leq \frac{p_c^t}{p_c^\tau} \leq \left(- \frac{\Delta c^\tau}{\Delta c^t} \right)^+ < \infty \, . \tag{5.7.1}$$

First, however, we must ask when intertemporal transformation makes sense, for, as already noted, there exist technological conditions under which either (1) a reduction of consumption in period t does not allow any future increase in consumption (so that the left-hand marginal rate of intertemporal substitution is zero), or (2) an increase in consumption now, period t, is impossible (so that the right-hand marginal rate of intertemporal substitution is infinity). Of course, in such cases we still have the trivial inequality

$$0 \leq \frac{p_c^t}{p_c^\tau} \leq \infty \, , \tag{5.7.2}$$

but obviously (5.7.1) must hold for the result to be of economic interest.

The issue of when intertemporal substitution is possible is highly technical and involves properties of the technology sets S^t. Moreover, as an empirical matter it is evident that the validity of these properties can depend crucially upon the length of the time period relative to the length of the production period. While it might be impossible to increase current consumption if one time period lasts a few seconds, it could be possible if time periods are of monthly or yearly durations. We shall not be concerned with a precise characterization of the conditions under which $(-\Delta c^t / \Delta c^\tau)^-$ and $(-\Delta c^t / \Delta c^\tau)^+$ exist, but rather simply note that our economic question makes sense when they do. The reader interested in technical details is referred to the list of sufficient conditions, given by Cass (1972a, pp. 232–6) (for $\tau = t + 1$), as well as his discussion of their economic interpretations.

We start by assuming the existence of some dynamic path that is always short-run efficient and hence, by Theorem 5.1, competitive. Let this path be denoted by

$$P = \{c^t, k^t, k^{t-1}, \ell^{t-1}\}_{t=1}^{\infty} \tag{5.7.3}$$

with associated dynamic equilibrium prices

$$\{p^t, w^t\}_{t=0}^{\infty} . \tag{5.7.4}$$

Let $\bar{P}$ be any alternative feasible path starting from the same initial capital-stock vector; $\bar{P}$ need not be competitive at the prices (5.7.4) for which P is competitive.

We assume that P and $\bar{P}$ have the following properties:

(P.1) $\quad \Delta c^t \equiv c^t - \bar{c}^t \neq 0$.
(P.2) $\quad \Delta c^\tau \equiv c^\tau - \bar{c}^\tau \neq 0, \qquad \tau \geq t + 1$.
(P.3) $\quad \Delta c^s \equiv c^s - \bar{c}^s \leq 0 \qquad$ for all $s \neq t, \tau$.
(P.4) $\quad \bar{k}^\tau \geq k^\tau \qquad$ for some finite $\tau \geq t + 1$.
(P.5) $\quad \ell^s \geq \bar{\ell}^s \qquad$ for all $s = 1, 2, \ldots$.

Note that the consumption along paths P and $\bar{P}$ need only differ in periods t and τ, although there may be other differences. However, by property (P.3) any such differences must yield greater consumption on the alternative path $\bar{P}$ than on the original path P. The fourth requirement ensures that the capital stock vector for period τ is at least as large (in every component) along $\bar{P}$ as along P, while property (P.5) ensures that path P uses at least as much of every primary factor in every time period as path $\bar{P}$. An immediate consequence of properties (P.3), (P.4), and (P.5) is that it is possible for these paths to be identical for all $s \geq \tau + 1$, and we lose no generality by assuming this to be the case.[14]

Accordingly, consider the two paths P and $\bar{P}$ for time periods 0, 1, 2, . . . , $\tau - 1$:

$$\{(c^1, k^1, k^0, \ell^0), \ldots, (c^t, k^t, k^{t-1}, \ell^{t-1}),$$
$$\ldots, (c^\tau, k^\tau, k^{\tau-1}, \ell^{\tau-1})\}$$
$$\{(\bar{c}^1, \bar{k}^1, \bar{k}^0, \bar{\ell}^0), \ldots, (\bar{c}^t, \bar{k}^t, \bar{k}^{t-1}, \bar{\ell}^{t-1}),$$
$$\ldots, (\bar{c}^\tau, \bar{k}^\tau, \bar{k}^{\tau-1}, \bar{\ell}^{\tau-1})\}.$$

Further, the sub-sequence of (5.7.4),

$$\{(p^1, p^0, w^0), \ldots, (p^{t+1}, p^t, w^t), \ldots, (p^\tau, p^{\tau-1}, w^\tau)\},$$

denotes dynamic equilibrium prices associated with the short-run efficient path P over time periods 0 to $\tau - 1$. Path $\bar{P}$ may or may not be competitive at these prices, but from the definition of a competitive path, the following inequalities are implied by equation (5.3.3):

$$\begin{aligned}
p^1 \cdot (c^1 + k^1) &- p^0 \cdot k^0 - w^0 \cdot \ell^0 \\
&\geqslant p^1 \cdot (\bar{c}^1 + \bar{k}^1) - p^0 \cdot \bar{k}^0 - w^0 \cdot \ell^0 \\
p^t \cdot (c^t + k^t) &- p^{t-1} \cdot k^{t-1} - w^{t-1} \cdot \ell^{t-1} \\
&\geqslant p^t \cdot (\bar{c}^t + \bar{k}^t) - p^{t-1} \cdot \bar{k}^{t-1} - w^{t-1} \cdot \bar{\ell}^{t-1} \quad (5.7.5) \\
p^{t+1} \cdot (c^{t+1} + k^{t+1}) &- p^t \cdot k^t - w^t \cdot \ell^t \\
&\geqslant p^{t+1} \cdot (\bar{c}^{t+1} + \bar{k}^{t+1}) - p^t \cdot \bar{k}^t - w^t \cdot \bar{\ell}^t \\
p^\tau \cdot (c^\tau + k^\tau) &- p^{\tau-1} \cdot k^{\tau-1} - w^{\tau-1} \cdot \ell^{\tau-1} \\
&\geqslant p^\tau \cdot (\bar{c}^\tau + \bar{k}^\tau) - p^{\tau-1} \cdot \bar{k}^{\tau-1} - w^{\tau-1} \cdot \bar{\ell}^{\tau-1}
\end{aligned}$$

or

$$\begin{aligned}
p_c^1(c^1 - \bar{c}^1) &\geqslant p^1 \cdot (\bar{k}^1 - k^1) + p^0 \cdot (k^0 - \bar{k}^0) \\
&\quad + w^0 \cdot (\ell^0 - \bar{\ell}^0) \\
p_c^t(c^t - \bar{c}^t) &\geqslant p^t \cdot (\bar{k}^t - k^t) + p^{t-1} \cdot (k^{t-1} - \bar{k}^{t-1}) \\
&\quad + w^{t-1} \cdot (\ell^{t-1} - \bar{\ell}^{t-1}) \\
p_c^{t+1}(c^{t+1} - \bar{c}^{t+1}) &\geqslant p^{t+1} \cdot (\bar{k}^{t+1} - k^{t+1}) \quad (5.7.6) \\
&\quad + p^t \cdot (k^t - \bar{k}^t) + w^t \cdot (\ell^t - \bar{\ell}^t) \\
p_c^\tau(c^\tau - \bar{c}^\tau) &\geqslant p^\tau \cdot (\bar{k}^\tau - k^\tau) + p^{\tau-1} \cdot (k^{\tau-1} - \bar{k}^{\tau-1}) \\
&\quad + w^{\tau-1} \cdot (\ell^{\tau-1} - \bar{\ell}^{\tau-1}).
\end{aligned}$$

Adding the inequalities above and rearranging yields

$$
\begin{aligned}
p_c^t(c^t - \bar{c}^t) + p_c^\tau(c^\tau - \bar{c}^\tau) \geq & \sum_{s=t,\tau} p_c^s(\bar{c}^s - c^s) \\
& + p^0 \cdot (k^0 - \bar{k}^0) \\
& + p^\tau \cdot (\bar{k}^\tau - k^\tau) \\
& + \sum_{s=0}^{\tau-1} w^s \cdot (\ell^s - \bar{\ell}^s).
\end{aligned} \tag{5.7.7}
$$

Using the fact that paths P and $\bar{P}$ start with the same initial capital-stock vector ($k^0 = \bar{k}^0$) and properties (P.1)–(P.5), we see that (5.7.7) implies that

$$
p_c^t \Delta c^t + p_c^\tau \Delta c^\tau \geq 0. \tag{5.7.8}
$$

Consider the "consumption sacrifice" case in which $\Delta c^t > 0$; we then have

$$
\frac{p_c^t}{p_c^\tau} \geq -\frac{\Delta c^\tau}{\Delta c^t}. \tag{5.7.9}
$$

The "consumption binge" case with $c^t < 0$ yields the analogous inequality

$$
\frac{p_c^t}{p_c^\tau} \leq -\frac{\Delta c^\tau}{\Delta c^t}. \tag{5.7.10}
$$

Taking the limits of the right-hand sides of (5.7.9) and (5.7.10) as $\Delta c^t \to 0^+$ and $\Delta c^t \to 0^-$, respectively, gives

$$
\left(-\frac{\Delta c^t}{\Delta c^\tau}\right)^- \leq \frac{p_c^t}{p_c^\tau} \leq \left(-\frac{\Delta c^t}{\Delta c^\tau}\right)^+. \tag{5.7.11}
$$

In view of assumptions (5.4.7) and (5.4.8), (5.7.11) is actually of the stronger form we have been seeking, namely the inequality (5.7.1).

This result is extremely broad, the numerical example given in the previous section being one simple example. It is valid despite the complications of (1) many heterogeneous types of capital goods and primary factors, and (2) the presence of a perhaps non-differentiable technology.

One additional special case will serve as an introduction to the next section. Suppose that the dynamic equilibrium price system is, in fact, a steady-state price system so that for some r satisfying $0 < r < \infty$ we may set

$$p_c^s = \left(\frac{1}{1+r}\right)^s \qquad \text{for all } s \tag{5.7.12}$$

where r is the consumption-good own rate of interest. We then have, from (5.7.1) and (5.7.12), that

$$0 < \left(-\frac{\Delta c^t}{\Delta c^\tau}\right)^- \leqslant (1+r)^{\tau-t} \leqslant \left(-\frac{\Delta c^t}{\Delta c^\tau}\right)^+ < \infty. \tag{5.7.13}$$

The important implication of (5.7.13) is that the possible values of the steady-state interest rate are restricted by the left- and right-hand marginal rates of intertemporal transformation.

Finally, we conclude by noting that one way to determine the equilibrium value of p_c^t/p_c^τ, rather than merely restricting it by the inequality (5.7.1), is to introduce preferences, as in the simple Fisherian model discussed in Section 2.4. Suppose that the technological options are as depicted in Figure 5.7a and b, analogous to Figure 5.6. To keep matters simple, assume that the only relevant choice to be made is between c^t and c^τ, $\tau \geqslant t+1$, with consumption in all other periods being identical. If the point (c^t, c^τ) is chosen, for whatever reasons, so as to maximize a well-behaved utility function $u(c^t, c^\tau)$, the equilibrium value of p_c^t/p_c^τ is determined and is equal to the slope of the highest indifference curve at the selected (c^t, c^τ) point. For example, at point E in Figure 5.7a, $p_c^t/p_c^\tau = 2$. Similarly, at point E in Figure 5.7b, p_c^t/p_c^τ is equal to the slope of the $u(c^t, c^\tau) = \bar{u}$ curve; and using (5.7.1), this value of p_c^t/p_c^τ satisfies

$$\frac{1}{2} \leqslant \frac{p_c^t}{p_c^\tau} \leqslant 2,$$

as is obvious from Figure 5.7b.

For example, under the stated assumptions and with the addition $\tau = t+1$, the preferences reflected by the intertemporal util-

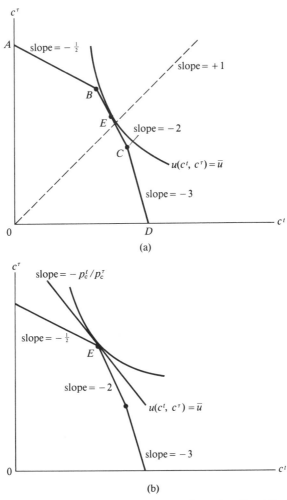

Figure 5.7. In (a) $p_c^t/p_c^\tau = 2$ at the point E, while in (b) $\frac{1}{2} = p_c^t/p_c^\tau \leqq 2$ at the point E.

ity function $u(c^t, c^{t+1})$ together with the technology determine the equilibrium (consumption) rate of interest, $r^t = (p_c^t/p_c^{t+1}) - 1$. Whether or not $p_c^t/p_c^{t+1} > 0$ (so that this interest rate is positive) depends upon both the properties of the technologically feasible options and intertemporal preferences.

Suppose, on the other hand, that (for whatever reasons) the intertemporal utility function $u(c^t, c^{t+1})$ does not exist. Consider production at point E in Figure 5.7b with $\tau = t + 1$. Under these circumstances the equilibrium (consumption) rate of interest is *indeterminate* without recourse to additional assumptions. The technology does impose the restriction

$$-\tfrac{1}{2} \le r^t = (p_c^t/p_c^{t+1}) - 1 \le +1,$$

leaving any r^t satisfying the latter inequality as a possible equilibrium interest rate. In these circumstances the actual value of r^t that prevails may have a substantial effect on the distribution of income. And if one "class of economic agents" ("capitalists"?) are net lenders and a second "class" ("workers"?) are net borrowers, the foundations are set for a legitimate "class struggle theory" of income distribution. Such issues are not our concern here, but rather we simply note that *any* such theory of income distribution must take into account the fundamental inequality imposed by the technology, namely (5.7.1).

5.8. Solow's concept of the rate of return

Robert M. Solow first introduced his concept of the *rate of return* in 1963, and subsequently it has sparked a number of papers.[15] However, much of the work on this subject is flawed by ideological preconceptions and erroneous interpretations of Solow's results. Our purpose here, rather than to review this unfortunate debate, is to present the issue concisely and to provide a simple economic interpretation of the results.

DEFINITION 5.4

Consider a competitive path P and an alternative feasible path $\bar{P}$ starting from the same initial capital stock-vector, where P is competitive at the dynamic equilibrium prices

$$p^t = \frac{p}{(1 + r)^t} \tag{5.8.1}$$

for some vector $p = (p_1, \ldots, p_n)$ and some r, $0 < r < \infty$. The *rate of return* associated with a transition from path P to $\bar{P}$ is defined as a number ρ satisfying

$$\sum_{t=1}^{\infty} \frac{p_c(c^t - \bar{c}^t)}{(1 + \rho)^t} = 0, \tag{5.8.2}$$

where, as before, we have set $p_c = p_1$ so that the consumption good is commodity 1.[16]

We then have the following result from Solow (1967):

THEOREM 5.3
Consider dynamic paths P and $\bar{P}$ as in Definition 5.4, and assume that

(a) $\ell^t = \bar{\ell}^t$ for all $t = 0, 1, \ldots$.
(b) $\bar{P}$ is also competitive at the prices (5.8.1).
(c) Both paths P and $\bar{P}$ have the properties that
$$\lim_{t \to \infty} p^t \cdot k^t = 0 \quad \text{and} \quad \lim_{t \to \infty} p^t \cdot \bar{k}^t = 0.$$

Then the rate of interest, r, is equal to the rate of return, ρ; that is, $r = \rho$.

Proof. Using (b) we have that

$$p_c^t(c^t - \bar{c}^t) = p^t \cdot (\bar{k}^t - k^t) + p^{t-1} \cdot (k^{t-1} - \bar{k}^{t-1}) \\ + w^{t-1} \cdot (\ell^{t-1} - \bar{\ell}^{t-1}) \tag{5.8.3}$$

for all $t = 1, 2, \ldots$. Since $k^0 = \bar{k}^0$, because both paths have the same initial capital-stock vectors, and since from (a) they both employ the same primary factors with $\ell^t = \bar{\ell}^t$, summing (5.8.3) over $t = 1, 2, \ldots, T$ yields

$$\sum_{t=1}^{T} p_c^t(c^t - \bar{c}^t) = p^T \cdot (\bar{k}^T - k^T). \tag{5.8.4}$$

Letting $T \to \infty$ and using (b), (5.8.1), and (c), equation (5.8.4) becomes

$$\sum_{t=1}^{\infty} \frac{p_c(c^t - \bar{c}^t)}{(1 + r)^t} = 0. \tag{5.8.5}$$

Comparing (5.8.2) with (5.8.5), the conclusion $r = \rho$ is immediate.

$$\text{Q.E.D.}$$

There are several special cases of Theorem 5.3, and one typical example is the following. Suppose that the technology consists of two Leontief–Sraffa techniques, α and β, and that both techniques are competitive at the steady-state prices

$$p^t = \frac{p}{(1 + r_1)^t}, \qquad w^t = \frac{w}{(1 + r_1)^t}. \tag{5.8.6}$$

Let P be the steady-state equilibrium using only technique α and generating consumption c^α. Path $\bar{P}$, assumed feasible, starts at time $t = 0$ with $\bar{k}^0 = k^0$ and $\bar{\ell}^0 = \ell^0$, but eventually reaches in a finite number of time periods (or asymptotically approaches) a steady state using only technique β. Then the interest rate r_1 is a rate of return for this transition.

The difficulty with the rate of return concept, as defined, is immediately evident from the reswitching examples discussed in Chapter 4. For suppose that α and β exhibit reswitching and that both are competitive for some $r_2 > r_1$. Then $r_2 = \rho$ also follows, and *the rate of return is not in general a unique number*.

What are we to make of such nonuniqueness? The answer is actually quite simple if we examine the feasible $\Delta c^t \equiv c^t - \bar{c}^t$ as pictured in Figure 5.8a and b.[17] Figure 5.8a depicts a *simple transition* in which Δc^t changes sign only once. The time period $0 < t < t'$ unambiguously can be identified as a "consumption sacrifice" period for which $\bar{c}^t < c^\alpha = c^t$, while the "benefits" of the transition are enjoyed in a second unambiguous time period with $\bar{c}^t > c^\alpha$ for all $t > t'$. Suppose that such a transition is feasible. We know from algebra (Descartes's rules of signs) that in this case the equation

$$\sum_{t=1}^{\infty} \frac{\Delta c^t}{(1 + \rho)^t} = 0 \tag{5.8.7}$$

has exactly one positive root. Conclusion: techniques α and β then cannot exhibit reswitching.

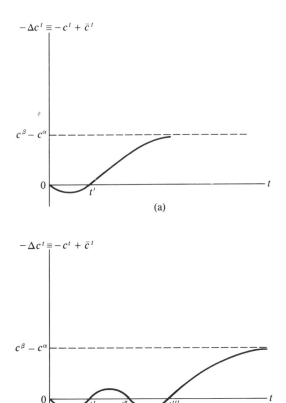

Figure 5.8. (a) Simple transition in which $\triangle c^t$ changes sign only once. The transition in (b) is not simple.

Conversely, suppose that techniques α and β do exhibit re-switching. Then a simple transition such as illustrated in Figure 5.8a *cannot exist,* but any feasible transition between techniques α and β must be as illustrated in Figure 5.8b, where there does not exist any unique ''consumption sacrifice'' period.

These results hold in general, and the existence of reswitching reveals that the dynamic choices open to an economy involve complicated Δc^t patterns (i.e., Figure 5.8b rather than Figure 5.8a).[18] Indeed, all of the "paradoxical (steady-state) behavior" discussed in Chapter 4 is now seen to be a reflection of the complicated intertemporal choices that potentially are available to an economy with heterogeneous capital goods. Moreover, it is evident that which of the patterns exemplified by Figure 5.8a and b prevails depends in part upon the choice of time period; even when "simple transitions" do not exist for some choice of time periods, say 1 day, they may exist for longer time periods, say 1 month. The reason is quite simple: the multiple "consumption sacrifice" periods in Figure 5.8b may "average out" with a longer time period to yield Figure 5.8a.

It is evident, therefore, that Solow's rate of return is a useful concept if we limit it to cases in which "simple transitions" are technologically feasible, a condition that is seen to involve the practical issue of the length of the time period.[19] Suppose, for example, that we take as given the intertemporal welfare function

$$W = \sum_{s=1}^{\infty} \frac{c^s}{(1 + \rho^*)^s} \tag{5.8.8}$$

where ρ^* $(0 < \rho^* < \infty)$ is the exogenously determined social rate of time preference, and consider an economy that is in a steady-state equilibrium with $c^s = c$ at an interest rate r. Suppose also, for a choice of an economically relevant time period (a practical matter in applications), that a "simple transition" is feasible to a new steady-state equilibrium with consumption $\bar{c} > c$, and that the transition path is competitive at the same prices as the original steady state.

Should the economy undertake this transition on welfare-maximization grounds? If the economy remains in the original steady state, welfare as measured by (5.8.8) is

$$W_1 = \sum_{s=1}^{\infty} \frac{c}{(1 + \rho^*)^s}. \tag{5.8.9}$$

If we follow the transition path, welfare is

$$W_2 = \sum_{s=1}^{\infty} \frac{\bar{c}^s}{(1 + \rho^*)^s}. \tag{5.8.10}$$

However, we know that

$$\sum_{s=1}^{\infty} \frac{c^s - \bar{c}^s}{(1 + \rho)^s} = \sum_{s=1}^{\infty} \frac{c - \bar{c}^s}{(1 + \rho)^s} = 0 \tag{5.8.11}$$

has a root $\rho = r$ that is unique because the transition is simple. Therefore,

$$W_2 - W_1 = \sum_{s=1}^{\infty} \frac{\bar{c}^s - c}{(1 + \rho^*)^s} > 0 \tag{5.8.12}$$

if, and only if, $\rho^* < r$.[20] In other words, the transition should be undertaken on the grounds of welfare maximization if and only if the steady-state rate of interest exceeds the social rate of time preference.

Now, of course, it is clear that what we have found are simply sufficient conditions that make the rate of return an operational concept. It is exactly analogous to the problem of when ''an internal rate of return criterion'' gives the correct answer to a problem that on economic grounds is one of ''maximize present discounted value.'' When there exist multiple internal rates of return for investment alternatives, one can make an economically correct choice by maximizing present discounted value. Similarly, when simple transitions do not exist and the rate of return is not unique, one must solve the more complex problem of maximizing the welfare function (5.8.8) directly, subject to the feasible option open to the economy.

However, as anyone who has looked at cost–benefit studies is aware, in applications economists often are forced to make approximations and employ methods not always justifiable on rigorous theoretical grounds, if the alternatives (such as making a random decision) are judged inferior. For these reasons there seems to be no doubt that Solow's rate of return concept is useful, but one must recognize that its usefulness hinges upon the conditions stated. The role of a good economist is to ascertain whether or not those conditions prevail in a particular application of the concept. But in any event, it must be stressed that the validity of the rate-of-return concept *does* extend to many cases of interest where there exist heterogeneous capital goods.

5.9. Consumption efficient paths and the Cass theorem

There remains one issue: When is an infinite-time-horizon dynamic path consumption efficient? This problem is identical to the one addressed in Section 3.5, except that now heterogeneous capital goods and primary factors are allowed. Upon reflection it is clear that the question of consumption efficiency makes sense only if the technology allows sufficient "intertemporal substitution." If a path is consumption inefficient, what we *mean* is that an alternative allocation of resources over time is capable of increasing consumption in some time period, without lowering it in any other, and this question can arise in a meaningful way only if intertemporal substitution of consumption is technologically possible.

Under essentially the same assumptions stated in this chapter – and in particular under the conditions sufficient to ensure that left-hand and right-hand marginal rates of intertemporal transformation exist – Cass has proven the following theorem (1972a):

THEOREM 5.4

Consider a dynamic path P that is short-run efficient with $c^t > 0$ for all t and with an associated consumption price sequence $\{p_c^t\}_{t=0}^\infty$ whose components are not identically zero. Then the path is consumption inefficient if and only if the price sequence grows too fast, that is, if and only if

$$\lim_{t \to \infty} \frac{p_c^0}{p_c^t} < \infty. \tag{5.9.1}$$

Subsequent authors have proven extensions of the basic Cass result,[21] but we confine ourselves to the following observations:

(1) When there is one primary factor, growing at an exogenous rate g, all the Golden Rule results proved in Section 3.5 for the one-capital-good case remain valid. In particular, with k_i^*, $i = 1, \ldots, n$, denoting the Golden Rule value of the ith-type capital good, a path or program for which

$$k_i^t \geqslant k_i^* + \epsilon, \qquad \text{some } \epsilon > 0, \quad \text{all } i, \text{ all } t, \tag{5.9.2}$$

is consumption inefficient.

(2) The convergence of capital value to zero implies consumption efficiency, that is, if

$$\lim_{t \to \infty} v^t = 0 \qquad (\text{where } v^t \equiv p^t \cdot k^t \equiv \sum_{i=1}^{n} p_i^t k_i^t), \tag{5.9.3}$$

then the associated path is consumption efficient.

(3) However, (5.9.3) is not necessary, as the Golden Rule path with $k_i^t = k_i^*$ for all i and t provides a counterexample exactly as in Section 3.5.

(4) Conditions (5.9.2) and (5.9.3) are but special cases of the general Cass theorem, which provides a complete characterization of consumption efficiency.

5.10. Concluding remarks

We started this chapter with the observation that one should not restrict attention to alternative steady-state equilibria, for these do not reflect the relevant dynamic options available to any economy starting from prescribed initial conditions with a given technology. The various concepts of "efficiency" introduced in Chapter 3 for a one-capital-good world generalize to one with many heterogeneous capital goods. However, complications arise primarily because we must make certain the technology is such that types of intertemporal questions we are asking are meaningful, and this complication involves technical details concerning the specification of the technology set which we have largely ignored, instead referring the reader to the relevant literature.

Two results are so fundamental that they merit emphasis here.

(1) Right- and left-hand marginal rates of intertemporal substitution limit the range of dynamic equilibrium prices according to the inequality (5.7.1). Also, prices do measure the relevant

intertemporal consumption trade-offs that are feasible, but only to inequality approximations unless there is "sufficient smoothness" in the technology [as, for example, when the technology can be described by a function with neoclassical properties such as equation (2.2.1)]. For technologies lacking "sufficient smoothness" – say for those exhibiting "kinks" as illustrated by Figures 5.6 and 5.7a and b – in equilibrium the (consumption) rate of interest may not be determined from the technology alone. In Section 5.7 we saw how the introduction of an intertemporal utility function could resolve such indeterminancies and made the brief observation that the indeterminancy of the interest rate raises issues of income distribution.

(2) Under assumptions that make the question meaningful, the necessary and sufficient condition for consumption efficiency in an infinite-time-horizon problem – the Cass condition that the consumption price sequence does not grow too fast – is exactly the same as for the one-capital-good case.

Perhaps the primary conclusion to be drawn is that economic theory is able to provide useful results even when the existence of heterogeneous goods makes the task more difficult. All too often, though, these complications are worsened by posing irrelevant questions rather than examining only the feasible dynamic options stressed here. In Chapter 6 we study a subset of these feasible options defined by (1) imposing descriptive rules on the actions of economic agents (e.g., save a constant fraction of income), and (2) explicitly maximizing some intertemporal criterion functions.

Exercises

5.1 Derive equations (5.2.10a) and (5.2.10b).

5.2 Prove that the slope of the EE locus in general does not give relative prices when $r > 0$.

5.3 Let $\bar{P}$ denote a competitive path.

(a) Prove that if $\bar{\ell}_i^t < L_i^t$, then $w_i^t = 0$.

(b) Prove that $p^{t+1} \cdot \bar{c}^{t+1} + p^{t+1} \cdot \bar{k}^{t+1} - p^t \cdot \bar{k}^t - w^y \cdot \ell^t \leq 0$.

(c) Prove that if $\bar{y}_i^{t+1} > \bar{c}_i^{t+1} + \bar{k}_i^{t+1}$, then $\bar{p}_i^{t+1} = 0$. [*Hint:* Use Assumption 5.4 with $\lambda > 1$ (constant returns) and Assumption 5.5 (free disposal) to contradict the inequality (5.3.3) if $p^{t+1} \cdot \bar{c}^{t+1} + p^{t+1} \cdot \bar{k}^{t+1} - p^t \cdot \bar{k}^t - w^t \cdot \bar{\ell}^t > 0$ holds.]

(d) Use the property $(0, 0, 0) \in S^t$ of Assumption 5.2 to strengthen ≤ 0 in (b) above to $= 0$.

5.4 Given the technology consisting of activities (5.6.1) and (5.6.2), derive the production function (5.6.3). [*Hint:* For any $0 \leq \lambda \leq 1$, output is

$$y^t = \min \left[\lambda 3 k_\alpha^{t-1}, \lambda \ell_\alpha^{t-1} \right] + \min \left[(1 - \lambda) 2 k_\beta^{t-1}, (1 - \lambda) \tfrac{3}{2} \ell_\beta^{t-1} \right]$$

where

$$k_\alpha^{t-1} + k_\beta^{t-1} = k^{t-1} \quad \text{and} \quad \ell_\beta^{t-1} + \ell_\beta^{t-1} = \ell^{t-1}.]$$

5.5 Consider the technology consisting of production activities (5.6.1) and (5.6.2). Show that (5.6.5) and (5.6.6) provide dynamic equilibrium prices for the steady-state (5.6.4) for all $0 < r \leq 2$.

6

Descriptive and optimal models with heterogeneous commodities

6.1. Introduction to models with heterogeneous commodities

How does a multisector economy with heterogeneous capital goods evolve over time? In this chapter the question is analyzed for both *descriptive* models (in which assumptions are made concerning the behavior of economic agents) and for *optimal* models (in which a specified intertemporal criterion function is maximized). We have seen from the descriptive models with one capital good that the decisions of economic agents facing competitive markets may result in dynamic paths that are not consumption efficient; the life-cycle model studied in Section 3.4c clearly shows this. Since the one-capital-good model is but a special case of a more general multisector model, obviously such intertemporal Pareto inefficiency can also occur when there are heterogeneous commodities[1] (i.e., some of the descriptive models we shall study may generate consumption efficient paths).

The central difficulty with multisector models is dynamic stability. That is, given at time $t = 0$ an arbitrary starting vector $k^0 = (k_1^0, \ldots, k_n^0) > 0$ of the n per capita capital stocks, under what conditions is it true that

$$\lim_{t \to \infty} k^t = k^*, \tag{6.1.1}$$

where $k^* = (k_1^*, \ldots, k_n^*)$ is some vector of per capita stocks representing a rest point to the dynamic equations of the model?

213

The problem, as we shall discover, is that in general (6.1.1) does not hold. Recall the one-capital-good model with money studied in Section 3.7. There we saw that the capital–labor ratio converged to a rest point with positive real money balances only for particular choices of initial conditions (k^0, x^0) lying on the stable arm of the saddlepoint equilibrium (the curve labelled AA in Figure 3.8). Analogously, we shall find that the rest points for the dynamic equations of multisector models generally are saddlepoints in the space of capital good prices (in terms of a single consumption good as *numéraire*) and per capita capital stocks. When this saddlepoint property exists, for any given initial vector k^0, the model converges – that is, (6.1.1) holds – only for a *particular* choice of the initial price vector $p^0 = (p_1^0, \ldots, p_n^0)$.

This saddlepoint behavior has far-reaching economic implications, and we shall see that fundamental issues have not been resolved satisfactorily. Indeed, a satisfactory resolution that is realistic necessitates the explicit introduction of stochastic features into the model, a problem to which we turn in Chapter 7.

The two features of descriptive multisector models just discussed – the possibility of intertemporal inefficiency and the problem of dynamic stability – do not arise in optimal multisector models. In the first place, it is obvious that a consumption inefficient path cannot be optimal with respect to any sensible intertemporal criterion function, for additional consumption can only be beneficial except in contrived cases. Second, the dynamic path of the price vector p^t is determined by the solution to a maximization problem in optimal models. Thus if the optimal solution requires that equation (6.1.1) hold, that solution will also ensure that the initial price vector p^0 is selected so that convergence to a saddlepoint equilibrium will occur. The existence of some market mechanisms that determine p^0 is not an issue here because prices are set by the optimal solution.[2]

The celebrated *turnpike theorem* emerges from our study of optimal multisector models in the special case of finite-time horizons.[3] However, even the turnpike results have certain cyclic exceptions. Indeed, this is only a part of the general difficulty we face. As our models become more complex, we find that new behavior can arise; all too often "nearly anything can happen" is the only possible unqualified conclusion. In such circumstances it is desirable to consider more carefully what economic questions we would like to ask and to modify our approaches to focus clearly on the relevant issues. Some advances in this direction are made in Chapter 7, but we must first concentrate on precisely why the current state of affairs is unsatisfactory from an economic perspective.

6.2. Descriptive models with heterogeneous capital

The exact specification of any particular model may have important consequences for the various types of dynamic behavior that may arise, but it would be a tedious and an unrewarding task to catalog every possibility. Our objective here is to illustrate some principles, and to do this, a relatively simple model will suffice. In particular, we shall work in continuous time, postulate a single primary factor (labor), and assume that there is a single (possibly composite) consumption good. The output of this consumption good is given by a production-possibilities frontier

$$C = F(Y_1, \ldots, Y_n; K_1, \ldots, K_n, L) \qquad (6.2.1)$$

where Y_i = gross output of the ith-type capital good, $i = 1, \ldots, n$,

K_i = stock of the ith-type capital good, $i = 1, \ldots, n$,

L = labor input.

As is conventional, the outputs $C, Y_1, \ldots, Y_n$ are flows, while the inputs $K_1, \ldots, K_n$, and L are stocks. No time variable is included in the notation, but it is understood that all variables are at time t unless otherwise indicated.

It is assumed that (6.2.1) exhibits the standard neoclassical properties; in particular, it is homogeneous of degree 1. Denoting per capita magnitudes with lowercase letters, we have

$$c = F(y_1, \ldots, y_n; k_1, \ldots, k_n, 1). \qquad (6.2.2)$$

Similarly, designating the consumption good as *numéraire*, along a competitive path current output prices $(p_1, \ldots, p_n)$, current factor prices or rental rates $(q_1, \ldots, q_n)$, and the current wage rate satisfy

$$p_i = -\frac{\partial F}{\partial y_i}, \qquad i = 1, \ldots, n, \tag{6.2.3a}$$

$$q_i = +\frac{\partial F}{\partial k_i}, \qquad i = 1, \ldots, n, \tag{6.2.3b}$$

$$w = +\frac{\partial F}{\partial L}. \tag{6.2.3c}$$

It is also postulated that capital of type i depreciates at the exponential rate δ_i, independently of usage. Allowing for growth of the labor supply at an exogenous rate $g \geq 0$, we thus arrive at the dynamic equations for the growth of per capita capital stocks, namely

$$\dot{k}_i = y_i - (g + \delta_i)k_i, \qquad i = 1, \ldots, n. \tag{6.2.4}$$

The derivation of (6.2.4) is left as Exercise 6.1.

It is assumed that asset markets are perfectly competitive, and we have the portfolio equilibrium condition

$$\frac{\dot{p}_1}{p_1} + \left(\frac{q_1}{p_1} - \delta_1\right) = \cdots = \frac{\dot{p}_n}{p_n} + \left(\frac{q_n}{p_n} - \delta_n\right) = r,$$

or, equivalently,

$$\dot{p}_i = -q_i + p_i(r + \delta_i), \qquad i = 1, \ldots, n. \tag{6.2.5}$$

This portfolio equilibrium condition, a continuous-time version of equation (3.3.7) has the usual interpretation: in the absence of uncertainty, the net returns on alternative means of holding wealth must be equal in equilibrium. Here $\dot{p}_i/p_i$ is capital gains or losses, while $(q_i/p_i) - \delta_i$ is net rental return allowing for depreciation. The sum of the latter is the total net return on the ith asset, a machine of type i, and for every i this net return is equal to the interest rate, r.

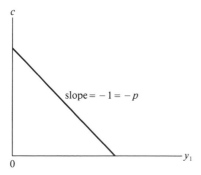

Figure 6.1. In the two-sector or $n = 1$ case the per capita production-possibilities frontier is $c = F(y_1; k_1, 1)$. If the capital–labor ratios in the two sectors are always equal, for any given value of k_1 this frontier defines a straight line with slope -1 in y_1–c space. If we are also given $p_1 = 1$, output levels are indeterminate without additional information; *any* (y_1, c) point on the pictured straight line is consistent with a competitive equilibrium having

$$-p_1 = -1 = \frac{\partial F}{\partial y_1} \equiv \frac{\partial c}{\partial y_1}.$$

Suppose, now, that we are given a vector of per capita capital stocks $k = (k_1, \ldots, k_n)$ and a vector of current prices, in terms of the consumption good as *numéraire,* $p = (p_1, \ldots, p_n)$. Denote these vectors by $\hat{k}$ and $\bar{p}$, respectively. Is a unique output vector $\bar{y} = (\bar{y}_1, \ldots, \bar{y}_n)$ then determined? In general, of, course, the answer is "no." For example, when $n = 1$ this model reduces to the two-sector case studied in Section 3.6. If the technology is such that the capital–labor ratios in both sectors are always equal, the per capita production-possibilities frontier

$$c = F(y_1; k_1, 1) \tag{6.2.6}$$

is a straight line having a slope of -1 in y_1–c space, as pictured in Figure 6.1. Thus given any value $\hat{k}_1$ and given $\bar{p}_1 = 1$, *any* output point (y_1, c) lying on the straight line in Figure 6.1 is consistent with a competitive equilibrium, because any such point satisfies

$$-\bar{p}_1 = -1 = \frac{\partial F(y_1; \hat{k}_1, 1)}{\partial y_1} \equiv \frac{\partial c}{\partial y_1}. \tag{6.2.7}$$

However, if $\bar{p}_1 \neq 1$, the equation

$$\bar{p}_1 = -\frac{\partial F(y_1; \hat{k}_1, 1)}{\partial y_1}$$

cannot be satisfied. In such circumstances one would have to study a more general system of *inequalities,* and equilibrium would entail "corner solutions" with either $\bar{c} = 0$ or $\bar{y}_1 = 0$.

All of this merely illustrates the technical complexities of the problem. However, given the objective of developing general economic principles, these details are more annoyance than substance. Accordingly, we shall make strong assumptions that will allow us to circumvent most of the technical problems that can arise in the general case. In particular, we shall assume that *for any given vector $k > 0$, the function F defines a strictly concave hypersurface in $(c, y_1, \ldots, y_n)$.* Further, we shall assume that *for any given vector $p > 0$, equations (6.2.3a) have a solution $y \geqslant 0$, $y \neq 0$.*

The convenience of these assumptions is illustrated in Figure 6.2. The tangency conditions implied by equations (6.2.3a), which we assume have a solution, uniquely determine the outputs $\bar{y}_1, \ldots, \bar{y}_n$ and the corresponding output of the consumption good

$$c = F(\bar{y}_1, \ldots, \bar{y}_n; \hat{k}_1, \ldots, \hat{k}_n, 1).$$

Given our strict concavity assumption, and given that we assume solutions with equalities [rather than reformulating equations (6.2.3a) as more general inequalities], then for any given vectors $\hat{k} > 0$ and $\bar{p} > 0$ the corresponding equilibrium outputs $\bar{c}$, $\bar{y}_1, \ldots,$ and $\bar{y}_n$ are all *uniquely* determined. Moreover, *unique* $\bar{q}_1, \ldots, \bar{q}_n$ and $\bar{w}$ are determined via equations (6.2.3b) and (6.2.3c) because the partial derivatives $\partial F/\partial k_i$ and $\partial F/\partial L$ are functions only of $(\bar{y}_1, \ldots, \bar{y}_n; \hat{k}_1, \ldots, \hat{k}_n, 1)$.

The remaining variable is the interest rate, r. Suppose that we complete the model by adding to it some type of consumption

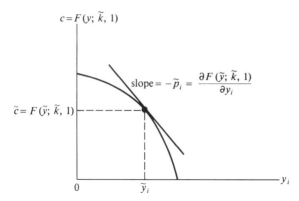

Figure 6.2. Under the assumptions stated in the text, for any given vector $\hat{k} > 0$, the equation $c = F(y_1, \ldots, y_n; \hat{k}_1, \ldots, \hat{k}_n, 1) \equiv F(y; \hat{k}, 1)$ defines a strictly concave hypersurface in $(c, y_1, \ldots, y_n)$. Thus for every $i = 1, \ldots, n$, we have the strictly concave y_i–c curve illustrated above. By assumption equations (6.2.3a) have a solution; this implies that the line with slope $-\tilde{p}_i$ is tangent to the y_i–c curve at the equilibrium output point $(\tilde{y}_i, \tilde{c})$. If we could draw an $(n + 1)$-dimensional diagram, the given vector p would define a hyperplane that is tangent to the strictly concave $(c, y_1, \ldots, y_n)$ hypersurface at the point of equilibrium outputs.

function, and suppose the resulting simultaneous equations imply the existence of a function

$$r = \psi(k_1, \ldots, k_n, p_1, \ldots, p_n). \tag{6.2.8}$$

Turning back to equations (6.2.4) and (6.2.5), we see that the dynamic equations for the model may be written in the causal, autonomous form

$$\left. \begin{array}{l} \dot{k}_i = f^i(k_1, \ldots, k_n, p_1, \ldots, p_n) \\ \dot{p}_i = h^i(k_1, \ldots, k_n, p_1, \ldots, p_n) \end{array} \right\} \quad i = 1, \ldots, n, \tag{6.2.9}$$

or, in vector notation,

$$\begin{array}{l} \dot{k} = f(k, p) \\ \dot{p} = h(k, p). \end{array} \tag{6.2.10}$$

Given vectors k^0 and p^0 as initial conditions (at time $t = 0$), equation (6.2.10) determines the evolution of the system over time.

The remaining issues are analogous to those for the one-capital-good cases studied in Chapter 3:

(1) Does there *exist* a steady-state vector of per capita capital stocks, $\bar{k}$, and a steady-state price vector, $\bar{p}$, such that

$$\dot{k} = \dot{p} = 0 \qquad \text{when } k = \bar{k} \text{ and } p = \bar{p}?$$

(2) Is such a $(\bar{k}, \bar{p})$ point *unique;* that is, is $(\bar{k}, \bar{p})$ the unique solution to

$$f(k, p) = h(k, p) = 0?$$

(3) Is the point $(\bar{k}, \bar{p})$ *stable;* that is, starting from any initial condition in some specified set, is it true that

$$\lim_{t \to \infty} k(t) = \bar{k}$$

and

$$\lim_{t \to \infty} p(t) = \bar{p}?$$

The answers to questions (1)–(3) depend, of course, upon what additional behavioral assumptions are used to specify the complete model. Existence of a steady-state point (k^*, p^*) is seldom an important issue; most likely cases of nonexistence can be attributed to a model that lacks economic interest. The uniqueness and stability questions, however, cannot be dismissed, and we shall now examine them by postulating a savings function of a very simple – though standard – form.

There are three components of income: capital gains or losses, $\sum_{i=1}^{n} \dot{p}_i K_i$; net rentals, $\sum_{i=1}^{n} (q_i - p_i \delta_i) K_i$; and labor income, wL. Making the common assumption that the propensities to save from these three types of incomes are given constants between zero and 1 (s_c, s_r, and s_w, respectively) we have that

$$total\ saving = S = s_c \sum_{i=1}^{n} \dot{p}_i K_i + s_r \sum_{i=1}^{n} (q_i - p_i \delta_i) K_i$$

$$+ s_w wL. \tag{6.2.11}$$

The value of capital, in terms of the consumption good as *numéraire,* is

$$V = \sum_{i=1}^{n} p_i K_i, \tag{6.2.12}$$

and the realized change in the real value of capital (wealth) is

$$\dot{V} = \sum_{i=1}^{n} \dot{p}_i K_i + \sum_{i=1}^{n} p_i \dot{K}_i. \tag{6.2.13}$$

As in Section 3.7, there is a flow-equilibrium condition that aggregate saving in real terms is equal to the change in real wealth: that is,

$$S = \dot{V}. \tag{6.2.14}$$

Accordingly, from (6.2.11), (6.2.13), and (6.2.14), we have that

$$\sum_{i=1}^{n} \dot{p}_i K_i + \sum_{i=1}^{n} p_i \dot{K}_i = s_c \sum_{i=1}^{n} \dot{p}_i K_i$$

$$+ s_r \sum_{i=1}^{n} (q_i - p_i \delta_i) K_i + s_w w L. \tag{6.2.15}$$

Now, as the reader is asked to show in Exercise 6.2, when $s_c \neq 1$, equation (6.2.15) can be solved for

$$r = \frac{c - w}{(1 - s_c)v} \tag{6.2.16a}$$

where $v \equiv V/L$ is the per capita value of capital. Similarly, when $s_c = s_r = s_w \equiv s$, $0 < s < 1$, we have

$$r = \frac{c - (1 - s)w}{(1 - s)v}. \tag{6.2.16b}$$

Now observe that every variable on the right-hand sides of both (6.2.16a) and (6.2.16b) is a function of $(k_1, \ldots, k_n, p_1, \ldots, p_n)$ under our assumptions; hence (6.2.16a) and (6.2.16b) define the function $\psi(k_1, \ldots, k_n, p_1, \ldots, p_n)$, given above as equation (6.2.8). Accordingly, in these two cases we have reduced our problem to the analysis of a $2n$-differential equation system of the form (6.2.10). However, this result necessitated the restriction that $s_c \neq 1$; when $s_c = 1$, (6.2.15) cannot be solved directly for r because the term

$$\sum_{i=1}^{n} \dot{p}_i K_i = \sum_{i=1}^{n} [-q_i + p_i(r + \delta_i)]K_i$$

appears on both sides of the equation and the variable r "drops out."

This feature complicates the dynamic structure of our problem. When $s_c = 1$, the flow equilibrium condition $\dot{V} = S$ expressed as (6.2.15) is of the form

$$\Phi(k_1, \ldots, k_n, p_1, \ldots, p_n) \equiv \Phi(k, p) = 0. \qquad (6.2.17)$$

We can derive a function of the form (6.2.8) by differentiating (6.2.17); this differentiation will introduce $\dot{p}_i$ terms and hence r via (6.2.5). However, given an initial vector of capital stocks k^0, the price vector at time zero must satisfy

$$\Phi(k^0, p^0) = 0, \qquad (6.2.18)$$

or the flow-equilibrium condition will not hold at time $t = 0$.

These results help to clarify the distinction between this formulation and the two-sector, one-capital-good model studied in Section 3.6. Those two-sector models are a special case of the general framework developed here; they are equivalent when $n = 1$ and $s_c = 1$.[4] We see, therefore, why we never had to introduce the price of capital, p_1, into the two-sector model. For this case the restriction (6.2.17) is

$$\Phi(k_1, p_1) = 0$$

which in general may be solved for

$$p_1 = \phi(k_1).$$

Thus given any initial capital–labor ratio k_1^0, the initial price p_1^0 is *not* open to choice; rather the price at time zero is determined by $p_1^0 = \phi(k_1^0)$. Also, the dynamic equations (6.2.10) reduce to

$$\dot{k}_1 = f_1(k_1, p_1) = f_1[k_1, \phi(k_1)],$$

which is identical in form to equation (3.6.15). We now see that this simplification necessitates the assumption $s_c = 1$.[5]

Since the two-sector model is a special case of our more general case, we know that neither uniqueness nor stability can hold without additional restrictive conditions. For example, it is evident that the behavior illustrated by Figure 3.6 (the existence of stable and unstable equilibria) and by Figure 3.7 (the existence of cyclical motions around an unstable equilibrium) can arise in the multisector model.

Suppose, however, that we are willing to make assumptions (perhaps unpalatable) that will ensure the existence of a unique dynamic equilibrium point $(\bar{k}, \bar{p})$. What can we then conclude about stability? The stability issue for heterogeneous capital good models dates to 1966 and Hahn's work (1966). Most of the published results have been proven for the special case with $s_c = 1$, $s_r = 1$, and $s_w = 0$, so that consumption and real wage income are always equal. However unrealistic this assumption may be, at least a definitive answer to the stability question has been given by Kuga (1977): *the equilibrium point $(\bar{k}, \bar{p})$ is a regular saddlepoint.* We now must explain the precise meaning of this result and provide an economic interpretation.

Consider the dynamic equations (6.2.10):

$$\dot{k} = f(k, p)$$
$$\dot{p} = h(k, p),$$

where $(\bar{k}, \bar{p})$ is the unique solution to

$$f(k, p) = h(k, p) = 0.$$

The dynamic equilibrium $(\bar{k}, \bar{p})$ is a *regular saddlepoint*[6] if there is an ϵ-neighborhood of $(\bar{k}, \bar{p})$ say $N(\epsilon)$, such that for all initial points $(k^0, p^0) \in N(\epsilon)$ the system asymptotically converges with

$$\lim_{t \to \infty} k^t = \bar{k}$$

and

$$\lim_{t \to \infty} p^t = \bar{p},$$

if and only if the point (k^0, p^0) in $2n$-dimensional (k, p)-space lies on a convergent manifold of dimension n.

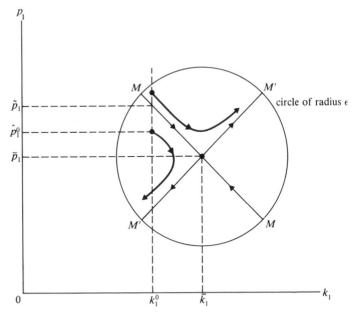

Figure 6.3. Regular saddlepoint.

Consider, for example, a case with $n = 1$ as illustrated in Figure 6.3. The circle is centered at $(\bar{k}, \bar{p})$ with a radius of ϵ; thus our attention is limited to initial points for which

$$\sqrt{(p_1^0 - \bar{p}_1)^2 + (k_1^0 - \bar{k}_1)^2} < \epsilon;$$

we have nothing to say about the motion of the system starting from points outside this circle. The point $(\bar{k}, \bar{p})$ is a *regular saddlepoint* because the convergent manifold, the curve labeled MM in Figure 6.3, has dimension $n = 1$. Given the value of k_1^0,

$$\lim_{t \to \infty} k_1^t = \bar{k}_1$$

and

$$\lim_{t \to \infty} p_1^t = \bar{p}_1$$

if and only if $p_1^0 = \tilde{p}_1^0$, the corresponding value of p_1^0 on the *MM* curve. In Figure 6.3, for example, the system does *not* converge to $(\bar{k}, \bar{p})$ starting from $(k_1^0, \hat{p}_1^0)$. The similarity between Figure 6.3 and Figure 3.8 is evident; both are illustrations of regular saddle-points for two-dimensional systems. For such two-dimensional systems the convergent manifold, *MM* in Figure 6.3, often is called the *stable arm* of the saddlepoint, and $M'M'$ is called the *unstable arm*.

Now consider the case $n = 2$ which is a four-dimensional system. Take $k^0 = (k_1^0, k_2^0)$ as given; then the system converges to $(\bar{k}, \bar{p})$ if and only if the initial price vector lies on a surface of dimension two in four-dimensional space [provided that we start sufficiently close to $(\bar{k}, \bar{p})$ with

$$\sqrt{(p_1^0 - \bar{p}_1)^2 + (p_2^0 - \bar{p})^2 + (k_1^0 - \bar{k}_1)^2 + (k_2^0 - \bar{k}_2)^2} < \epsilon$$

for some $\epsilon > 0$].

And, finally, we have the general conclusion proved by Kuga when $s_c = 1$, $s_r = 1$, and $s_w = 0$:[7]

> Provided that we restrict our attention to starting points in an ϵ-neighborhood of $(\bar{k}, \bar{p})$, for a given k^0 vector there is one and only one p^0 vector such that the system converges to $(\bar{k}, \bar{p})$.

In Section 6.3 we shall examine the profound economic implications of this result. First, however, we must note that often matters are even more complex than just stated. For example, suppose that we make the assumption that $s_c = s_r = s_w \equiv s$, $0 < s < 1$. With two capital goods and a Cobb–Douglas technology, the resulting four-dimensional system *does not* have a regular saddlepoint equilibrium, but rather the convergent manifold is of dimension *three*.[8] Suppose in this case that we are given an initial vector $k^0 = (k_1^0, k_2^0)$. Since the convergent manifold is of dimension three, we are now free to pick *one* of either p_1^0 or p_2^0, provided that we remain within an ϵ-neighborhood of $(\bar{k}, \bar{p})$. Suppose that we select p_1^0 arbitrarily. Since the convergent manifold is of dimension three, there is no remaining freedom; there is one and only one value of p_2^0 which lies on the convergent manifold.

This example conclusively demonstrates that the stability behavior of multisector models can depend crucially upon the precise specification of the model. From an economic perspective it is clear that when not all capital gains are saved, the economy may be "more stable" in the sense that the convergent manifold has a higher dimension.

On the other hand, whenever there are heterogeneous capital goods ($n > 1$), we have seen that given an initial vector of per capita capital stocks, the system will converge only for a *particular* choice of the initial price vector.

What are we to make of this result? In particular, what might happen to the system if initial prices are selected that do *not* lie on the convergent manifold? Is there any economic mechanism that would lead to the stable evolution of a multisector economy? We turn to these questions in the next section.

6.3. **Divergent paths, price expectations, and the maximizing behavior of economic agents**

It has been stated that in general a descriptive multisector model may exhibit many dynamic properties, including the existence of many steady-state equilibria and the possibility of cyclical motions. Suppose, however, that we confine ourselves to the simplest case in which there is a *unique* steady-state equilibrium that is a regular saddlepoint in the $2n$-dimensional space of $k_1, \ldots, k_n$ and $p_1, \ldots, p_n$. What happens if the initial vector (k^0, p^0) does not lie on the convergent manifold?

This saddlepoint instability property of multisector economic models, sometimes referred to as the *Hahn problem*,[9] would be resolved if all nonconvergent paths could be excluded on the grounds of an inconsistency with some economic criterion; if such a criterion could be found, the only remaining possibility would be that the economy follow a dynamically stable path. One such economic criterion was suggested by Samuelson (1967), who, arguing on the basis of known results for consumptionless capital accumulation models, posited that nonconvergent paths would contradict the assumptions of the model because some prices would become zero in finite time. Although definitive results have been established only for special cases, Samuelson's conjecture *is* correct in certain models for which $p_i^T = 0$ for some commodity at some finite time T has been proven.[10]

The reason for a contradiction in these circumstances can be illustrated in a two-capital-goods case. Suppose that we start with an initial vector $(k_1^0, k_2^0, p_1^0, p_2^0)$ not on the convergent manifold. In finite time the price of either commodity 1 or 2 will become zero, and without any less generality we may assume that $p_1^T = 0$ at some finite time T. As is standard, let capital goods be freely disposable, implying that negative prices are impossible; with free disposal no one would hold any capital good having a negative price. It follows, then, that if $p_1^T = 0$, the price of commodity 1 cannot be falling, and therefore $\dot{p}_1^T \geq 0$ must be true.

It can also be established that at time T

$$q_1 = \frac{\partial F}{\partial k_1} > 0 \qquad \text{[see equation (6.2.3a)]},$$

and hence, as $p_1^T = 0$, we have

$$\frac{q_1^T}{p_1^T} = + \infty. \tag{6.3.1}$$

Now consider the portfolio equilibrium condition at time T, namely

$$\frac{\dot{p}_1^T}{p_1^T} + \frac{q_1^T}{p_1^T} = \frac{\dot{p}_2^T}{p_2^T} + \frac{q_2^T}{p_2^T}. \tag{6.3.2}$$

Since $\dot{p}_1^T \geq 0$, (6.3.1) implies that the left-hand side of (6.3.2) is $+ \infty$. For the cases that have been studied it can be shown that $\dot{p}_2^T$, p_2^T, and q_2^T are all finite, and consequently the right-hand side of (6.3.2) is finite. We therefore have a contradiction: equation (6.3.2) cannot hold, and there is not equilibrium in the markets for commodities 1 and 2. In fact, everyone wants to hold capital of type 1 since it yields an *infinite* rate of return, whereas no one would be willing to hold commodity 2, which yields only a finite rate of return. Accordingly, for the special cases that have been examined, the models are consistent over an infinite-time horizon if and only if the initial vector (k^0, p^0) lies on the convergent manifold. Starting at any other point, the paths followed by the economy are, after a finite time, inconsistent with the assumptions of perfect competition, free disposal of capital goods, and portfolio equilibrium (equilibrium in the markets for capital assets).

Such "errant" nonconvergent paths generating this inconsistency can be ruled out if *all* contracts are made at time $t = 0$. If, as in Chapter 2, all intertemporal decisions are concluded at time zero, only initial vectors (k^0, p^0) consistent with the assumptions of the model are admissible. Therefore, nonconvergent paths along which equilibrium in the markets for capital assets is violated in finite time are not admissible. In such a fictitious world convergence to the unique saddlepoint equilibrium is assured.

Such "solutions" to the dynamic stability problem must be rejected if our objective is to better understand the operation of real-world economies, for obviously economic transactions are continually occurring. Also, we observe futures markets for few commodities, primarily metals and agricultural goods, and even these have relatively short time horizons (1 year or less in the case of most agricultural products).[11] Although a visit to the Chicago Board of Trade will show well-developed futures markets for such commodities as corn, wheat, or silver, there is no such market for futures in machine tools.[12]

Reality forces us to recognize that at time $t = 0$ (and at all other times $t > 0$) futures markets exist only for certain commodities and contracts are of only finite lengths. There is no sense in which the observable facts are approximately consistent with a model for which either (1) all contracts are concluded at time $t = 0$, or (2) there exist futures markets of infinite duration for every commodity. Therefore, we are left without any economic mechanism that will prevent our model economy from starting on a nonconvergent path, even though we know from specific examples that some nonconvergent paths violate the model after a finite time because a commodity price becomes zero.

This unsatisfactory state of affairs will be examined more closely in Chapter 7, where we shall analyze a macroeconomic model with an explicit stochastic process and assume that economic agents form *rational price expectations*. Although no satisfactory solution has been found, our investigation will suggest some areas of research that merit exploration. Here, however, we note that *the mere introduction of uncertainty will not "solve" the dynamic instability problem*.

We can imagine that the $2n$ deterministic variables $k_1^t, \ldots, k_n^t, p_1^t, \ldots, p_n^t$ at time τ are, for all $t > \tau$, *means* of underlying stochastic variables having certain probability distributions. In many instances the qualitative behavior of such a stochastic model is identical to the deterministic case, except that now "stability" refers to convergence of a random variable in various stochastic senses that we need not make precise here.[13] Unless we make other more fundamental changes in our multisector model, it will remain "unstable" in that, except for initial conditions lying on a convergent manifold, with probability 1 the dynamic behavior will be nonconvergent.[14]

Realistically, of course, we do live in a world with stochastic disturbances. The point is that we must not only introduce uncertainty explicitly, but we must also take into account how uncertainty modifies the behavior of economic agents. Without fundamental changes in the model, it will remain unstable in the sense that, except for initial conditions on a convergent manifold, the *means* of variables will diverge with probability 1.

Once it is recognized that future events are uncertain, it is clear that the portfolio equilibrium condition must be modified. As a first step, we define *expected prices* as a function of two dates, the date at which the expectation was formed and the date at which the expectation is to prevail:

$$p_i^*(s, t) = \text{expectation formed at time } t \text{ for the actual price of the } i\text{th commodity at time } s.$$

We shall assume that actual prices are known at time t and that price forecasts at time t for time t satisfy the Burmeister–Turnovsky *weak consistency axiom*[15] that

$$p_i^*(t, t) \equiv p_i^*(t) = p_i^t, \qquad i = 1, \ldots, n. \tag{6.3.3}$$

Define

$$\lim_{h \to 0} \left[\frac{p_i^*(t + h, t) - p_i^t}{h} \Big/ p_i^t \right] = \textit{expected instantaneous} \\ \textit{rate of change of the ith} \\ \textit{price at time } t, \tag{6.3.4}$$

$$p_{1i}^{*t} \equiv \lim_{h \to 0} \left[\frac{p_i^*(t + h, t) - p_i^*(t, t)}{h} \right], \tag{6.3.5}$$

and

$$p_{2i}^{*t} \equiv \lim_{h \to 0} \left[\frac{p_i^*(t, t + h) - p_i^*(t, t)}{h} \right]. \tag{6.3.6}$$

Exercise 6.3 asks the reader to verify that equations (6.3.3)–(6.3.5) imply that

$$\frac{p_{1i}^{*t}}{p_i^t} = \textit{expected instantaneous rate of change of the ith} \\ \textit{price at time } t. \tag{6.3.7}$$

The fact that economic agents make forecast errors implies that actual and expected rates of price change *differ* with

$$\frac{\dot{p}_i^t}{p_i^t} \neq \frac{p_{1i}^{*t}}{p_i^t}. \tag{6.3.8}$$

However, assuming that $p_i^*(t, t)$ has continuous partial derivatives, from the weak consistency axiom – equation (6.3.3) – we have that

$$\frac{dp_i^*(t, t)}{dt} \equiv \dot{p}_i^*(t) = p_{1i}^{*t} + p_{2i}^{*t} = \dot{p}_i^t, \tag{6.3.9}$$

and from (6.3.8) and (6.3.9) we see that

$$p_{2i}^{*t} \neq 0. \tag{6.3.10}$$

In view of (6.3.10) and (6.3.6), it must be that

$$p_i^*(t, t + h) \neq p_i(t) = p_i^*(t, t) \qquad \text{for } h > 0. \qquad (6.3.11)$$

Essentially, (6.3.11) is a *mathematical* condition required to capture the fact that economic agents do make forecast errors about instantaneous rates of price change. From an *economic* viewpoint the variable $p_i^*(s, t)$ for $s < t$ makes no sense; *expectations* must be *forward-looking* in time, and it is meaningless to ask what one *expects* yesterday's price to be. This discussion makes it evident that the proper interpretation of price expectations – especially in continuous-time models – can be treacherous. For example, as long as $p_i^*(s, t)$ never affects any economic decisions if $s < t$, there is no problem with equation (6.3.11). However, if past prices matter for decisions at time t, we would want to use actual prices p_i^s for $s < t$; using $p_i^*(s, t) \neq p_i^s$ for $s < t$ implies that people forget past prices and incorrectly remember them (or "forecast backward").

With this warning in mind, we may summarize our results by writing

$$\frac{\dot{p}_i^t}{p_i^t} = \frac{p_{1i}^{*t}}{p_i^t} + \frac{p_{2i}^{*t}}{p_i^t}, \qquad (6.3.12)$$

where, as before, p_{1i}^{*t}/p_i^t measures the *anticipated* rate of price change and

$$\frac{p_{2i}^{*t}}{p_i^t} = unanticipated\ rate\ of\ change\ of\ the\ ith\ price\ at\ time\ t$$

The previous deterministic results hold whenever $p_{2i}^{*t} \equiv 0$ for all t and all i.[16]

How, then, are we to modify our portfolio equilibrium condition, which for the deterministic case with $n = 2$ is

$$\frac{\dot{p}_1^t}{p_1^t} + \frac{q_1^t}{p_1^t} = \frac{\dot{p}_2^t}{p_2^t} + \frac{q_2^t}{p_2^t}? \qquad (6.3.13)$$

Clearly, asset markets will be in equilibrium if and only if *ex-*

pected yields on the two assets are equated; that is, in place of (6.3.13) we now have

$$\frac{p^{*t}_{11}}{p^t_1} + \frac{q^t_1}{p^t_1} = \frac{p^{*t}_{12}}{p^t_2} + \frac{q^t_2}{p^t_2}. \tag{6.3.14}$$

The model may then be closed by introducing an assumption about how price expectations are formed.

One convenient method is to postulate the adaptive mechanism

$$p^*_i(t + h, t) - p^*_i(t, t - h) = \beta_i[p^t_i - p^*_i(t, t - h)] \tag{6.3.15}$$

where

$0 < \beta = $ *constant rate of adaptation for the ith price equation.*

Although (6.3.15) is not derived from an explicit stochastic model, it will provide some useful insights; the theoretically more acceptable *rational expectations hypothesis* will be examined in Chapter 7.

Dividing both sides of (6.3.15) by h and letting $h \to 0$ yields

$$\dot{p}^*_i(t) = \beta_i p^{*t}_{2i} \tag{6.3.16}$$

which, in view of (6.3.9), implies that

$$p^{*t}_{1i} = \frac{\beta_i - 1}{\beta_i} \dot{p}^t_i; \tag{6.3.17}$$

these derivations are left as Exercise 6.4.

Note that as $\beta_i \to \infty$, we have that

$$p^{*t}_{1i} = \dot{p}^t_i, \tag{6.3.18}$$

the case of *perfect myopic foresight.*[17] Similarly, $\beta_i = 1$ corresponds to the case of *static expectations* in which expected price changes are zero (i.e., $p^{*t}_{1i} = 0$). It turns out that if $0 < \beta_i < 1$ – if expected rates of price change are always in the opposite direction from actual price changes – then our multisector economic model can exhibit stability provided that the technology satisfies certain generalized capital-intensity conditions similar to those stated for the two-sector case in Section 3.6.[18]

Obviously, it is foolish to believe that economic agents will *always* forecast every price change in the wrong direction. However, suppose that in addition market adjustment is sluggish with

$$\frac{\dot{p}_i^t}{p_i^t} = \alpha_i[H_i^t(\cdot) - G_i^t(\cdot)] \tag{6.3.19}$$

where H_i^t = demand for the ith commodity,
$\quad\quad\quad G_i^t$ = supply for the ith commodity,
$\quad\quad\quad (\cdot) = (p_1^t, \ldots, p_n^t)$,
$\quad 0 < \alpha_i$ = constant rate of market adjustment.

We must recognize that (6.3.19) is not satisfactory because it, like the adaptive price expectations mechanism, (6.3.15), is not derived from microeconomic principles. We really should like a theory to explain *why* markets adjust slowly (costly information?) and *how* the adjustment speeds, the α_i's, are determined. If, however, we do postulate both (6.3.15) and (6.3.19), it turns out that the adjustment coefficients always appear in the multiplicative form $\alpha_i(\beta_i - 1)/\beta_i$ with stability requiring (in addition to other conditions) that the inequalities

$$\alpha_i \frac{\beta_i - 1}{\beta_i} < A_i \tag{6.3.20}$$

hold for all i and given values of $A_i > 0$. This means that there is a trade-off between the rate of expected price adaptation and the rate of market adjustment; unlike the case of instantaneous market adjustment where $\alpha_i = \infty$ and $H_i^t \equiv G_i^t$, it is now possible to meet the stability conditions (6.3.20) even when $\beta_i > 1$ and price movements are always in the correct directions.[19]

These results, although not based upon a satisfactory theoretical foundation, at least provide us with one clue: frictions that cause markets to adjust slowly are potential stabilizing influences.

If we are willing to ignore reality, a more theoretically satisfactory solution to the Hahn saddlepoint instability problem has been provided by Becker (1977). Suppose that we consider a representative consumer who takes as given the path of capital good prices (in terms of a single consumption good as *numéraire*),

$$\{p^t\}_{t=0}^{\infty} \equiv \{p_1^t, \ldots, p_n^t\}_{t=0}^{\infty};$$

the path of net rental rates for capital goods,

$$\{q^t\}_{t=0}^{\infty} \equiv \{q_1^t, \ldots, q_n^t\}_{t=0}^{\infty};$$

and the path of profits paid to this consumer by a representative firm he or she owns,

$$\{\pi^t\}_{t=0}^{\infty}.$$

At every instant the consumer decides his or her consumption, c^t; net investment, $\dot{k}^t = (\dot{k}_1^t, \ldots, \dot{k}_n^t)$; and the quantity of capital rented, $k^t = (k_1^t, \ldots, k_n^t)$. Assuming that $q^t > 0$, the consumer will always rent all the capital he or she owns, and thus we need only determine c^t and $\dot{k}^t$, because

$$k^t = k^0 + \int_0^t \dot{k}(s) \, ds. \tag{6.3.21}$$

It is postulated that at time zero the consumer has an intertemporal utility function

$$W = \int_0^{\infty} u(c^t)e^{-\gamma t} \, dt \tag{6.3.22}$$

where

$$u'(c) > 0, \quad u''(c) < 0 \qquad \text{for all } c \geqslant 0, \quad \lim_{c \to 0} u'(c) = +\infty$$

and

$$0 < \gamma = \text{exogenous rate of time preference.}$$

The *consumer's problem* is to solve

$$\max_{\{c^t, \dot{k}^t\}} \int_0^{\infty} u(c^t)e^{-\gamma t} \, dt$$

subject to, for all $t \in [0, \infty)$, the budget constraint

$$c^t + p^t \cdot \dot{k}^t = \pi^t + q^t \cdot k^t,$$

the nonnegativity constraints

$$c^t \geq 0 \quad \text{and} \quad k^t \geq 0,$$

and the initial condition k^0.

The representative firm faces a neoclassical production function

$$c = F(\dot{k}, k) \equiv F(\dot{k}_1, \ldots, \dot{k}_n; k_1, \ldots, k_n), \qquad (6.3.23)$$

and makes an instantaneous profit

$$\pi^t = F(\dot{k}^t, k^t) + p^t \cdot \dot{k}^t - q^t \cdot k^t. \qquad (6.3.24)$$

The firm takes $\{p^t\}_{t=0}^{\infty}$, $\{q^t\}_{t=0}^{\infty}$, and the path of interest rates, $\{r^t\}_{t=0}^{\infty}$, as given. The *firm's problem* at time zero is to maximize the present discounted value of profits given these paths; that is,

$$\max_{\{\dot{k}^t\}} \int_0^{\infty} \pi^t e^{-I(t)} \, dt$$

where

$$I(t) \equiv \int_0^t e^{-rs} \, ds,$$

subject to (6.3.24), $k^t \geq 0$ for all $t \in [0, \infty)$, and given k^0.

Now, *assuming that consumers perfectly predict* the paths for p^t, q^t, and π^t, the solution to the consumer's problem implies demands c_d^t and $\dot{k}_d^t$, as well as the supply k_s^t. Also, given paths for p^t, q^t, and r^t, the solution to the firm's problem implies demand k_d^t and supply $\dot{k}_s^t$; given the latter demand and supply, c_s^t is determined from (6.3.23) and π^t is determined by (6.3.24).

Given an initial value of k^0, the paths

$$\{\hat{p}^t\}_{t=0}^{\infty}, \quad \{\hat{q}^t\}_{t=0}^{\infty}, \quad \{\hat{\pi}^t\}_{t=0}^{\infty}, \quad \text{and} \quad \{\hat{r}^t\}_{t=0}^{\infty}$$

are called a *perfect-foresight competitive equilibrium* if at these prices the solution of the firm's problem, which we denote by $\hat{k}_d^t$, $\dot{\hat{k}}_s^t$, and $\hat{c}_s^t$, is such that if

(1) $\hat{\pi}^t = F(\hat{k}_s^t, \hat{k}_d^t) + \hat{p}^t \cdot \dot{\hat{k}}_s^t - \hat{q}^t \cdot \hat{k}_d^t$, and
(2) $\hat{c}_d^t$, $\dot{\hat{k}}_d^t$, $\dot{\hat{k}}_s^t$ solve the consumer's problem, *then* for all
     $t \in [0, \infty)$ there is *flow equilibrium* with

$$\hat{c}_d^t = \hat{c}_s^t \tag{6.3.25a}$$

and

$$\dot{\hat{k}}_d^t = \dot{\hat{k}}_s^t, \tag{6.3.25b}$$

as well as *stock equilibrium* with

$$\hat{k}_d^t = \hat{k}_s^t. \tag{6.3.25c}$$

Given this framework, Becker proves that for all perfect-foresight competitive equilibrium paths, the initial price vector, $\hat{p}^0$, is such that the *transversality condition* holds;[20] that is,

$$\lim_{t \to \infty} (p^t k^t e^{-\gamma t}) = 0. \tag{6.3.26}$$

Becker's results rely upon the fact that with $\gamma > 0$ the transversality condition is *necessary* if a path is to solve the consumer's problem.[21] Thus within this framework, which incorporates explicit maximizing behavior on the part of economic agents, the imposition of *perfect-foresight competitive equilibrium* as a criterion that dynamic paths must satisfy serves to eliminate nonconvergent paths.[22] This result follows mainly from the fact that perfect-foresight competitive equilibrium paths allow only certain initial price vectors.[23]

However, it does *not* follow that the economy converges to a unique steady-state equilibrium. There is nothing yet to preclude either multiple steady states or the possibility that a perfect-foresight competitive equilibrium path converges to a *limit cycle* with p^t and k^t oscillating in an orbit in (k, p) space.[24] The possibility of such cyclical motion will be examined more closely in the next section. Note, however, that perfect foresight competitive equilibrium paths *cannot* exhibit a zero price in finite time. As already stated, with free disposal the yield on a free capital good is $+\infty$, and hence the stock equilibrium condition (6.3.25c) is violated.

The assumption that consumers have identical tastes enables formulation of the model in terms of "a representative consumer." If there are H consumers having different intertemporal welfare functions

$$W_h = \int_{t=0}^{\infty} u_h(c^t)e^{-\gamma_h t}\, dt, \qquad h = 1, 2, \ldots, H, \quad (6.3.27)$$

the problem becomes more complex. When $n = 1$ (i.e., when there is only one capital good) and when tastes are given by (6.3.27), there exist perfect-foresight competitive equilibrium paths that converge to a steady-state equilibrium where the consumer having the *lowest* rate of time preference (the lowest value of γ_h over all $h = 1, \ldots, H$) owns the entire capital stock![25] Such intuitively unappealing results might be avoided if we allow tastes to change as wealth is accumulated, but undoubtedly such a problem would be technically formidable.

This observation, as well as the fact that we live in economies with very imperfect foresight, makes the concept of a perfect-foresight competitive equilibrium of dubious usefulness for understanding the dynamic behavior of the multisector economies we observe in the real world. Indeed, this will be even more evident from the results derived in the next section; we shall see that a perfect-foresight competitive equilibrium path is always the solution to an optimization problem for a *planned* economy. Nevertheless, the results that we have stated are crucially important for us if we are to gain some understanding about how to approach the problem of constructing more economically reasonable models. We return to this largely ignored problem in Chapter 7.

6.4. Optimizing models of multisector economies

In contrast to descriptive models which generate dynamic paths that may or may not have desirable economic properties, *optimal control models* have solution paths that maximize some social criterion function subject to the given technology and a given initial vector of capital stocks. There are two cases to distinguish. In an infinite-time horizon problem, no "terminal" capital stocks are specified and the value of $\lim_{t \to \infty} k^t$ (if this limit exists) is determined by the solution to the maximizing problem. For finite-time horizons, on the other hand, the capital stocks at the terminal time T are taken as given, entering the maximization problem as a constraint. Although in both instances the dynamic properties of the optimal paths are of interest, dynamic stability is not here an *economic* issue; even if an optimal path diverges, by definition it solves the maximization problem and consequently is a desirable path.

a. *Infinite-horizon problems*

There is a vast economic literature using optimal control theory as a mathematical technique to solve continuous-time intertemporal optimization problems, and our objective here is merely to provide a brief introduction to selected issues of economic significance. For illustrative purposes we shall consider a technology consisting of $n + 1$ production functions

$$
\begin{aligned}
c &= f^0(k_{00}, k_{10}, \ldots, k_{n0}) \\
\dot{k}_1 &= f^1(k_{01}, k_{11}, \ldots, k_{n1}) \\
&\quad\cdot \\
&\quad\cdot \quad\quad\quad\quad\quad\quad\quad\quad\quad (6.4.1) \\
&\quad\cdot \\
\dot{k}_n &= f^n(k_{0n}, k_{1n}, \ldots, k_{nn})
\end{aligned}
$$

where

k_{00} = quantity of labor used to produce the consumption good whose output is denoted by c,

k_{i0} = quantity of the ith-type capital good used to produce the consumption good,

k_{0j} = quantity of labor used to produce capital of type $j, j = 1, \ldots, n$,

k_{ij} = quantity of the ith-type capital good used to produce capital of type $j, i, j = 1, \ldots, n$.

We shall assume that the production functions $f^0, f^1, \ldots, f^n$ exhibit all the standard neoclassical properties, and also postulate that the labor supply is fixed; thus all quantities are per capita. Every variable depends upon time, but to simplify the notation we shall now write c for c^t, k_i for k_i^t, and so on.

A standard and convenient intertemporal welfare function is

$$W = \int_0^\infty u(c)e^{-\gamma t}\, dt \tag{6.4.2}$$

where $u(c)$ is a concave function and where

$$0 < \gamma = \text{social rate of time preference.}$$

The infinite-time optimal control problem is to maximize (6.4.2) subject to the technology described by (6.4.1) and a given initial vector of capital stocks, $k^0 = (k_1^0, \ldots, k_n^0)$. At every instant we must also impose the nonnegativity constraints $k_{ij} \geqslant 0$ ($i, j = 0, 1, \ldots, n$), the labor constraint $1 - \sum_{j=0}^n k_{0j} \geqslant 0$, and the capital constraints $k_i - \sum_{j=0}^n k_{ij} \geqslant 0$ ($i = 1, \ldots, n$).

This maximization problem may be solved by a straightforward application of optimal control theory.[26] The *discounted value Hamiltonian*[27] for our case is

$$H = \max_{\{k_{ij}\}} \left[L(\cdot)e^{-\gamma t} + \sum_{i=1}^n f^i(k_{0i}, k_{1i}, \ldots, k_{ni})q_i e^{-\gamma t} \right] \tag{6.4.3}$$

where the Lagrangian $L(\cdot)$ is

$$L(\cdot) = u[f^0(k_{00}, k_{10}, \ldots, k_{n0})] + \sum_{i=0}^n \sum_{j=0}^n \alpha_{ij} k_{ij} + \sum_{i=1}^n w_i \left(k_i - \sum_{j=0}^n k_{ij} \right) + w_0 \left(1 - \sum_{j=0}^n k_{0j} \right). \tag{6.4.4}$$

The α_{ij}'s are Lagrangian multipliers associated with the nonnegativity constraints $k_{ij} \geqslant 0$, w_i are Lagrangian multipliers associated with the capital constraints, and w_0 is the Lagrangian multiplier associated with the labor constraint. The maximization in (6.4.3) with respect to the *control variables,* the k_{ij}'s, must hold for all t.

Defining

$$f_j^i \equiv \frac{\partial f^i(k_{0i}, k_{1i}, \ldots, k_{ni})}{\partial k_{ji}}, \qquad i, j = 0, 1, \ldots, n,$$

this maximization with respect to the control variables implies the necessary conditions[28]

$$u'f_i^0 + \alpha_{i0} - w_i = 0, \qquad i = 1, \ldots, n, \tag{6.4.5}$$

$$\alpha_{ij} - w_i + q_j f_i^j = 0, \qquad i = 0, 1, \ldots, n; j = 1, \ldots, n, \tag{6.4.6}$$

with the side conditions

$$\alpha_{ij} \geq 0, \quad k_{ij} \geq 0, \quad \alpha_{ij} k_{ij} = 0, \qquad i, j = 0, 1, \ldots, n, \tag{6.4.7a}$$

$$w_i \geq 0, \quad \left(k_i - \sum_{j=0}^{n} k_{ij}\right) \geq 0, \quad w_i \left(k_i - \sum_{j=0}^{n} k_{ij}\right) = 0$$
$$i = 1, \ldots, n, \tag{6.4.7b}$$

and

$$w_0 \geq 0, \quad \left(1 - \sum_{j=0}^{n} k_{0j}\right) \geq 0, \quad w_0 \left(1 - \sum_{j=0}^{n} k_{0j}\right) = 0. \tag{6.4.7c}$$

Equations (6.4.6) and (6.4.7a)–(6.4.7c) have an economic interpretation. Suppose first that $k_{ij} > 0$; then (6.4.7a) implies that $\alpha_{ij} = 0$, and hence from (6.4.6),

$$q_j f_i^j = w_i. \tag{6.4.8}$$

But interpreting q_j as the price of commodity j and w_i as the factor price of the ith input,[29] (6.4.8) is simply the familiar condition for cost minimization under perfect competition. Next, suppose that $k_{ij} = 0$: then (6.4.7a) implies that $\alpha_{ij} > 0$, and hence from (6.4.6),

$$q_j f_i^j - w_i = -\alpha_{ij} < 0. \tag{6.4.8a}$$

Equation (6.4.8a) shows that when the marginal revenue product, $q_j f_i^j$, is less than the corresponding factor price, w_i, then that factor is not employed (i.e., $k_{ij} = 0$).

Moreover, multiplying (6.4.6) by k_{ij}, using (6.4.7a), and summing over i yields

$$\sum_{i=0}^{n} w_i k_{ij} = q_j \sum_{i=0}^{n} f_i^j k_{ij}. \tag{6.4.9}$$

Since the production functions are homogeneous of degree 1, Euler's theorem gives

$$f^j = \sum_{i=0}^{n} f_i^j k_{ij}, \qquad j = 0, 1, \dots, n, \tag{6.4.10}$$

and consequently, substituting (6.4.10) into (6.4.9), we have

$$\sum_{i=0}^{n} w_i k_{ij} = q_j f^j. \tag{6.4.11}$$

That is, the total cost of production is equal to total revenue for every $j = 0, 1, \dots, n$.

Finally, we may relate the prices q_j and w_j to the prices in Section 6.3, which were in terms of the consumption good as *numéraire*. Let the latter commodity prices and factor prices (rental rates) in terms of the consumption good be denoted by Q_j and W_j, respectively, with $Q_0 \equiv 1$. The same procedure which led to (6.4.11) gives

$$u'(c) = \frac{\sum_{i=0}^{n} w_i k_{i0}}{c}. \tag{6.4.12}$$

The derivation of (6.4.12) is left as Exercise 6.5. We wish to find a factor of proportionality, $\lambda > 0$, such that

$$q_i = \lambda Q_i \tag{6.4.13a}$$

and

$$w_i = \lambda W_i, \qquad i = 1, \dots, n. \tag{6.4.13b}$$

But with the consumption good as *numéraire,*

$$f_i^0 = W_i \quad \text{when } k_{i0} > 0, \qquad i = 1, \ldots, n. \tag{6.4.14}$$

Thus multiplying by k_{i0}, summing over i, and applying Euler's theorem, we have

$$c = \sum_{i=0}^{n} W_i k_{i0}. \tag{6.4.15}$$

Substitute (6.4.15) and (6.4.13b) into (6.4.12); this yields

$$u'(c) = \frac{\lambda \sum_{i=0}^{n} W_i k_{i0}}{\sum_{i=0}^{n} W_i k_{i0}} = \lambda. \tag{6.4.16}$$

We thus arrive at an interpretation of the variables q_i and w_i: *q_i is equal to the current price of the ith commodity in terms of the consumption good as numéraire times the marginal utility of consumption; w_i* has an analogous interpretation.

With these details understood, we are better able to understand the role of H, as defined by equation (6.4.3). In view of (6.4.7a) and (6.4.7b), we may write

$$H = u(c)e^{-\gamma t} + \sum_{i=1}^{n} \dot{k}_i q_i e^{-\gamma t}. \tag{6.4.17}$$

Let

$$\hat{H} \equiv H e^{\gamma t}$$

denote the *current value Hamiltonian;* we then have

$$\hat{H} = u(c) + \sum_{i=1}^{n} q_i \dot{k}_i = u(c) + u'(c) \sum_{i=1}^{n} Q_i \dot{k}_1. \tag{6.4.18}$$

Thus $\hat{H}$ is *the current value of net national product expressed in utility units.* When the utility function is linear with $u(c) = c$ and $u'(c) = 1$, $\hat{H}$ is equal to the current value of ordinary net national product in terms of the consumption good as *numéraire.* Because both H and $\hat{H}$ are maximized – see (6.4.3) – we reach the important conclusion that along an optimal path both the discounted and current value of net national product expressed in utility units are maximized.[30]

Returning now to our optimal control problem, the necessary conditions for an optimal policy are that there exist n piecewise continuous functions of time, q_i for $i = 1, \ldots, n$ such that

$$\frac{d}{dt}(q_i e^{-\gamma t}) = -\frac{\partial H}{\partial k_i}, \qquad i = 1, \ldots, n. \tag{6.4.19}$$

From (6.4.3) and (6.4.4) we may calculate

$$-\frac{\partial H}{\partial k_i} = -w_i e^{-\gamma t}, \tag{6.4.20}$$

and thus, differentiating the left-hand side of (6.4.19), the necessary conditions for an optimal path can be expressed as

$$\dot{q}_i e^{-\gamma t} - \gamma q_i e^{-\gamma t} = -w_i e^{-\gamma t}$$

or

$$\dot{q}_i + w_i = \gamma q_i, \qquad i = 1, \ldots, n. \tag{6.4.21}$$

If in addition the *transversality condition*

$$\lim_{t \to \infty} (q_i e^{-\gamma t}) = 0, \qquad i = 1, \ldots, n \tag{6.4.22}$$

is satisfied, the necessary conditions (6.4.21) are also sufficient. Moreover, with regularity conditions on the technology and the welfare functions that are economically reasonable, the transversality condition (6.4.22) is also *necessary*. These technical details are left for the interested reader to pursue.[31]

From equations (6.4.13a), (6.4.13b), and (6.4.16), we may rewrite the necessary conditions (6.4.21) as

$$\frac{du'(c)}{dt} Q_i + \dot{Q}_i u'(c) + u'(c) W_i = \gamma u'(c) Q_i, \qquad i = 1, \ldots, n$$

or

$$\frac{\dot{Q}_i}{Q_i} + \frac{W_i}{Q_i} = \gamma - \frac{du'(c)/dt}{u'(c)} \equiv r, \qquad i = 1, \ldots, n. \tag{6.4.23}$$

But (6.4.23) is simply our portfolio equilibrium condition expressed in current prices in terms of the consumption good as *numéraire!* Thus we see that along an optimal path the interest rate is equal to the social rate of time preference minus the rate of change of marginal utility. If c approaches a constant, or if marginal utility is constant, the rate of interest is constant and equal to γ.

The current value Hamiltonian, $\hat{H}$ given by equation (6.4.18), plays a central role in optimal control theory. It is clear from (6.4.18), (6.4.3), and (6.4.4) that, at each t, $\hat{H}$ is a function of $q \equiv (q_1, \ldots, q_n)$ and $k \equiv (k_1, \ldots, k_n)$. *The cannonical equations*

$$\dot{q} = -\frac{\partial \hat{H}(q, k)}{\partial k} + \gamma q \equiv -\hat{H}_k(q, k) + \gamma q \qquad (6.4.24a)$$

and

$$\dot{k} = +\frac{\partial \hat{H}(q, k)}{\partial q} \equiv +\hat{H}_q(q, k) \qquad (6.4.24b)$$

are necessary conditions which an optimal path must satisfy.[32] Note that (6.4.24a) and (6.4.19) are equivalent.

A *rest point* or steady-state equilibrium for an optimal control path is a point $(\bar{q}, \bar{k})$ such that

$$\dot{q} = 0 = -\hat{H}_k(\bar{q}, \bar{k}) + \gamma \bar{q} \qquad (6.4.25a)$$

and

$$\dot{k} = 0 = +\hat{H}_q(\bar{q}, \bar{k}). \qquad (6.4.25b)$$

Defining the *deviation vectors*

$$\xi \equiv q - \bar{q} \qquad (6.4.26a)$$

and

$$\eta \equiv k - \bar{k}, \qquad (6.4.26b)$$

the *associated linear system* to the nonlinear system (6.4.25a)–(6.4.25b) is

$$\dot{\xi} = [-\hat{H}_{kq}(\bar{q}, \bar{k}) + \gamma]\xi - \hat{H}_{kk}\eta \qquad (6.4.27a)$$

and

$$\dot{\eta} = [+\hat{H}_{qq}(\bar{q}, \bar{k})]\xi + \hat{H}_{qk}(\bar{q}, \bar{k})\eta. \qquad (6.4.27b)$$

The latter may be written more compactly as

$$\begin{bmatrix} \dot{\xi} \\ \dot{\eta} \end{bmatrix} = \bar{J} \begin{bmatrix} \xi \\ \eta \end{bmatrix}, \qquad (6.4.28)$$

where the matrix $\bar{J}$ is

$$\bar{J} \equiv \begin{bmatrix} -\hat{H}_{kq}(\bar{q}, \bar{k}) + \gamma I & -\hat{H}_{kk}(\bar{q}, \bar{k}) \\ +\hat{H}_{qq}(\bar{q}, \bar{k}) & +\hat{H}_{qk}(\bar{q}, \bar{k}) \end{bmatrix}. \qquad (6.4.29)$$

The characteristic roots of this Jacobian matrix $\bar{J}$ are the solutions to the characteristic equation

$$\det [\lambda I - \bar{J}] = 0. \qquad (6.4.30)$$

Provided that $\det \bar{J} \neq 0$ and there are no purely imaginary characteristic roots, then whenever (q, k) is in a sufficiently small neighborhood of the rest point $(\bar{q}, \bar{k})$, the stability properties of the linear system (6.4.28) are identical to those of the nonlinear system (6.4.25a)–(6.4.25b). We shall assume that the characteristic roots to (6.4.30) (denoted by λ_i, $i = 1, \ldots, 2n$) all have nonvanishing real parts.[33] Thus the local stability properties of (6.4.25a)–(6.4.25b) are completely characterized by the signs of Re λ_i, $i = 1, \ldots, 2n$.

Recall from note 6 that a rest point to an autonomous (i.e., time invariant) system of differential equations in $2n$ dimensions is a *regular saddlepoint* if the associated linear system has n characteristic roots with negative real parts and the other n roots have positive real parts. It has been proven that if λ is a characteristic root of J^*, then $-\lambda + \gamma$ is another characteristic root.[34] The following important conclusion is immediate: *whenever the social rate of time preference, γ, is sufficiently near zero, the rest point $(\bar{q}, \bar{k})$ is a regular saddlepoint.*

Unfortunately, matters are not always this simple, and in general there may exist dynamic equilibria that are not regular saddlepoints.[35] Here we merely note that the characteristic roots as-

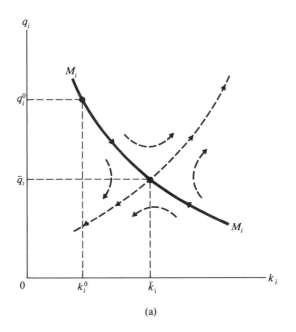

(a)

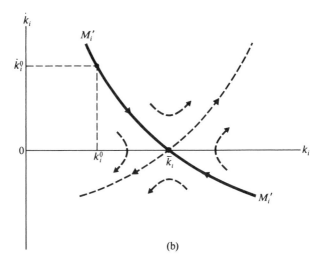

(b)

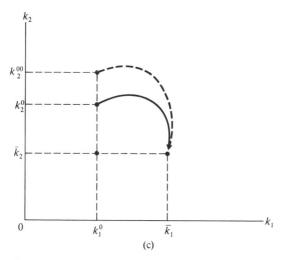

Figure 6.4. Convergence to the capital stocks k_i occurs only along the M_iM_i curve in (a) and the M_iM_i curve in (b). Examples of such convergent paths are illustrated in (c).

sociated with a rest point may have from 0 to n characteristic roots with negative real parts (and with $2n$ to n positive real parts, respectively).[36] This means that the types of dynamic behavior exhibited by optimal control solutions can be very complex. Indeed, an optimal path may exhibit cyclical behavior with the solution converging to a limit cycle in (q, k) space.[37]

Let us suppose, however, that our optimal control problem has a *unique*, regular saddlepoint at $(q, k) = (\bar{q}, \bar{k})$.[38] The optimal trajectory sufficiently near $(\bar{q}, \bar{k})$ then lies on an n-dimensional manifold in $2n$-dimensional (q, k)-space. The dynamic properties illustrated by Figure 6.4a are familiar by now; for any given initial vector k^0, there exists a unique value of q^0 that leads to the optimal path that maximizes the criterion function (6.4.2). Since q is open to choice, there is no issue of stability. Given a vector of capital stocks, $k = (k_1, \ldots, k_n)$, the optimal policy at each t is to select q_i on the stable M_iM_i curve for every $i = 1, \ldots, n$, as illustrated by Figure 6.4a. However, this figure is misleading because the optimal choice of any q_i depends upon *all* capital stocks, not on just k_i as the diagram suggests. In general, the solution to our optimal control problem may be written as

$$q_i = \psi_i(k_1, \ldots, k_n), \qquad i = 1, \ldots, n,$$

or, in more compact vector notation,

$$q = \psi(k). \tag{6.4.31}$$

The current value Hamiltonian, $\hat{H}$, is a function of q and k; thus from (6.4.25b) we have that, at each t,

$$\dot{k} = \hat{H}_q(q, k) = \hat{H}_q[\psi(k), k] \equiv \phi(k). \tag{6.4.32}$$

The function $\dot{k} = \phi(k)$ is the *feedback control law* represented by the curve $M'_i M'_i$ in Figure 6.4b. This control law describes the change in the state variables – the k_i's – which must occur at each t to realize an optimal policy.

The dashed trajectories in Figure 6.4a – and, analogously in Figure 6.4b – represent solutions to the necessary differential equations (6.4.24a) and (6.4.25b) with incorrect initial price vectors. Such paths are not optimal because the necessary transversality condition (6.4.22) is violated. Therefore, for this simple case under consideration, optimal policies, starting from any initial k^0 vector, converge to a unique rest point $(\bar{q}, \bar{k})$. Accordingly, in k-space the optimal path for a given k^0 consists of a single curve, as illustrated in Figure 6.4c. The dashed curve in Figure 6.4c illustrates the optimal path in (k_1, k_2)-space starting from a different initial condition with $k_1^0 = k_1^{00}$ but $k_2^0 \neq k_2^{00}$.

All of the stability results stated so far have been derived from a linearization of the necessary differential equations (6.4.24a)–(6.4.24b) and are valid only for (q, k) in a sufficiently small neighborhood of $(\bar{q}, \bar{k})$. Brock and Scheinkman, Cass and Shell, Rockafellar, and others have studied the problem of *global stability* for optimal control problems.[39] The primary result is that an optimal path converges to a unique $(\bar{q}, \bar{k})$ along an n-dimensional manifold in $2n$-dimensional (q, k)-space, provided that the Hamiltonian satisfies certain curvature conditions relative to the size of the social rate of time preference. One such sufficient condition is that the matrix

$$Q(q, k) \equiv \begin{bmatrix} \hat{H}_{qq}(q, k) & \frac{1}{2}\gamma I \\ \frac{1}{2}\gamma I & -\hat{H}_{kk}(q, k) \end{bmatrix} \tag{6.4.33}$$

be positive definite.[40] When $\gamma = 0$, this sufficient global stability condition is satisfied provided that $\hat{H}(q, k)$ is strictly convex in q and strictly concave in k. If the Hamiltonian has sufficient curvature, Q will also be positive definite for sufficiently small $\gamma > 0$. Under these circumstances the qualitative dynamic behavior illustrated in Figure 6.4a through c is valid globally [i.e., for all $(q, k) > 0$].

When $\gamma \leq 0$, the improper integral measuring intertemporal welfare – equation (6.4.2) – may not converge; there may exist many paths for which $W = +\infty$, and some other criterion is necessary to identify an optimal path.

One such criterion is the *overtaking principle:*

DEFINITION 6.1
A path $\{\hat{c}, \hat{k}, \dot{\hat{k}}\}$ *overtakes* the path $\{c, k, \dot{k}\}$ if (a) for all $\epsilon > 0$ there exists a time $T(\epsilon)$ such that for all $T \geq T(\epsilon)$ we have

$$\int_0^T [u(\hat{c}) - u(c)]e^{-\gamma t}\, dt \geq -\epsilon,$$

or, equivalently, if (b)[41]

$$\lim_{T \to \infty} \int_0^T [u(\hat{c}) - u(c)]e^{-\gamma t}\, dt \geq 0.$$

A feasible path $\{\hat{c}, \hat{k}, \dot{\hat{k}}\}$ is *optimal* if it overtakes *all* other feasible paths.

Cases of $\gamma \leq 0$ can arise if population grows at the exponential rate $g > 0$ and we measure intertemporal social welfare by weighting per capita utility at every instant by the existing population at that instant. Letting ρ denote a rate of time discount, this measure of social welfare is

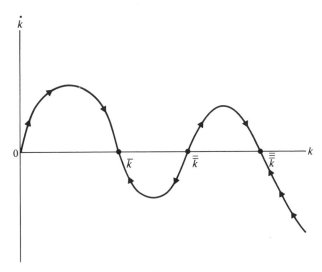

Figure 6.5. Multiple rest points with $n = 1$.

$$\int_0^\infty u(c)e^{(-\rho+g)t}\, dt, \tag{6.4.34}$$

which is identical to W given by (6.4.2) with $\gamma \equiv \rho - g$. Now, however, we see that $\gamma \le 0$ when $\rho \le g$. Gale (1967), McFadden (1967), Weizsäcker (1965), and others have used the overtaking principle to study capital accumulation problems when $\gamma \le 0$.

Another approach when $\gamma = 0$ is to assume that there is *utility saturation* at a per capita consumption level $\bar{c}$ and to define a *Bliss point B* by

$$B \equiv u(\bar{c}) = \sup_{c \ge 0} u(c).$$

One then selects a policy that *minimizes* the expression

$$\int_0^\infty [B - u(c)]e^{-\gamma t}\, dt. \tag{6.4.35}$$

Assumptions regarding the technology assure that there exist feasible paths along which $u(c) = B$ at some finite time. Thus the improper integral (6.4.35) has finite values for a set of feasible

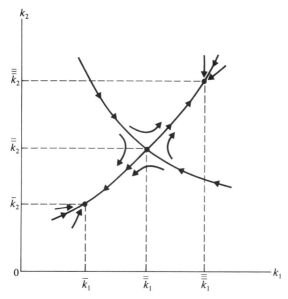

Figure 6.6. Multiple rest points with $n = 2$.

paths, and an optimal path becomes one that minimizes (6.4.35). This formulation of the optimal capital accumulation problem is motivated by the 1928 work of Ramsey.[42]

We now return briefly to our original problem with $\gamma > 0$. Instead of the production functions (6.4.1), let the technology be described by

$$c = F(\dot{k}, k). \tag{6.4.36}$$

Even when there is a single capital good ($n = 1$), the optimal capital accumulation problem can exhibit multiple rest points when $\gamma > 0$.[43] In such instances the optimal policy is shown by the curve in Figure 6.5, which is analogous to Figure 6.4b. Note that $\bar{k}$ and $\bar{\bar{k}}$ are stable, while $\bar{\bar{k}}$ is unstable; that is, unless $k^0 = \bar{\bar{k}}$, the optimal path will converge to $\bar{k}$ when $0 < k^0 < \bar{\bar{k}}$, and it will converge to $\bar{\bar{k}}$ when $k^0 > \bar{\bar{k}}$. Thus the point toward which an optimal policy converges depends on the initial capital stock.

This result generalizes when $n > 1$, as illustrated by Figure 6.6, which is analogous to Figure 6.4c. Through any initial point (k_1^0, k_2^0) in Figure 6.6, there is a unique optimal trajectory. We see that $\bar{k}$ and $\bar{\bar{\bar{k}}}$ are stable, while $\bar{\bar{k}}$ is a regular saddlepoint in the (k_1, k_2)-space of optimal paths. Given an initial value of k_1^0, there is one and only one value of k_2^0 for which it is optimal to converge to $\bar{\bar{k}}$.

Similar results emerge when we retain the technology (6.4.1), but postulate heterogeneous consumption goods with $u(c)$ replaced by $u(c_1, \ldots, c_n)$. Unless the utility function satisfies a *normality condition,* multiple rest points will exist.[44] However, even when a unique rest point to an optimal capital accumulation problem does exist, the optimal path may not converge to it. *There exist cases in which an orbit is optimal.*[45] Further, for values of $\gamma > 0$ this phenomenon can occur even with the technology given by (6.4.1), $n = 2$ (two capital goods and one consumption good), Cobb–Douglas production functions, and the intertemporal welfare function (6.4.2). For precisely this simple case Benhabib and Nishimura have proved that the unique rest point $(\bar{q}_1, \bar{q}_2, \bar{k}_1, \bar{k}_2)$ has an associated linear system with four complex roots all having *positive* real parts.[46] Moreover, they show that a periodic closed orbit exists satisfying the necessary differential equations (6.4.24a) and (6.4.24b). Because q and k are bounded on this orbit, the transversality condition

$$\lim_{t \to \infty} qke^{-\gamma t} = 0 \qquad (6.4.37)$$

is also satisfied, implying that the orbital motion is optimal. The solutions here are illustrated in Figure 6.7, which is analogous to Figures 6.4c and 6.6, which depict optimal paths in k-space. Observe that for any initial (k_1^0, k_2^0), the optimal path converges to the limit cycle indicated by the thick closed curve. In four-dimensional (q_1, q_2, k_1, k_2)-space, there exists a two-dimensional manifold along which paths converge to a cycle in (q, k)-space. In this sense the limit cycle itself has a generalized saddlepoint property. The mathematics required to completely analyze the dynamic behavior in such a case involves advanced topological concepts, and the interested reader is referred to the

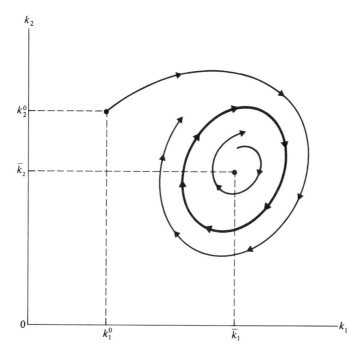

Figure 6.7. The optimal policy in (k_1, k_2)-space converges to the limit cycle indicated by the thick closed curve.

paper by Benhabib and Nishimura cited above. We may conclude, however, that an optimal path can be extremely complex.[47]

This observation is of considerable economic significance in view of the following theorem proved by Becker (1977, 1979b):

THEOREM 6.1 (EQUIVALENCE THEOREM)
A perfect-foresight competitive equilibrium, as defined in Section 6.3, is *equivalent* to an optimal path which maximizes (6.4.2).

Thus an optimal path is a perfect-foresight competitive equilibrium, and vice versa. Accordingly, we see that some perfect-foresight competitive equilibria are limit cycles.

b. *Finite-time problems*

Intertemporal maximization problems with a finite-time horizon, T, can be solved using similar techniques. As before, the initial condition k^0 is given, but now we *also* impose the inequality constraint

$$k^T \geq \kappa, \qquad \kappa > 0 \text{ given}, \tag{6.4.38}$$

at the terminal time T. Our problem is to find a path that maximizes

$$\int_0^T u(c)e^{-\gamma t}\, dt \tag{6.4.39}$$

subject to given k^0, the terminal condition (6.4.38), and the technology (6.4.1). Since c will be bounded on all feasible paths, the improper integral (6.4.39) converges even if $\gamma \leq 0$.

As before, the differential equations (6.4.24a) and (6.4.24b) are necessary conditions, while the finite-time transversality condition is

$$q^T e^{-\gamma T}(k^T - \bar{k}) = 0 \quad \text{and} \quad q^T e^{-\gamma T} \geq 0. \tag{6.4.40}$$

From (6.4.40) we see that if the terminal condition (6.4.38) is met with inequality and $k_i^T > \kappa_i$ for the ith capital good, then $q_i^T = 0$.

The *turnpike theorems* for consumptionless economies generalize to *consumption turnpike theorems*.[48] The name "turnpike" is motivated by the observation that if one wished to travel from point A to point B by automobile, the fastest route is not necessarily the one that minimizes the road distance between points A and B; if A and B are sufficiently distant, it may be quicker to start out from A and proceed toward a "turnpike" (interstate highway) that may not involve moving closer to B initially. One could then take advantage of the presumably higher speed possible on the turnpike compared with a direct (distance minimizing) route between A and B along which there are frequent traffic lights. One would leave the turnpike at the exit closest to B and then proceed directly to the terminal target. Moreover, for long trips – for example, New York City to San Francisco – a large percentage of the total travel time would be spent on the turnpike.

The analogy to consumption turnpike theorems is evident when considering the path (route) between a given initial condition, k^0 (point A), and a given terminal condition, $k^T = \kappa$ (point B), such that (6.4.39) is maximized. For given k^0, let $[\bar{q}(k^0), \bar{k}(k^0)]$ denote the rest-point solution to the corresponding *infinite*-time problem. This notation reflects our previous observation that infinite-time problems may have multiple rest points and that the optimal path is sensitive to initial conditions, as illustrated by Figures 6.5 and 6.6. We now state the fundamental result.

THEOREM 6.2 (CONSUMPTION TURNPIKE THEOREM)
Assume that the optimal solution for the infinite-time problem converges to the rest point $[\bar{q}(k^0), \bar{k}(k^0)]$. For any $\epsilon > 0$ define

$$N(\epsilon) = \{(q, k): \|q - \bar{q}_0\| < \epsilon, \quad \|k - \bar{k}_0\| < \epsilon\}$$

where $\|\cdot\|$ denotes the Euclidean norm. For all sufficiently large but finite values of T, the optimal paths from k^0 to $k^T = \bar{k}$ have the property that the point (q, k) is in the neighborhood $N(\epsilon)$ for all t satisfying

$$T_1(\epsilon) \leq t \leq T - T_2(\epsilon)$$

where $T_1(\epsilon)$ and $T_2(\epsilon)$ are finite.

The proportion of the time T that this optimal path spends in the ϵ-neighborhood of the "turnpike" $[\bar{q}(k^0), \bar{k}(k^0)]$ is

$$\theta = 1 - \frac{T_1(\epsilon) + T_2(\epsilon)}{T}.$$

Thus for any given $\epsilon > 0$, we can make θ as close to unity as desired by choosing a sufficiently large T.

We have seen that an optimal solution may converge to a periodic closed orbit. The consumption turnpike theorem generalizes to include such cases. If the optimal path from k^0 in the infinite-time problem converges to a limit cycle Γ, the fraction of time that the solution to a finite-time problem spends in a specified neighborhood of Γ approaches unity as the finite time T ap-

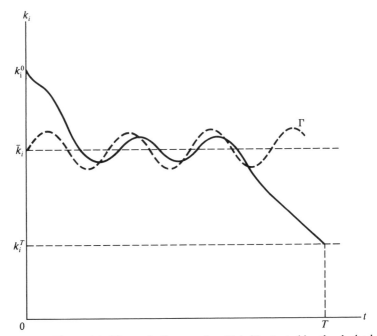

Figure 6.8. The periodic turnpike, Γ, is illustrated by the dashed curve; it oscillates around an unstable rest point, $\bar{k}$. The optimal path from k^0 to k^T is illustrated by the solid curve; as T becomes larger it will spend longer fractions of the planning horizon in any specified neighborhood of Γ.

proaches $+\infty$.[49] Figure 6.8 illustrates a periodic turnpike. Thus we again see that periodic closed orbits may play exactly the same role as rest points.

c. *Other issues in optimizing models*

In conclusion, we shall briefly discuss the issues of (1) uncertainty, (2) exhaustible resources, and (3) sensitivity of optimal solutions.

Uncertainty. Consider a discrete-time model with one capital good and a technology

$$c^{t+1} + k^{t+1} = f(k^t; w^{t+1}), \qquad t = 0, 1, \ldots, \qquad (6.4.41)$$

where for each value of w, $f(k; w)$ is a strictly concave production function having the standard neoclassical properties. Uncertainty arises because w^t are random variables, assumed independent and identically distributed.

The initial value $c^0 + k^0$ is taken as given, and a program $\{k^t; c^t\} = \{k^0, k^1, \ldots; c^0, c^1, \ldots\}$ satisfying (6.4.41) is called *feasible*. The optimization problem is to select a feasible program that is optimal (in some sense) with respect to the *expected* intertemporal welfare criterion

$$\sum_{t=0}^{\infty} \frac{E[u(c^t)]}{(1 + \gamma)^t} \tag{6.4.42}$$

where E denotes the expectation operator and where $\gamma \geq 0$ is the social rate of time discount. As in deterministic cases, an optimal path may be one that maximizes (6.4.42), or, when $\gamma \leq 0$ and the infinite sum does not converge, the overtaking principle may be used to define optimality.

The dynamic properties of an optimal path are now stochastic, and in place of a rest point there now is a stationary *distribution* associated with an optimal stationary program. *Competitive programs* are feasible programs for which expected profits are nonpositive. An expected value version of the transversality condition is necessary and sufficient for the optimality of a competitive program. More precisely, let $\{\hat{k}^t; \hat{c}^t\}$ be a competitive program with initial condition $(k^0; c^0)$; Mirman and Zilcha (1977, p. 397) have proved that such a program is optimal if and only if there exists a constant M such that

$$E[u'(\hat{c}^t)(\hat{c}^t + \hat{k}^t)] \leq M \qquad \text{for all } t. \tag{6.4.43}$$

Since the price of homogeneous output $(c^t + k^t)$ is $u'(c^t)$, (6.4.3) shows that the expected value of output must be bounded.

The literature on optimal capital accumulation under uncertainty is both large and technically difficult; below we refer the interested reader to some representative work.[50]

Exhaustible Resources. The models we have considered so far allow for a per capita interpretation, and it is trivial to generalize them to the case in which labor, the single primary factor, grows at the exponential rate $g > 0$. In fact, however, there exist many primary factors which are presumably fixed in total supply (e.g., oil). To capture the issues involved, consider a simple technology for which

$$\dot{k}^t + c^t = f(k^t, x^t), \tag{6.4.44}$$

where f is a strictly concave production function and x^t is the *flow* of a single exhaustible resource at time t.[51] The flow, x^t, is constrained by the total stock available at time zero, S^0; that is,

$$\int_{t=0}^{\infty} x^t \, dt \leq S^0. \tag{6.4.45}$$

The intertemporal maximization is now modified to

$$\max \int_0^{\infty} u(c^t)e^{-\gamma t} \, dt \tag{6.4.46}$$

subject to (6.4.44), (6.4.45), $c^t > 0$, $k^t \geq 0$, $x^t \geq 0$, and given $k^0 > 0$, $S^0 > 0$. The Hamiltonian for this problem is (dropping the superscripts)

$$H = \max_{c,x} \left[u(c)e^{-\gamma t} + qe^{-\gamma t}[f(k, x) - c] - \lambda x + \mu e^{-\gamma t}x \right] \tag{6.4.47}$$

where

$$\mu \geq 0 \quad \text{and} \quad \mu x = 0 \tag{6.4.48}$$

and

$$\lambda \geq 0 \quad \text{and} \quad \left(S^0 - \int_{t=0}^{\infty} x \, dt\right) = 0. \tag{6.4.49}$$

Maximization with respect to c and x yields the necessary condition

$$q = u'(c) \tag{6.4.50a}$$

and

$$\lambda = e^{-\gamma t}(\mu + qf_x) = \text{constant} > 0, \qquad (6.4.50\text{b})$$

respectively, where $f_x \equiv \partial f / \partial x$. From (6.4.48) and (6.4.50b) we reach the important economic conclusion that when $x > 0$ on an optimal path, then

$$\lambda = qe^{-\gamma t}f_x. \qquad (6.4.51)$$

That is, λ is the *present value utility price of the exhaustible resource*. Moreover, if

$$\lim_{x \to 0} f_x(k, x) = +\infty \qquad \text{for all } k > 0, \qquad (6.4.52)$$

then an optimal path, if one exists, has the property $x > 0$; that is, the resource is never depleted in finite time.

As before, we have the necessary conditions

$$-H_k \equiv -\frac{\partial H}{\partial k} = \frac{d(qe^{-\gamma t})}{dt} \qquad (6.4.53)$$

or

$$-qe^{-\gamma t}f_k = \dot{q}e^{-\gamma t} - \gamma qe^{-\gamma t}$$

or

$$\frac{\dot{q}}{q} + \frac{f_k}{q} = \gamma, \qquad (6.4.54)$$

as well as

$$+\frac{\partial H}{\partial q} e^{\gamma t} \equiv +H_q e^{\gamma t} = \dot{k}. \qquad (6.4.55)$$

Moreover, differentiating (6.4.51) yields

$$0 = \frac{\dot{q}}{q} - \gamma + \frac{\partial f_x / \partial t}{f_x}, \qquad (6.4.56)$$

and, combining (6.4.54) with (6.4.56), we see that

$$\frac{\dot{q}}{q} + \frac{\partial f_x / \partial t}{f_x} = \frac{\dot{q}}{q} + \frac{f_k}{q} = \gamma. \qquad (6.4.57)$$

Interpreting the exhaustible resource as an asset, condition (6.4.57) is simply the portfolio equilibrium condition that the rates of return in utility prices on the two assets – the resource and the capital good – must be equalized.

The existence of an optimal policy and the dynamic properties of an optimal path depend upon the properties of the production function $f(k, x)$. We have seen, though, that the same economic principles emerge despite the existence of exhaustible primary factors.[52]

However, it should be observed that many crucially important features of the real world are not incorporated into models of this type. Indeed, important sources of uncertainty involve the value of S^0 – the amount of an exhaustible resource actually available – as well as the form of the production function for $t > 0$. Uncertainty, as described by (6.4.41), for example, does not allow – through luck or research and development projects – the set of technologically feasible options to change over time.

Moreover, expectations about what resources may be rapidly depleted influence the direction of research and development, implying that the evolution of technological knowledge is not necessarily independent of initial resource stocks. Despite these complications, our simple models do serve to qualify pessimistic "doomsday predictions," and, in any event, are an invaluable guide to the development of economically sound intuition.

Sensitivity. In all of the optimizing models we have considered, computation and implementation costs have been ignored. How much is gained by following an optimal trajectory instead of following other competitive paths? Is the answer robust with respect to a misspecification of the utility function $u(c)$? That is, if an optimal policy is computed using the wrong utility function, might the resulting path be very poor compared with alternative paths evaluated by the correct utility function? The precise sense in which these questions may be meaningful – and some tentative answers to them – are given by Burmeister, Jackson, and Ross (1977). Their preliminary finding is that, in a wide range of circumstances, simple "rule-of-thumb policies" that violate the portfolio equilibrium condition do quite badly as measured by a variety of criteria. This finding again underscores the importance of the portfolio equilibrium condition as a requirement for a desirable intertemporal allocation of resources.

Another sensitivity question concerns the properties of optimal paths for very long, but finite, time horizons. One would expect that as T becomes large, the behavior of the path near $t = 0$ would not be very sensitive to the terminal capital-stock condition, $k^T \geq \bar{k}$ for a given $\bar{k} > 0$. Indeed, the consumption turnpike theorem suggests this result, and it has been confirmed for special cases.[53]

Finally, we note that the significance of the consumption turnpike theorem involves a sensitivity issue. For example, if we select an ϵ so that a point $(q, k) \in N(\epsilon)$ differs (in every component) by no more than 10% from $[q^*(k^0), k^*(k^0)]$, how large must T become for an optimal T-horizon plan to spend half the horizon in this neighborhood? If the answer to this question is $T > 10,000$ years, the qualitative dynamic behavior suggested by the consumption turnpike theorem might become irrelevant. Unfortunately, no adequate analyses of such questions currently exist, and we must leave the issue unresolved.[54]

6.5. Concluding remarks

The primary conclusion to emerge from this chapter is that descriptive models of economic growth having heterogeneous capital goods often possess steady-state equilibria that exhibit saddlepoint instability. In such cases, if we are given arbitrary initial stocks of the various capital goods, convergence to a steady-state equilibrium occurs only for very special choices of initial capital-good prices. Various mechanisms do allow us to select the "correct" initial prices which assure convergence, as discussed in Section 6.3; however, none of these are satisfactory in an economically realistic framework.

Optimizing models of multisector economies, surveyed in Section 6.4, are related to descriptive models of economic growth if we impose the assumption that descriptive economies always exhibit a perfect-foresight competitive equilibrium; Becker's equivalence theorem, stated in Section 6.4, guarantees that a path which is a perfect-foresight competitive equilibrium is identical to the path generated by some optimizing problem, and vice versa. Accordingly, since we know that optimal paths might oscillate, we also know that some perfect foresight competitive equilibrium paths will oscillate rather than converge.

Thus the question of dynamic stability remains an important but unresolved economic issue. Moreover, to analyze realistic stability questions, one must explicitly recognize that the future is uncertain. We now turn, in Chapter 7, to simple models that serve as an introduction to stochastic models and to the important notion of *rational expectations*. As we see, no definitive answers are reached; rather we identify a list of unresolved issues that apparently are relevant for the extremely complex question of how actual economies evolve over time.

Exercises

6.1 Derive (6.2.4), the dynamic equations for the per capita capital stocks, under the assumptions stated in the text.

6.2 **(a)** Derive equation (6.2.16a).

(b) Derive equation (6.2.16b). [*Hint:* Substitute (6.2.5), $\dot{K}_i = Y_i - \delta_i K_i$, and the income identity

$$C + \sum_{i=1}^{n} p_i Y_i = \sum_{i=1}^{n} q_i K_i + wL$$

into equation (6.2.15) and manipulate.]

6.3 Prove that equations (6.3.3) through (6.3.5) imply (6.3.7).

6.4 Derive equations (6.3.16) and (6.3.17).

6.5 Derive equation (6.4.12) from (6.4.5), (6.4.7a), and (6.4.10).

6.6 **(a)** Consider the problem of selecting c and $\dot{k}_i$, $i = 1, \ldots, n$, at given prices $Q = (Q_1, \ldots, Q_n)$ so as to maximize ordinary net national product $C + Q\dot{k}$ subject to the technological constraint $c = F(\dot{k}, k)$. Show that $Q = -F_{\dot{k}_i}$ is a necessary condition.

(b) Similarly, maximize net national product in utility units, $u(c) + q\dot{k}$, at given utility prices q, and derive the necessary condition $q = -u'(c)F_{\dot{k}}$.

(c) Conclude from (a) and (b) that $c + Q\dot{k}$ and $u(c) + q\dot{k}$ are simultaneously maximized when q and Q satisfy $q = u'(c)Q$. [*Hint:* Form the Lagrangian expressions

$$L(c, \dot{k}) = c + Q\dot{k} + \lambda[F(\dot{k}, k) - c]$$

and

$$\bar{L}(c, \dot{k}) = u(c) + q\dot{k} + \mu[F(\dot{k}, k) - c].$$

The necessary conditions for a constrained maxima are $L_c = L_{\dot{k}} = 0$ and $\bar{L}_c = \bar{L}_{\dot{k}} = 0$, respectively.]

6.7 Prove that any rest point $(\bar{q}, \bar{k})$, if one exists, satisfying (6.4.25a) and (6.4.25b) is *unique*. [*Hint:* Use the fact that $\bar{r} = \gamma$; also see Theorem 1 of Burmeister and Graham (1974, p. 328).]

7

Introduction to stochastic models and rational expectations

7.1. Dynamic instability and "tulip-mania phenomena"

We have seen that economic models with heterogeneous assets can exhibit saddlepoint instability. Models having money and a single capital good (see Section 3.7), as well as the models with several types of capital goods studied in Chapter 6, share the property that asymptotic convergence to a steady-state equilibrium is obtained only from certain initial conditions. Thus given exogenous stocks of the assets at time zero, convergence necessitates the selection of particular prices at time zero to start the economy along a dynamic path that lies on a convergent manifold. This feature is not worrisome in a planning context where initial prices are assigned to assure such convergence along an optimal path or where convergence is not in itself an economic issue. In the context of descriptive models, though, we must be concerned whether or not there exist any economic mechanisms that select initial prices consistent with dynamic stability.

This fundamental problem has been recognized for over 20 years.[1] Writing in 1957, Samuelson discussed the issue of nonconvergent paths:

> So much for the avoidable difficulties introduced by infinite time. Now to return to the intrinsic difficulty. I shall call it the "tulip-mania phenomenon." Let the

264

market maximize over any finite time, adding in at the end into the thing to be maximized a value for the terminal amount of grain left. At what level should this terminal grain be valued? We could extend the period in order to find out how much it is really worth in the remaining time left; but this obviously leads us back into our infinite regression, since there is always time left beyond any extended time. We are back into maximizing over infinite time.

But suppose we do what the market itself does in evaluating any stock $Q(t)$ at any given date; suppose we simply evaluate it at the then ruling market price $P_0(t)$. Then we immediately run into the paradox that any speculative bidding up of prices at a rate equal to carrying costs can last *forever*. This is precisely what happens in a tulip mania or new-era bull stock market. The market literally lives on its own dreams, and each individual at every moment of time is perfectly rational to be doing what he is doing.

Of course, history tells us that all tulip manias have ended in finite time. Every ''Ponzi scheme'' and every chain letter scheme finally runs out. Every bubble is some day pricked. But I have long been struck by the fact, and puzzled by it too, that in all the arsenal of economic theory we have absolutely no way of predicting how long such a ''Stage (i)'' will last. To say that prices will fall back to earth after they reach ridiculous heights represents safe but empty prediction. Why do some manias end when prices have become ridiculous by 10 per cent, while others persist until they are ridiculous to the tune of hundreds of per cent? Moreover, we do not need the recent Harrod–Domar models to raise in our minds the question whether social progress and secular growth themselves are not self-fulfilling acts of faith which, once interrupted by a serious enough breakdown in the economic and political fabric, may not give way to self-perpetuating trends of disorganization.

The above paradoxes are even more important for general business cycle theory at the macro-level than for a particular grain market, and they play a prominent role in the psychological theories of Bagehot, Pigou, and others. I mention them here because, quite without my suspecting it, the mathematical analysis of perturbations of the equilibrium paths by crop changes revealed some of the same phenomena. (1957, pp. 215–16)

Samuelson's position a decade later, addressing himself specifically to the "Hahn problem," is very little changed:

Heuristically, I feel that the fact underlying the Furuya–Inada theorem about permanent inefficiency may provide something of an answer. In the long, long future, any path but the convergent one is going to frustrate somebody's expectations and, crudely, is going to lead to bankruptcy for someone and to reaiming for the system. "Whom the Gods would destroy, they first make mad." And, I may add, "There will generally be a sharp-shooting speculator around, both to pick up the pieces after the debacle and – by foreseeing the debacle – to make money by doing some of the things that keep it from happening."

The image in my mind is that of a bicycle. The rider of the bicycle is the bulk of the market, a somewhat mystical concept to be sure – like its analogue, the well-informed speculator who gets his way in the end because his way is the correctly discerned way of the future; and those who think differently are bankrupted by their bets against (him and) the future. (It is easier to identify the well-informed speculator *ex post* than *ex ante*, and the image can easily dissolve into an empty tautology.) For a time, the less than omniscient market may chase down a false path emanating from A; but when the system is led too far from the balanced-growth configuration, some entrepreneurs begin to foresee the shoals ahead at Z, and they act to push the system back toward the turnpike. (1967, p. 229)

I leave this heuristic discussion with a reminder that it lacks both analytical rigor and empirical documentation. And I must give warning that, in at least one economic model, there exists an *infinity* of self-fulfilling motions that are *permanently* explosive. I refer to the tulip-mania phenomenon. If people think tulips will appreciate at 10 per cent per month, they can be motivated to act so that this will happen. Happen for how long? As far as the theory can tell, forever. Even though every tulip mania and stock-market bubble have come to an end in history, economists have no good theory to explain why they last as long as they do and not twice or half as long.

One feels that the real world of tools, plants, and inventory contrasts with the purely financial dream world of indefinite group self-fulfillment. But can this feeling be given documentation and plausible explication? (1967, p. 230)

In principle this "tulip-mania phenomenon" arises in *all* dynamic macroeconomic models, and the only reason it has not received wider recognition in the macroeconomic literature is that typically expected capital gains are either ignored or treated in a naive fashion (e.g., static expectations). For example, this dynamic instability problem arises in typical macroeconomic models containing money, bonds, and a homogeneous capital good, provided that capital gains and losses on the three assets are properly included in a portfolio equilibrium condition that arises when there are heterogeneous *assets*. Likewise, we have seen that saddlepoint instability arises in the simple monetary growth model discussed in Section 3.7.

For expositional purposes it shall be convenient here to examine very simple models with only one asset, money. However, unlike one-good models where the current price of homogeneous output is always unity (see, e.g., Section 3.2), we now let P denote the price of homogeneous output, assumed fixed, in terms of money as *numéraire*. Suppose that the demand for real cash balances is given by

$$\frac{M^d}{P} = Be^{-a(\dot{P}/P)} \tag{7.1.1}$$

where B and a are exogenously given positive constants. Equation (7.1.1) plays the role of the previous portfolio equilibrium condition because it involves the rate of inflation, $\dot{P}/P$. The simple postulate reflected in (7.1.1) is that the demand for real cash balances will decrease with increases in $\dot{P}/P$ because in an inflationary world nominal money holdings lose purchasing power in terms of real goods, and the real return on nominal money balances is $-\dot{P}/P$.

It will be convenient to transform (7.1.1) by taking natural logarithms. Define

$$m^d \equiv \log M^d,$$
$$p \equiv \log P,$$

and

$$b \equiv \log B,$$

and, using the fact that

$$\dot{p} = \frac{d \log P}{dt} = \frac{\dot{P}}{P},$$

we may write (7.1.1) as

$$m^d - p = b - a\dot{p}. \tag{7.1.2}$$

Throughout the remainder of this chapter lowercase letters will denote the natural logarithms of the corresponding uppercase variable (i.e., $x \equiv \log_e X$). Thus letting m denote the "money supply,'' we mean that the money supply measured in dollars (or any other unit of account) is $M = e^m$.

We assume money market equilibrium with $m^d = m$, and hence from (7.1.2) we have that

$$\dot{p} = \frac{b - m + p}{a}. \tag{7.1.3}$$

Let the money supply be constant; we lose no generality by setting $m = 0$ ($M = 1$). Then

$$\dot{p} = \frac{b}{a} + \frac{p}{a}. \tag{7.1.4}$$

Clearly, (7.1.4) has a unique rest point $p^* = -b$ at which $\dot{p} = 0$.[2] Moreover, since

$$\frac{d\dot{p}}{dp} = \frac{1}{a} > 0,$$

p^* is *unstable;* p will diverge unless the initial price, p^0, is set equal to the dynamic equilibrium price (i.e., unless $p^0 = p^*$).

These results are analogous to the previous saddlepoint behavior if we interpret p^* as a degenerate saddlepoint in one-dimensional p-space having a convergent manifold of dimension zero; that is, the convergent manifold consists only of the single point $p = p^*$. Were we to construct a more realistic model with other assets, genuine saddlepoint behavior would emerge in a higher-dimensional space; see, for example, Figure 3.8. Also note that the definition of a steady-state equilibrium involves constant real money balances with $M/P =$ constant in dynamic equilibrium. Thus when the money supply is growing at a constant rate θ, in steady-state equilibrium the rate of inflation is also θ (see Exercise 7.1).

In the remainder of this chapter we shall continue to restrict our attention to systems in one-dimensional p-space; this trick simplifies the model enormously without sacrificing any economic insights to the fundamental saddlepoint instability problem for macroeconomic models.[3]

7.2 A stochastic money supply

We have seen several times that in any realistic model the future is uncertain. The difficulty is to develop stochastic models that accurately reflect the types of economic uncertainties actually encountered. While realism is recognized as an ultimate objective, we will use a simple stochastic model to illustrate important economic concepts and to reveal the basic economic issues that could be overlooked in more complex formulations.

It is technically easier to handle uncertainty in a discrete-time formulation, and in place of (7.1.2) we now postulate that the demand for real money balances is given by

$$m^d(t) - p(t) = b - a[p^*(t + 1, t) - p^*(t, t)] \qquad (7.2.1)$$

where lowercase letters denoted natural logarithms and where

$$p^*(t + j, t) = \text{expectation formed at time } t \text{ for the price}$$
$$\text{level at time } t + j, \quad j = 0, 1, 2, \ldots$$

(see Exercise 7.2). The money supply is now governed by the stochastic process

$$m(t) = m(t - 1) + \epsilon(t) \qquad (7.2.2)$$

where the $\epsilon(t)$'s are stochastic disturbances independently distributed over time and where, for each t, $\epsilon(t)$ is a normally distributed random variable with mean zero and variance σ^2. *Money market equilibrium* requires that the demand for and supply of real cash balances be equal:

$$m^d(t) - p(t) = m(t) - p(t). \qquad (7.2.3)$$

This condition, of course, implies that nominal demand and supply are equal with $m^d(t) = m(t)$.

It is easy to see that the property $p^*(t, t) = p(t)$ holds when $m(t)$ is known at time t and expectations are formed *rationally*. Equations (7.2.1) and (7.2.3) imply that

$$m(t) - p(t) = b - a[p^*(t + 1, t) - p^*(t, t)], \qquad (7.2.4)$$

and the *rational expectations hypothesis* is simply that all the information available at time t, including equation (7.2.4), be used to form the expectation

$$p^*(t, t) = E_t[p(t)|I(t)]$$

where

$E_t[p(t)|I(t)]$ = mathematical expectation of $p(t)$, calculated at time t, conditional upon the information set available at time t, $I(t)$.

Thus, since $m(t)$ is known at time t, the expectation, taken at time t, of (7.2.4) is

$$m(t) - p^*(t, t) = b - a[p^*(t + 1, t) - p^*(t, t)]. \quad (7.2.5)$$

Thus (6.2.4) and (6.2.5) imply that

$$p^*(t, t) = p(t). \quad (7.2.6)$$

This case is called *full current information*.

On the other hand, suppose that $m(t)$ is *not* known at time t; in view of the stochastic process (7.2.2), this is equivalent to not knowing the disturbance term $\epsilon(t)$ at time t. The expectation formed at time t for $m(t)$ is

$$m^*(t, t) = m(t - 1)$$

since $\epsilon(t)$ has a zero expected value. Accordingly, in place of (7.2.5) we now have

$$m(t - 1) - p^*(t, t) = b - a[p^*(t + 1, t) - p^*(t, t)], \quad (7.2.7)$$

and combining the latter with (7.2.4) and then using (7.2.2) yields

$$\begin{aligned} p^*(t, t) &= p(t) + m(t) - m(t - 1) \\ &= p(t) - \epsilon(t). \end{aligned} \quad (7.2.8)$$

Whether or not $\epsilon(t)$ is known at time t, the dynamic behavior of expectations is determined by

$$m^*(t, t) - p^*(t, t) = b - a[p^*(t + 1, t) - p^*(t, t)], \quad (7.2.9)$$

which is derived by taking expectations at time t of equation (7.2.4). Note that both (7.2.5) and (7.2.7) are equivalent to (7.2.9) under the two different hypotheses about $\epsilon(t)$.

Equation (7.2.9) can be solved for

$$p^*(t + 1, t) = (1 - \beta)p^*(t, t) - \beta b + \beta m^*(t, t) \tag{7.2.10}$$

where

$$\beta \equiv -\frac{1}{a}.$$

It will be convenient to designate $t = 0$ as the initial time at which *all* future expectations are formed and to simplify our notation by defining

$$p^*(t) \equiv p^*(t, 0), \qquad t = 0, 1, \ldots$$

and

$$m^*(t) \equiv m^*(t, 0), \qquad t = 0, 1, \ldots .$$

We may thus rewrite (7.2.10) as

$$p^*(t + 1) = (1 - \beta)p^*(t) - \beta b + \beta m^*(t). \tag{7.2.11}$$

Observe that (7.2.11) is an ordinary linear difference equation in $p^*(t)$ with a forcing function $m^*(t)$. Also note that the solution will be deterministic since (7.2.11) does not contain any stochastic terms.

Let us consider the case of full current information in which $m^*(t, t) = m(t)$ and $p^*(t, t) = p(t)$. We then have

$$m^*(t) \equiv m^*(t, 0) = m(0) \qquad \text{for all } t = 0, 1, \ldots , \tag{7.2.12}$$

so that (7.2.11) may be expressed as

$$\begin{aligned} p^*(t + 1) = (1 - \beta)p^*(t) \\ + \beta[m(0) - b], \qquad t = 0, 1, \ldots . \end{aligned} \tag{7.2.13}$$

Observe that (7.2.13) has a unique rest point where

$$p^*(t + 1) = p^*(t) = \bar{p} = m(0) - b. \qquad (7.2.14)$$

A necessary and sufficient condition for

$$\lim_{t \to \infty} p^*(t) = \bar{p}$$

from an arbitrary initial $p^*(0)$ is that

$$-1 < (1 - \beta) < +1. \qquad (7.2.15)$$

However, for the case under consideration $\beta \equiv -1/a$ and $a > 0$; hence (7.2.14) is dynamically unstable. The only possibility for "stability" is to select

$$p^*(0) = \bar{p} = m(0) - b. \qquad (7.2.16)$$

The situation is analogous to the deterministic continuous-time model studied in Section 7.1. There we also found that "stability" required setting the initial price at the dynamic rest point. Likewise, setting the initial price as given by (7.2.16) is a special example of selecting free initial conditions that place the system on a convergent manifold. As before, our one-dimensional system is a degenerate saddlepoint with a convergent manifold consisting of the single point $\bar{p}$.

For the moment, *let us assume that expectations taken at every* $t = 0, 1, 2, \ldots$ *are stable.* This assumption, which we shall discuss subsequently, necessitates that (7.2.16) hold, and we then see from (7.2.13) that

$$p^*(t, 0) \equiv p^*(t) = m(0) - b \qquad \text{for all } t = 0, 1, \ldots.$$
$$(7.2.17)$$

By exactly the same reasoning

$$p^*(t, t) = m(t) - b \qquad \text{for all } t = 0, 1, \ldots$$
$$(7.2.17a)$$

and

$$p^*(t + 1, t) = m(t) - b \qquad \text{for all } t = 0, 1, \ldots.$$
$$(7.2.17b)$$

The derivations of (7.2.17a) and (7.2.17b) are left as Exercise 7.3. It follows from (7.2.17a) and (7.2.17b) that the expected inflation rate, $p^*(t + 1, t) - p^*(t, t)$, equals zero for all $t = 0, 1, 2, \ldots$. Thus from equations (7.2.2) and (7.2.4) we find that actual prices are given by

$$p(t) = m(t) - b = m(0)$$
$$+ \sum_{i=1}^{t} \epsilon(i) - b, \qquad t = 0, 1, 2, \ldots. \tag{7.2.18}$$

It follows that the inflation rate is

$$x(t) \equiv p(t + 1) - p(t) = \epsilon(t + 1). \tag{7.2.19}$$

Thus, the inflation rate, viewed from time zero, is a random variable with the same properties as $\epsilon(t)$; in particular, $x(t)$ is normally distributed with mean zero and variance σ^2. However, from (7.2.18) we see that the variance of the price level is $t\sigma^2$. Moreover, from (7.2.18) we may calculate that

$$p^*(t, s) = m(0) + \sum_{i=1}^{s} \epsilon(i) + E_s \left[\sum_{i=s+1}^{t} \epsilon(i) \right] - b$$
$$= m(s) + 0 - b \qquad \text{for } s = t, t - 1, \ldots, 0 \tag{7.2.20}$$

since the expectation taken at time $s < \theta$ for $\epsilon(\theta)$ is equal to 0; that is,

$$E_s \left[\sum_{i=s+1}^{t} \epsilon(i) \right] = 0 \tag{7.2.21}$$

where E_s denotes the expectation taken at time s. Observe that (7.2.20) is simply a generalization of (7.2.17a) and (7.2.17b) and thus confirms our hypothesis that expectations have been taken rationally.

But what of the *assumption* that expectations are stable? One argument is that we do not observe divergent expectations, and consequently any economic model that is consistent with the real world must exhibit stable expectations. Such reasoning, even if based on valid evidence, does not confront the basic theoretical

issue of *why* expectations are stable. A more theoretically satisfactory method is to assume that a representative individual maximizes the expected value of an intertemporal criterion function
subject to the expected value of his or her intertemporal budget
constraint. Money may be introduced by postulating that real balances enter the utility function. For example, we may assume
that for each $t = 0, 1, 2, \ldots$, a representative individual solves
the problem

$$\max_{\{C^i, M^i/P^i\}} E_t \left[\sum_{i=t}^{T} \frac{u(C^i, M^i/P^i)}{(1 + \gamma)^{i-t}} \right] \qquad (7.2.22)$$

where $\gamma > 0$ is the rate of time discount. With certain assumptions it will be possible to invoke a transversality condition for the
maximization problem (7.2.22).[4] Under such circumstances the
assumption that expected prices converge may be justified because it is a *necessary* implication of the postulated maximizing
behavior on the part of economic agents.

There are several worrisome aspects to this approach:

(1) It does not necessarily settle the original question because
the solution to (7.2.22) may not imply the demand for money
function (7.1.2). Moreover, equation (7.1.2) is supported by considerable empirical evidence.[5]

(2) The assumption that economic agents have identical
preferences – which is required for the "representative individual" approach – is most unrealistic. However, it appears that allowing for heterogeneous preferences will introduce formidable
technical difficulties.[6]

(3) The postulated criterion function raises the familiar monetary theory issue of whether or not real money balances should be
included in the utility function. A more satisfactory solution
would explain *why* people want to hold money rather than implicitly assume that they do because it is in their utility functions.
That is, the demand for money may stem primarily from the fact
that money holdings increase expected utility because a wider
range of future consumption options are then feasible. Such arguments are especially persuasive if various transactions costs are
included in the analysis.

(4) A related problem concerns the terminal time T. If T is finite, one must find some method to fix the terminal stock of real balances, M^T/P^T. If $T = \infty$, on the other hand, we must either assume that economic agents live forever, or else it is necessary to answer the question of why finite-lived individuals plan for the infinite future.

We must conclude, therefore, that the assumption of convergent expectations has not yet been rigorously justified on suitable *economic* grounds. Indeed, in the next section we shall see how this assumption implies a contradiction if the money market is not always in equilibrium with $m^d = m$ for every t. In the final section some research strategies that may resolve these economic issues will be suggested.

7.3. A stochastic disequilibrium model[7]

In Section 7.2 money market equilibrium necessitated that

$$m^d(t) = m(t) \qquad \text{for all } t = 0, 1, 2, \ldots . \tag{7.3.1}$$

Alternatively, we now assume that

$$p(t + 1) - p(t) = \alpha[m(t) - m^d(t)] \tag{7.3.2}$$

where the parameter $\alpha > 0$ is an exogenously given market adjustment speed. This hypothesis allows for disequilibrium in the money market, and when money supply (demand) exceeds money demand (supply), there will be excess demand (supply) for goods and a positive (negative) rate of inflation with $p(t + 1) > (<) p(t)$. We may obtain (7.3.1) as a special case of (7.3.2) by setting $\alpha = +\infty$.

It is important to recognize that this formulation, simple as it is, constitutes a *partial equilibrium* model whenever α is finite. A general equilibrium formulation would necessitate a derivation of the price-adjustment mechanism (7.3.2) in which α is determined as an endogenous variable. A rigorous approach to this price-adjustment problem would have to take into account realities such as the existence of transactions costs and the fact that different economic agents do not possess the same information. These features suggest that prices do not adjust instantaneously, and recent econometric work is addressed to the question of which specification – equation (7.3.2) or (7.3.1) – is more consistent with existing data.[8] Moreover, we observe that many commodities are sold by contracts in which there is a guaranteed future delivery of specified quantities at designated prices. This fact implies that if we interpret $p(t)$ as a price index of actual market transactions at time t, some of which will be at terms specified by *previous* contracts, then in general the dynamic behavior of $p(t)$ will be inconsistent with instantaneous money market adjustment. This conclusion follows from the fact that there is excess demand (supply) in the money market if and only if there is excess supply (demand) in the "goods market," and the goods market is based upon the aggregate of current transactions at prices which would not necessarily prevail if there were not binding commitments to deliver commodities at previously determined prices.[9]

One justification of (7.3.1) as an appropriate assumption is to argue that despite the facts just stated, actual markets do "adjust very fast" and consequently market equilibrium is a "satisfactory approximation" of reality. As we shall see, this rationale is not legitimate for our model. As proved below, the properties of the model change discontinuously at $\alpha = +\infty$. Thus the behavior of the model is drastically different for the cases (1) $\alpha = +\infty$ (market equilibrium) and (2) $\alpha = \bar{\alpha} > 0$, where $\bar{\alpha}$ is any positive, finite value (that is, there exists market disequilibrium with a market adjustment speed that is only restricted to be finite). Accordingly, in our case market equilibrium is *not* a "satisfactory approximation" to market disequilibrium with very fast but finite speeds of adjustment. It follows that those conclusions which depend crucially upon assumption (7.3.1), if in fact this assumption is incorrect, may be dangerously misleading.

The demand for money function is still given by (7.2.1) and the money supply is generated by the stochastic process (7.2.2); the latter combined with (7.3.2) constitute the complete model:

$$p(t + 1) - p(t) = \alpha\{m(t) - p^*(t, t) - b$$
$$+ a[p^*(t + 1, t) - p^*(t, t)]\} \quad (7.3.3)$$

where

$$m(t) = m(t - 1) + \epsilon(t) \quad (7.3.4)$$

and $\epsilon(t)$ has the previously stated properties. Let us suppose further that

$$E_t[\epsilon(t)] = 0. \quad (7.3.5)$$

That is, $\epsilon(t)$ is not known at time t, so that, taking expectations of (7.3.4) at time t, we have

$$m^*(t, t) = m(t - 1). \quad (7.3.6)$$

In general, because at time t all future disturbance terms have zero expected values,

$$m^*(s, t) = m(t - 1) \quad \text{for all } s = t, t + 1, \ldots . \quad (7.3.7)$$

The hypothesis of rational expectations requires that all the information available at time t be used to form the expectations $p^*(t, t)$ and $p^*(t + 1, t)$. However, unlike the $\alpha = +\infty$ case in the previous section, we now have that

$$p^*(t, t) = p(t) \quad (7.3.8)$$

despite (7.3.5). That is, even though $m(t)$ is not known at time t, $p(t)$ is known at time t when α is finite, whereas $p(t) = p^*(t, t) + \epsilon(t)$ [equation (7.2.8)] holds when $\alpha = +\infty$ and $m(t)$ is not known at time t.

To prove (7.3.8) we rewrite (7.3.2) as

$$p(t) - p(t - 1) = \alpha[m(t - 1) - m^d(t - 1)] \quad (7.3.9)$$

and observe that

$$m^d(t - 1) = p^*(t - 1, t - 1) + b - a[p^*(t, t - 1)$$
$$- p^*(t - 1, t - 1)]$$

is known at time t. Thus taking expectations of (7.3.9) at time t we find that

$$p^*(t, t) - p(t - 1) = \alpha[m(t - 1) - m^d(t - 1)]. \quad (7.3.10)$$

Equations (7.3.9) and (7.3.10) together imply the conclusion (7.3.8). The economic reason $p(t)$ is known at time t, even though $m(t)$ is not, can be traced to the finite market adjustment speed; because $p(t)$ must satisfy the market adjustment equation (7.3.9), it is determined by variables at time $t - 1$ that are known at time t.

To calculate $p^*(t + 1, t)$ we take expectations of (7.3.3) at time t and use (7.3.6):

$$p^*(t + 1, t) - p^*(t, t) = \alpha\{m(t - 1) - p^*(t, t) - b \\ + a[p^*(t + 1, t) - p^*(t, t)]\}. \quad (7.3.11)$$

Equation (7.3.11) may be solved for

$$p^*(t + 1, t) = (1 - \beta)p^*(t, t) - \beta b + \beta m(t - 1) \quad (7.3.12)$$

where

$$\beta \equiv \frac{\alpha}{1 - \alpha a} \neq 0 \quad (7.3.13)$$

(see Exercise 7.4). Again we have a simple linear difference equation with a rest point

$$\bar{p} = m(t - 1) - b \quad (7.3.14)$$

which is stable if and only if

$$-1 < (1 - \beta) < +1,$$

or, equivalently,

$$0 < \beta < 2. \quad (7.3.15)$$

In view of (7.3.13) the necessary and sufficient stability condition is

$$\alpha < \frac{2}{1 + 2a} \quad (7.3.16)$$

(see Exercise 7.5).

Let us first consider the case in which α, the market-adjustment speed, is sufficiently large to violate (7.3.16) and the rest point (7.3.14) is unstable. Exactly as was the case in Section 7.2, the *assumption* of convergent expectations necessitates that the expected price always be at the rest point (7.3.14); that is, we must have

$$p^*(t, t) = m(t - 1) - b. \tag{7.3.17}$$

Using (7.3.8) we see, therefore, that the assumption of convergent price expectations implies that the actual price is

$$p(t) = m(t - 1) - b \qquad \text{for all } t. \tag{7.3.18}$$

In particular, (7.3.18) implies that

$$p(t + 1) = m(t) - b, \tag{7.3.19}$$

and subtracting (7.3.18) from (7.3.19) yields

$$p(t + 1) - p(t) = m(t) - m(t - 1) = \epsilon(t), \tag{7.3.20}$$

while taking expectations of (7.3.20) at time t gives

$$p^*(t + 1, t) - p^*(t, t) = 0. \tag{7.3.21}$$

Now substitute (7.3.21) and (7.3.17) into (7.3.3) to derive

$$p(t + 1) - p(t) = \alpha\{m(t) - [m(t - 1) - b] - b + a[0]\}$$

or

$$p(t + 1) - p(t) = \alpha\epsilon(t). \tag{7.3.22}$$

Unless $\alpha = 1$, equations (7.3.20) and (7.3.22) stand in *contradiction* except for the freak case when

$$(1 - \alpha)\epsilon(t) = 0 \qquad \text{for all } t, \tag{7.3.23}$$

that is, except when *all* the stochastic disturbance terms are zero!

The explanation for this contradiction is simple. The assumption of convergent expectations, when α is large enough to violate (7.3.16), implies that the inflation rate must satisfy (7.3.20). However, by assumption the inflation rate satisfies (7.3.3), and these two results are not equal unless either $\alpha = 1$ or $\epsilon(t) = 0$. When $\epsilon(t) = 0$, the system remains at the dynamic equilibrium point with

$$p(t) = \bar{m} - b \qquad \text{for all } t = 1, 2, \ldots \tag{7.3.24}$$

and $\bar{m} \equiv m(0) = m(t)$. When $\alpha = 1$ the inflation rate is the random variable

$$p(t + 1) - p(t) = \epsilon(t), \tag{7.3.25}$$

and the stochastic disturbances exactly ''cancel out'' to satisfy (7.3.22) with $\alpha = 1$.

The contradiction that arises when convergent expectations are assumed and when the market adjustment speed is large enough to violate the condition (7.3.16) does not arise without uncertainty, for that is precisely the case in which the random disturbances are identically zero. With uncertainty, however, the contradiction remains, even with several changes in the specification of the model. In particular, it arises when the market adjustment mechanism is stochastic (see Exercise 7.7), when $m(t)$ is known at time t (see Exercise 7.8), or when a continuous-time formulation is used and the money supply is generated by a Wiener process.[10] We shall discuss some other implications of this contradiction in the next section, but first we turn briefly to cases of slow adjustment speeds.

Now assume that the market speed of adjustment is small enough to satisfy the condition (7.3.16). In this case one need not *assume* that expectations are stable because they *are* stable; starting from any initial condition $p^*(t, t) = p(t)$, the solution to (7.3.12) will converge with

$$\lim_{\tau \to \infty} p^*(\tau, t) = m(t - 1) - b. \tag{7.3.26}$$

From (7.3.8) and (7.3.12) we have that

$$p^*(t + 1, t) - p^*(t, t) = -\beta[p(t) + b - m(t - 1)], \tag{7.3.27}$$

and substituting (7.3.27) into (7.3.3) yields the equation for the rate of inflation:

$$p(t + 1) - p(t) = -\beta p(t) - \beta b + \beta m(t - 1) + \alpha \epsilon(t).$$
(7.3.28)

Although tedious, it is straightforward to prove that the inflation rate $p(t + 1) - p(t)$, viewed from time 0, converges in various stochastic senses (e.g., almost certain convergence, convergence in probability, and convergence in quadratic mean[11]) to a stationary, normally distributed random variable with zero mean and a finite variance that increases with the parameter β. Proofs of this result for a continuous-time formulation have been given by Burmeister, Flood, and Turnovsky (1978).

Finally, suppose that the condition (7.3.16) is violated, but we drop the assumption of convergent expectations which led to the contradiction. In this case we start from an arbitrarily given $p(0) = p^*(0, 0)$, and the expectations formed at each t diverge with

$$\lim_{\tau \to \infty} [p^*(\tau + 1, t) - p^*(\tau, t)] = \pm \infty.$$
(7.3.29)

Similarly, as $t \to +\infty$ the inflation rate, which is a random variable viewed from time zero, diverges to $+\infty$ if $p(0) > m(0) - b$ and to $-\infty$ if $p(0) < m(0) - b$, while the variance of the inflation rate approaches $+\infty$. Thus while there is no contradiction when expectations are not assumed convergent, the resulting model is *stochastically unstable*.

We now turn to the very difficult question of the relevance these results have for the evolution of a dynamic economy over time.

7.4. A synthesis of unresolved issues

The simple monetary models of inflation studied in this chapter provide several new clues in the search for a realistic and theoretically rigorous economic solution to the general problem of dynamic stability:

(1) The mere introduction of uncertainty does not resolve the

saddlepoint instability problem. Although our exposition has been in terms of a one-dimensional system with a "degenerate saddlepoint" having a convergent manifold of dimension zero – the dynamic equilibrium point itself – it is evident that the results generalize to more complex systems in higher dimensions.[12] In general the assumption that price expectations are stable necessitates that, at each t, the system be positioned on a convergent manifold.

Suppose, for example, that there is a regular saddlepoint in a $2n$-dimensional space of expected prices and expected capital stocks. At each t, expected stocks equal actual and known magnitudes, and the restriction that expected prices converge necessitates that, for every t, the n expected prices are such that the system is on an n-dimensional convergent manifold. If $p_i^*(t, t) = p_i(t)$, actual prices are also determined; on the other hand, it may be that $p_i^*(t, t) \neq p_i(t)$ with actual prices being determined only after random disturbances have occurred. In both cases the evolution of the system is governed by the fact that after each random disturbance is observed, expected prices must be repositioned to place them on a convergent manifold.

(2) Disequilibrium with "slow" speeds of market adjustment may be stabilizing. For example, given any positive value of the parameter a in the money demand function, any positive value of $\alpha < 2/(1 + 2a)$ satisfies condition (7.2.16) and ensures stability. Moreover, this stabilizing feature arises both in deterministic models and in stochastic models with rationally formed expectations.[13]

(3) The very simple model we analyzed in the previous section gives rise to a fundamental contradiction when the market adjustment speed is sufficiently fast but finite and convergent expectations are assumed. This contradiction suggests that the specification of the model requires a careful examination. In particular, instead of (7.2.1) suppose that the money demand function is of the form

$$
\begin{aligned}
m^d(t) - p(t) = b &- a_1[p^*(t + 1, t) - p^*(t, t)] \\
&- a_2[p^*(t + 2, t) - p^*(t + 1, t)]
\end{aligned} \quad (7.4.1)
$$

where a_1 and a_2 are positive parameters. The justification for the last term on the right-hand side of (7.4.1) involves a crude notion of transactions costs. If, for example, trips to the bank every time period are costly – perhaps in terms of foregone leisure – then money demand at time t may depend on the expected inflation rate over the time period from $t + 1$ to $t + 2$.

No contradiction arises when (7.2.1) is replaced by (7.4.1) because the difference equation in expected prices is now of second order. This means that for any value of $p^*(t, t)$, we can find a value of $p^*(t + 1, t)$ which is consistent with the assumption of convergent expectations. Previously, $p^*(t, t) = p(t)$ was determined at each t by (7.3.18) since only then would expectations converge, and this implied (7.3.23) – a contradiction – except in freak circumstances. Now, however, convergent expectations can be assured by a proper choice of $p^*(t + 1, t)$, and hence the contradiction does not arise.[14]

The basic issue, in which the choice between (7.2.1) and (7.4.1) is a special case, is the appropriate length of a planning horizon for economic agents. In an uncertain world the length of an individual's planning horizon, T, may be determined endogenously. That is, in some models the choice of T may be determined by the requirement that planning for any longer horizon does not increase expected utility.

A related issue concerns the probability distribution of expectations. We have implicitly assumed that expectations are means held with subjective probability 1, but in reality economic behavior is affected by higher moments. For example, a risk-averse individual may avoid situations in which he or she anticipates a positive, although perhaps small, probability of large losses. The distribution of expectations may also influence the choice of T because, loosely speaking, the more "noise" there is in the system, the less may be the gains in welfare (appropriately defined to account for risk aversion) due to a lengthening of the planning horizon.

(4) *Any* economic model that is *always* on a dynamically stable path cannot shed light on the more fundamental questions raised

by the quotations from Samuelson in Section 7.1. All of the known "solutions" to the instability problem – including cases where transversality conditions are invoked to justify convergence – *exclude the possibility of speculative booms rather than provide an economic explanation for them.* The much more difficult and perhaps more significant problem is to formulate a model that allows the possibility of speculative, tulip-mania booms, and then *to provide a theory of when the bubble bursts.* Upon reflection it is evident that an appropriate answer to the latter question may crucially involve the issue of an endogenous time horizon. Heuristically speaking, one of Samuelson's shrewd speculators may possess better information than other economic agents; consequently, he may look further ahead and via decisions based upon this longer time horizon, take actions that "force the bubble to burst."

Of course, even if different people initially possess different information, trades and repeated experiments may result in convergence to a situation in which everyone has the same information set.[15] Unfortunately, many uncertain economic phenomena are not repeated experiments. For example, weather is a repeated experiment, and from past observations we can ascertain the probability distribution of rainfall and the associated probability distribution of crop yields. On the other hand, innovations may cause "the rules of the game" to change. For example, a new type of seed may be developed for which one would have to learn the distribution of expected crop yields associated with any given distribution of rainfall. Thus innovations cause the experiments which we observe to change, and in such a world, one would expect economic agents to possess heterogeneous information.

It is evident that our analysis has left many fundamental economic questions unanswered. This should be a source of encouragement rather than frustration, however, because our objective has been to stimulate rigorous thought on unresolved but relevant economic issues. Ultimately, any particular model can be judged satisfactory only if we specify those economic questions to which we wish to address ourselves, and it is meaningless to ask how *best* to model a dynamic economy in an uncertain world with many assets.

Exercises

7.1 Let money demand be given by equation (7.1.2), but assume that the money supply grows at the constant rate $\theta > 0$ with

$$\frac{\dot{M}}{M} = \frac{d(\log M)}{dt} = \dot{m} = \theta.$$

Define $X \equiv M/P$ and $x \equiv m - p$.

(a) Derive the differential equation for $\dot{x}$ assuming $m^d = m$.
(b) Show there exists a unique rest point $x^* = b - a\theta$ which is unstable.
(c) Prove that $\dot{p}/p = \theta$ when $x = x^*$.

7.2 Use $e^x \doteq 1 + x$ for small x to prove $\log Y \doteq Y - 1$ for Y near 1. Use this approximation to show that

$$\frac{M^d(t)}{P(t)} = B \exp\left\{-a\left[\frac{P(t + 1) - P(t)}{P(t)}\right]\right\}$$

is approximated by

$$m^d(t) - p(t) = b - a[p(t + 1) - p(t)]$$

for $P(t + 1)/P(t)$ near 1.

7.3 Derive equations (7.2.17a) and (7.2.17b) under the assumptions stated in the text.
7.4 Derive equation (7.3.12).
7.5 Derive the necessary and sufficient stability condition (7.3.16) from (7.3.13) and (7.3.15).
7.6 Show that the actual price $p(t + 1)$ is given by

$$p(t + 1) = p^*(t + 1, t) + \alpha\epsilon(t).$$

[*Hint:* Using (7.3.8) and (7.3.12), we have

$$p^*(t + 1, t) - p(t) = -\beta[p(t) + b - m(t - 1)].$$

Substituting this result into (7.3.3) gives

$$p(t + 1) - p(t) = \alpha\{m(t) - p(t) - b - \beta a[p(t) + b - m(t - 1)]\}.$$

Subtract the latter from the former to obtain an expression for

$$p^*(t + 1, t) - p(t + 1),$$

and simplify using the definition of β and (7.3.4).]

7.7 Assume that the market-adjustment mechanism is stochastic with

$$p(t + 1) - p(t) = \alpha\{m(t) - p^*(t, t) - b$$
$$+ a[p^*(t + 1, t) - p^*(t, t)]\} + \mu(t)$$

where the disturbance term $\mu(t)$ has the same stochastic properties as $\epsilon(t)$. Show that the expectations equation is still given by (7.3.12). Repeat the steps leading to (7.3.23) to prove that in this case a contradiction arises except in the razor's edge case when

$$\mu(t) = (1 - \alpha)\epsilon(t) \qquad \text{for all } t.$$

7.8 Suppose that $m(t)$ is known at time t, that is, that

$$E_t[\epsilon(t)] = \epsilon(t).$$

Prove that there is still a contradiction when α is sufficiently large to violate the condition (7.3.16) and convergent expectations are assumed. [*Hint:* Show that (7.3.18) and (7.3.19) are now replaced by

$$p(t) = m(t) - b \tag{A}$$

and

$$p(t + 1) = m(t + 1) - b. \tag{B}$$

Taking expectations of the latter at time t gives $p^*(t + 1, t) - p^*(t, t) = 0$, and substituting this expression and (A) into (7.3.3) yields

$$p(t + 1) - p(t) = \alpha\{m(t) - [m(t) - b] - b + a[0]\} = 0.$$

Subtract (A) from (B) to show a contradiction unless $\epsilon(t + 1) = 0$.]
7.9 Derive equation (7.3.28).

NOTES

Chapter 1. Introduction and overview

1   A precise and elegant treatment of these results is given by Debreu (1959).

Chapter 2. The pure role of time

1   A more advanced and comprehensive treatment of the intertemporal model presented here is contained in Chapters 2 and 3 of Bliss (1975).

2   Note we have implicitly assumed that this *numéraire* good is not free, for otherwise it would have a zero price. It should be stressed that any commodity with a positive price in period 1 could serve equally well as *numéraire,* and no special economic significance should be attached to "commodity 1." Indeed, there are many alternative price normalization rules that would suffice; for example, one could select some basket of commodities delivered at the beginning of period 1 as a *numéraire.*

3   If the time period is a small time interval of length h,

$$hr_i^t \doteq \frac{p_i^t - p_i^{t+h}}{p_i^{t+h}} \quad \text{implies that} \quad -r_i^t = \lim_{h \to 0} \frac{p_i^{t+h} - p_i^t}{hp_i^{t+h}} = \frac{\dot{p}_i^t}{p_i^t}$$

where the "·" denotes total differentiation with respect to time (e.g., $\dot{x} \equiv dx/dt$).

4   "Own interest rate" must be distinguished from "money interest rates." A person loaning 1 unit of commodity i at the beginning of period t is repaid $1 + r_i^t$ units *of the same commodity* at the end of period t. By contrast, a person loaning p_i^t dollars at the beginning of period t receives $p_i^t(1 + r_0^t)$ dollars at the end of period t, where r_0^t denotes the money rate of interest over period t; but whether or not these $p_i^t(1 + r_0^t)$ dollars can purchase more or less than 1 unit of commodity i at the beginning of period $t + 1$ (which coincides with the end of period t) depends upon whether or not $p_i^t(1 + r_0^t) \gtrless p_i^{t+1}$, respectively.

288

5 This concept of dynamic efficiency was introduced in Samuelson (1960) and Dorfman, Samuelson, and Solow (1958).

6 *A neoclassical production function* has continuous second partial derivatives, is homogeneous of degree 1 (constant returns to scale), and exhibits generalized diminishing returns. These conditions imply that the function $F^t(\cdot)$ has a Hessian matrix of second partial derivatives which is negative semidefinite and of one less than full rank.

7 As quoted by Paul A. Samuelson in his famous introductory text *Economics* (1976a, p. 41). Also see Edwin Cannan's edition of *The Wealth of Nations* (1937, p. 423).

8 These same dynamic efficiency conditions and their relationship to the "invisible hand" principle are discussed in the path-breaking book by Dorfman, Samuelson, and Solow (1958); see Chapter 12 ("Efficient Programs of Capital Accumulation"), especially pages 319–21, where the "invisible hand" is explicitly mentioned. Also relevant to this discussion is Samuelson's seminal paper (1960), as well as the paper by Samuelson and Solow (1956).

9 It is convenient to think of the unit of account as money, but the reader is cautioned that this device is for expositional purposes only, and at this point we shall not become involved in any of the substantive issues of a monetary economy.

10 Of course, the "bank" is a fictitious construct used only as an expository device; see note 9.

11 Although the distinction between firms that own, rather than rent, capital may be important in some contexts, it is of no consequence to our model. As we shall see, given the assumption of profit maximization, firms owning capital must take into account capital gains and losses in exactly the same way that a pure investor does via the portfolio equilibrium condition (2.3.7).

12 This formulation of the problem also makes it trivial to prove that the discounted value of capital in every time period is a *constant* along a dynamically efficient accumulation path. Since the production functions

$$k_1^{t+1} = F^t(k_2^{t+1}; k_1^t, k_2^t) \tag{2N.1}$$

are homogeneous of degree 1 by assumption, Euler's theorem enables us to write

$$k_1^{t+1} = \frac{\partial F^t}{\partial k_2^{t+1}} k_2^{t+1} + \frac{\partial F^t}{\partial k_1^t} k_1^t + \frac{\partial F^t}{\partial k_2^t} k_2^t. \tag{2N.2}$$

Substitution of (2.3.17a) through (2.3.17c) into (2.3.20) implies that

$$p_1^{t+1}k_1^{t+1} + p_2^{t+1}k_2^{t+1} = p_1^t k_1^t + p_2^t k_2^t. \tag{2N.3}$$

Thus whatever the initial values of prices $\bar{p}_1^1$, $\bar{p}_2^1$ and capital stocks $\bar{k}_1^1$, $\bar{k}_2^1$, we have

$$p_1^t k_1^t + p_2^t k_2^t = \bar{p}_1^1 \bar{k}_1^1 + \bar{p}_2^1 \bar{k}_2^1 = \text{constant} \qquad \text{for all } t = 2, 3, \ldots . \tag{2N.4}$$

An analogous result holds in current prices. Use (2.3.1) to express (2.3.17b) as

$$(1 + r_0^t) \frac{P_1^t}{P_1^{t+1}} = \frac{\partial F^t}{\partial k_1^t}, \tag{2N.5}$$

and substitute (2.3.17a), (2N.5), and (2.3.17c) into (2N.2); then multiplication by P_1^{t+1} gives

$$P_1^{t+1} k_1^{t+1} + \frac{p_2^{t+1}}{p_1^{t+1}} P_1^{t+1} k_2^{t+1} = (1 + r_0^t) P_1^t k_1^t + \frac{P_1^{t+1} p_2^t}{p_1^{t+1}} k_2^t. \tag{2N.6}$$

But since

$$\frac{p_1^t}{p_2^t} = \frac{P_1^t}{P_2^t} \quad \text{[see equation (2.1.5)]},$$
$$\frac{p_2^{t+1}}{p_1^{t+1}} P_1^{t+1} = P_2^{t+1}; \tag{2N.7}$$

it is also true that

$$\begin{aligned}
\frac{P_1^{t+1} p_2^t}{p_1^{t+1}} &= P_2^t \left(\frac{P_1^{t+1}}{p_1^{t+1}} \frac{p_2^t}{P_2^t} \right) \\
&= P_2^t \left(\frac{P_2^{t+1}}{p_2^{t+1}} \frac{p_2^t}{P_2^t} \right) \\
&= P_2^t (1 + r_0^t) \quad \text{[using (2.3.1) and Definition 2.2]}.
\end{aligned} \tag{2N.8}$$

Thus from (2N.6)–(2N.8), we find that

$$\frac{P_1^{t+1} k_1^{t+1} + P_2^{t+1} k_2^{t+1}}{1 + r_0^t} = P_1^t k_1^t + P_2^t k_2^t. \tag{2N.9}$$

That is, the discounted value of current capital at the beginning of period $t + 1$ is equal to the current value of capital at the beginning of period t, with r_0^t being the "money" rate of interest over period t.

13 The term "Fisherian" is used because the model presented in this section is based upon Irving Fisher's 1930 classic, *The Theory of Interest*. A similar model formulated in continuous time has been analyzed by Uzawa (1968).

14 By a "well-behaved" utility function we mean one that is defined for all $(c^1, c^2) > (0, 0)$, has continuous second partial derivatives, and is strictly quasi-concave. For our purposes here it is sufficient to assume that any indifference curve in the c^1-c^2 plane has the ordinary textbook shape.

15 Discounted profits $p^2 y^2 - p^1 k^1 = p^2 [f(k^1) - (1 + r)k^1]$ are always positive due to the regularity conditions imposed on the production function; since $f'' < 0$, $[f(k^1) - f(0)]/k^1 > f'(k^1)$, and the conclusion follows by substitution of $f(0) = 0$ and the profit-maximization condition $f'(k^1) = 1 + r$ into the latter inequality. Note, however, there need not be "production" in the technological sense that one unit of input may "produce" *less* than one *physical* unit of output a time period later (i.e., it is possible that $y^2 < k^1$). Such cases

can be termed *storage processes,* and they may be profitable provided that $p^2 > p^1$ or $(p^2/p^1) - 1 = r < 0$.

On the other hand, suppose that there is a second type of commodity which is required as another input into the production function, its only use, and suppose every individual has an exogenous endowment of this commodity at the beginning of period 1. Denoting the quantity of this input by z and its market price (at the beginning of period 1) by p_z, an individual's discounted profits now become $p^2y^2 - (p^1k^1 + p_zz)$. If every new production function of the form $y^2 = f(k^1, z)$ exhibits constant returns to scale [i.e., if $f(\lambda k^1, \lambda z) = \lambda y^2$ for all $\lambda > 0$], then the new profit maximization conditions

$$p^2 \frac{\partial f}{\partial k^1} - p^1 = 0, \qquad p^2 \frac{\partial f}{\partial z} - p_z = 0$$

and Euler's theorem $[y^2 \equiv (\partial f/\partial k^1) \, k^1 + (\partial f/\partial z) \, z]$ together imply that discounted profits are zero in equilibrium. Accordingly, we may interpret positive profits in our one-commodity model as the return to some nonproduced factor of production (e.g., labor) that we have ignored.

Chapter 3. Introduction to dynamic economics

1 Output Q is a flow – it is measured as units of output per unit of time just as the flow of water from a pipe is measured in units such as gallons per minute. The production function $F(K, L)$ should be interpreted as stating the maximum *flow* of output for specified *stocks* of capital, K, and workers, L. Thus it is implicitly assumed that the utilization rates for both capital and labor are unity.

2 See Arrow (1964) for a justification of this very common and convenient assumption.

3 Throughout this book a dot above a variable indicates total differentiation with respect to time (e.g., $\dot{x} \equiv dx/dt$).

4 These "stylized facts" were suggested by Kaldor (1961). Although their validity is questionable [see, e.g., Atkinson (1975, chap. 9, especially pp. 165–8)], one nevertheless would like a model that is at least capable of generating some of the "facts" (e.g., a rising real wage rate in dynamic equilibrium).

5 *Embodied* technological changes require investment in new inputs, presumably technologically advanced in some appropriate sense, if increases in output are to be realized. In some important respects the long-run behavior of embodied technological change models cannot be distinguished from the long-run behavior of models with disembodied technological change. The reason is that in a steady-state equilibrium with constant rate of technological change, the amount of new investment that "embodies" technological improvements may exactly match the depreciation of old equipment at a constant growth rate of per capita output.

6 This assertion must be interpreted precisely; it says that if all the "stylized facts" (1)–(4) are valid as $t \to \infty$, then equation (3.3.2) must be satisfied. However, as first proved by Whitaker (1970a), there do exist balanced growth paths consistent with a subset of the "facts" (1)–(4) even when (3.3.2) does not

hold. References relevant to the question of Harrod neutrality and balanced growth also include Burmeister and Dobell (1969b, 1970), Chilosi and Gomulka (1974), Diamond (1965a, 1965b), Gomulka (1976), Swan (1970), Uzawa (1961), and Whitaker (1977).

7 See Chapter 3 of Burmeister and Dobell (1970), as well as the references there cited, for discussions of induced technological change.

8 The reader interested in pursuing a one-sector model with an alternative specification of the consumption function involving a distributed log, and/or with consumption decisions based upon the utility maximization of immortal economic agents with identical preferences, is referred to Whitaker (1970b).

9 Kurz (1968) has analyzed "the inverse optimum" problem of finding when the consumption function $c = (1 - s) f(k)$ is the solution to the intertemporal maximization problem

$$\max_{\{c(t)\}} \int_{t=0}^{\infty} u(c)e^{-\gamma t}\, dt \qquad \text{subject to} \quad \dot{k} = f(k) - gk - c \quad \text{and} \quad k(0) = k^0 > 0.$$

The conditions $u(c) = -\, c^{-[(1-s)/s]}$, $f(k) = k^\alpha$, $\gamma = (\alpha - s)/s$, $0 < s < 1$, $0 < \alpha < 1$, and $s < \alpha$ are sufficient. We shall consider such problems of optimal economic growth in Chapter 6.

10 The particular version presented here is nearly identical to that studied by Diamond (1965c), and it may be regarded as an extension of the Fisherian model discussed in Section 2.4.

11 We have assumed $c^{t+1} + k^{t+1} = f(k^t)$. As an alternative option, we may specify the technology by $c^{t+1} + k^{t+1} - k^t = h(k^t)$. Since $f(k^t) \equiv h(k^t) + k^t$, $r^t = f'(k^t) - 1 = h'(k^t)$. If one postulates $f(k^t) = (k^t)^\alpha$, on the one hand, and $h(k^t) = (k^t)^\alpha$, on the other, the two alternative specifications imply *different* Golden Rule capital–labor ratios, say k^* and k^{**}, respectively, with corresponding Golden Rule interest rates $r^* = f'(k^*) - 1$ and $r^{**} = h'(k^{**})$. Note that $r^{**} \neq r^* - 1$.

12 The consumption denoted by C^{t+1} is from output of the production process taking place during period t using K^t and L^t as factor inputs, and this output occurs at the *beginning* of period $t + 1$. Alternatively, one could change the timing convention and write $K^{t+1} = F(K^t, L^t) - C^t$, but now this C^t is not available until the *end* of period t.

13 Note that C^{t+1} is the consumption available at the beginning of period $t + 1$, whereas wage income $\bar{w}L^t$ is received at the end of period t; see the preceding note for an alternative timing convention.

14 *Joint production* exists when two or more different commodities are produced jointly by the same production process; for example, gasoline, kerosene, heating oil, and other petroleum products can be produced jointly by a crude oil distilling operation. In the two-sector model discussed in Section 3.6, separate production functions are assumed for each of the two commodities, and hence there is no joint production.

15 See page 109 and Samuelson (1961). Also see Theorems 1 and 6 in Chapter 9 of Burmeister and Dobell (1970).

16 This theorem was proved by Phelps and Koopmans (Phelps, 1965).

17 Various modifications can be introduced without altering the basic results; for example, we could admit technological change or a continuous-time formulation. More important, as we shall observe below, generalizations to many commodities are possible.

18 A simplified proof of slightly more general results can be found in Benveniste and Gale (1974), as well as in Benveniste (1976b). The results stated in the text rely on the implicit assumption that investment is reversible (i.e., that the capital stock can be consumed). If, on the other hand, investments in physical capital goods cannot be converted into consumption, then the necessary and sufficient conditions stated in Theorem 3.1 must be modified; the interested reader is referred to Mitra (1978).

19 See Malinvaud (1953); also, Malinvaud (1962) and Benveniste (1976b).

20 See Benveniste and Gale (1975, pp. 232–3).

21 One must be cautious not to confuse *current* and *discounted prices*. The prices $p(t)$ in this section are *discounted prices* for the single commodity, while in the next two sections the same variable will denote the *current relative price* of a single capital good to another *numéraire* commodity.

Of course, for a single-commodity model, no *relative* price exists, but the price normalization rule $p^0 = 1$ implies that the current price in every period is unity. More generally, if the current price (which must be the same in every period for this one-commodity world) is set at P, discounted prices are given by

$$p^t = \frac{P}{(1 + r^0)(1 + r^1)(1 + r^2) \cdots (1 + r^{t-1})}$$

where r^t denotes the commodity own interest rate over the tth period.

Some economic insight into the Cass necessary and sufficient consumption efficiency condition can be obtained by examining $\lim_{t \to \infty} p^t$ for the infinite price sequence $\{p^t\}_{t=0}^{\infty}$ associated with a program $\{k^t\}_{t=0}^{\infty}$. Recall that

$$r^t = f'(k^t) - 1 \gtreqless 0 \quad \text{if and only if} \quad \frac{\partial F(K^t, L^t)}{\partial K^t} - \delta \gtreqless g;$$

[see equations (3.5.26)–(3.5.28).] Assume that $k(t) = k^*$ for $t \geq T$, in which case

$$r^t = r^* \equiv f'(k^*) - 1 \quad \text{for } t \geq T.$$

Setting $P = 1$, we have that prices are

$$p^t = \frac{1}{(1 + r^*)^t} \quad \text{for } t = 0, 1, 2, \ldots.$$

Now clearly, if $r^* < 0$ (which is equivalent to $[\partial F(k^*, 1)/\partial K^t] - \delta < g$), then

$$\lim_{t \to \infty} p^t = \infty.$$

In this case, since $-1 < 1 + r^* < +1$,

$$\sum_{t=0}^{\infty} \frac{1}{p^t} = \sum_{t=0}^{\infty} (1 + r^*)^t = \frac{1}{1 - (1 + r^*)} = \frac{1}{r^*} < \infty,$$

that is, the price sequence $\{p^t\}_{t=0}^{\infty}$ grows too fast, and hence there is capital overaccumulation. Of course, we knew this result beforehand because $r^* < 0$ or $[\partial F(k^*, 1)/\partial K^t] - \delta < g$ implies that k^* is above the Golden Rule value.

On the other hand, if $r^* > 0$, then

$$\lim_{t \to \infty} p^t = 0$$

and

$$\lim_{t \to \infty} v^t = \lim_{t \to \infty} p^t k^* = 0.$$

The Cass theorem enables us to handle the borderline case when $r^* = 0$ and k^* is equal to the Golden Rule value; for then $p^t = 1$ for all t, and hence

$$\sum_{t=0}^{\infty} \frac{1}{p^t} = \infty,$$

implying that the program for which k^t is equal to the Golden Rule value is consumption efficient. Note, however, that the transversality condition

$$\lim_{t \to \infty} v^t = 0$$

fails as an appropriate *necessary* signal for consumption efficiency, because in this case

$$\lim_{t \to \infty} v^t = k^* > 0.$$

22 As before, δ is the exponential depreciation rate for capital.
23 See Burmeister and Dobell (1970, chap. 4); and Burmeister (1968b).
24 Equivalently, condition (3.6.17b) must hold for every (admissible) value of the wage–rental ratio, ω.
25 The "stylized facts" discussed in Section 3.3 are also consistent with this two-sector model modified to include labor-augmenting technological progress *at the same rate* in both the consumption and investment good sectors. However, other possibilities now arise; for example, we may ask whether the capital–labor ratio k is constant or, alternatively, ask whether the *value* of the capital–labor ratio pk is constant. The interested reader is referred to the table on page 145 of Burmeister and Dobell (1970), where some of the various cases are summarized.
26 The cyclic motion $A-B-C-D$ is analogous to a stable limit cycle in two-dimensional differential equation systems of the form $\dot{x} = \dot{x}(x, y)$ and $\dot{y} = \dot{y}(x, y)$. Note that the "limit cycle" $A-B-C-D$ results from starting from all initial points $(k, \dot{k}/k)$ except the dynamic rest point $(k^*, 0)$, which is an *unstable* steady state. The cyclic $A-B-C-D$ motion with discontinuous "jumps" provides a simple example of a so-called *catastrophe* in the theory of dynamical systems; since our model exhibits stability properties (S) when $\sigma_c = 1$, the discontinuous behavior of $\dot{k}$ exemplified by the $A-B-C-D$ cycle

eventually may rise as the parameter σ_c is reduced, and thus there may exist a discontinuous change in outcome as a parameter is continuously changed. Readers interested in catastrophe theory are referred to Hirsch and Smale (1974), Thom (1976), Zeeman (1968), and Lu (1976). An application of catastrophe theory to the business cycle is provided by Varian (1979).

27 In other words, p units of money are required to purchase 1 unit of the commodity.

28 In actuality, the assumption of perfect myopic foresight can imply perfect foresight into the infinite future for some models, depending in part upon one's notion of ''equilibrium.'' This observation shall be important in Chapters 6 and 7.

29 Indeed, we have already seen in Section 2.3 that the ''dynamic invisible hand'' principle obtains both when firms rent and when they own their capital stock.

30 Note that since

$$x(t) = \frac{m(t)}{p(t)} = \frac{m(0)e^{(\theta - g)t}}{p(t)}$$

follows from (3.7.29), then for $\theta \geqslant g$, $\lim_{t \to \infty} x(t) = 0$ implies that $\lim_{t \to \infty} p(t) = \infty$. On the other hand, for $\theta < g$, $\lim_{t \to \infty} x(t) = 0$ implies only that $\lim_{t \to \infty} p(t)$ is nonzero.

31 Note 30 suggests that $\theta \geqslant g$ may be one necessary condition if this property is to hold.

32 Suppose that we consider a maximization problem over any finite-time horizon $[0, T]$. The solution to such a problem depends upon what values for the economic variables are specified to hold at time T. If there exists any future time beyond T, the economically appropriate terminal values depend upon what will happen in the future beyond T. Since there is no natural time horizon, at least in models without uncertainty, and since there are no economically natural terminal valuations at any finite stopping time, it is logical to avoid these difficulties by postulating an infinite-time horizon.

   An elementary discussion of terminal conditions and the rationale for infinite-time horizons can be found in Burmeister and Dobell (1970, pp. 379–91).

33 The literature relevant to ''speculative boom'' questions includes: Keynes, (1936, Chap. 12), Hahn (1966), Samuelson (1957, 1967), Heckscher (1930), and Burmeister, Caton, Dobell, and Ross (1973).

34 The robustness of this conclusion is confirmed by the results of Gale (1977). He analyzes a model with money, but economic agents cannot hold capital; all capital is owned by ''the State,'' and private saving can only take the form of money holdings. The resulting dynamic equilibria may be stable or unstable, but no saddlepoint equilibria exist.

   One must, however, recognize that not every rest point of a multiasset perfect-foresight model need be a saddlepoint. For example, Burmeister and Phelps (1971) have constructed models with a single type of capital good and many financial assets which are featured by nonunique rest points, not all of which are saddlepoints. In general, suppose that any two-dimensional differential equation system has more than one dynamic equilibrium; then clearly *every* rest point cannot be a saddle. However, existing results suggest the following proposition: in economic models with perfect foresight and alternative means for holding wealth, *at least one* of the dynamic equilibria must be a saddlepoint (so that if there exists a *unique* rest point, *t*, it must be a saddle).

Chapter 4. Cambridge controversies in capital theory

1 If labor were also paid at the beginning of the production period, we would simply replace W by $(1 + r)W$ to reflect the opportunity cost of advanced wages.

2 The simple linear equations (4.2.10) may be written in vector-matrix notation as

$$p = a_0 + (1 + r)pa$$

where $p = (p_1, \ldots, p_n)$,
$$a_0 = (a_{01}, \ldots, a_{0n}),$$

$$a = \begin{bmatrix} a_{11} \cdots a_{1n} \\ \cdot \quad \cdot \\ \cdot \quad \cdot \\ \cdot \quad \cdot \\ a_{n1} \cdots a_{nn} \end{bmatrix}.$$

Clearly, they have a solution

$$p = a_0[I - (1 + r)a]^{-1}$$

provided that $[I - (1 + r)a]^{-1}$ exists.

The matrix a is *indecomposable* if every commodity is required, either directly or indirectly, to produce every other commodity. Under this condition the matrix a has a *dominant characteristic root* λ_a^*, also called the *Frobenius root*, which is positive and not less in modules than any other characteristic root of a. It is then a theorem in linear algebra that

$$[\lambda I - a]^{-1} > 0 \quad \text{if and only if} \quad \lambda > \lambda_a^*.$$

Accordingly, assuming that $a_{0j} > 0$ for all j, it follows immediately that

$$p = a_0[I - (1 + r)a]^{-1} > 0 \quad \text{if and only if} \quad r < r_a^* \equiv \frac{1}{\lambda_a^*} - 1.$$

Of course, such solutions are economically meaningful only if we restrict our attention to nonnegative values of r, and hence the assumption that r_a^* is positive is required to ensure that technique a is economically viable (i.e., that it is capable of generating positive prices, p_j's, at least some positive interest rates satisfying $0 \leqslant r < r_a^*$).

Readers interested in pursuing these mathematical details, as well as other generalizations to ensure nonnegative prices, are referred to Chapter 8 of Burmeister and Dobell (1970), as well as to the references cited there.

3 Equations (4.2.8) are said to have a pole at r_a^*; they have mathematical – but economically meaningless – solutions with the property that p_j approaches $-\infty$ as r approaches r_a^* from above.

4 Clearly, when there exist m_j alternative activities for producing the jth commodity, there exist $\Pi_{j=1}^n m_j$ technique matrices in the economy.

5 The reader interested in details of the proof is referred to Theorems 7 and 8 in Chapter 8 and Theorem 1 in Chapter 9 of Burmeister and Dobell (1970).

6 It can be shown that switch points are positive roots to a polynomial of the form $\alpha_0 + \alpha_1 r + \alpha_2 r^2 + \cdots + \alpha_{n-1} r^{n-1} = 0$, and it is well known that there may exist as many as n such roots. For a more complete discussion, the reader is referred to Bruno, Burmeister, and Sheshinski (1966, pp. 524–5) and to Burmeister and Dobell (1970, pp. 245–50).

7 Its relevance to the present discussion has been pointed out by Velapillai (1975, pp. 679–80).

8 See the papers by Pasinetti; Levhari and Samuelson; Morishima; Bruno, Burmeister, and Sheshinski; Garegnani; and Samuelson, all appearing in *The Quarterly Journal of Economics,* "Paradoxes in Capital Theory: A Symposium," Vol. 80, No. 4 (November), 1966, pp. 503–84.

9 The interested reader is referred to Burmeister (1977b), as well as to Robinson (1975b) and to "Comments" by Paul A. Samuelson and Robert M. Solow (1975) and a "Response" by Joan Robinson (1975a) in the same issue of the *Quarterly Journal of Economics.*

10 This section includes excerpts from Sections 3 and 4 of Burmeister (1977b).

11 Here we use the standard notation that T_i is the partial derivative of the function T with respect to its ith argument; for example,

$$T_i \equiv \frac{\partial T(c_1 + \dot{k}_1, \ldots, c_n + \dot{k}_n; k_1, \ldots, k_n)}{\partial (c_i + \dot{k}_i)}$$

and

$$T_{n+i} \equiv \frac{\partial T(c_1 + \dot{k}_1, \ldots, c_n + \dot{k}_n; k_1, \ldots, k_n)}{\partial k_i}.$$

12 See Burmeister and Dobell (1970, pp. 293–4) and Brock and Burmeister (1976).

13 See Burmeister (1976b).

14 See Pasinetti (1969, 1970). Also see Solow (1970).

15 Burmeister and Dobell (1970, pp. 289–92) have found such numerical examples for an economy with one consumption good, two capital goods, and Cobb–Douglas production functions.

16 This section includes excerpts from Sections 7 and 8 of Burmeister (1977b).

17 See Brock and Burmeister (1976).

18 See Brock and Burmeister (1976).

19 See Burmeister and Long (1977).

20 Burmeister and Hammond (1977).

21 Here we are assuming that both k_1^0 and k_2^0 are below their Golden Rule values (corresponding to the point labeled $r = 0$ in Figure 4.11).

22 Except that the existence of neoclassical production functions *precludes* the possibility of reswitching; see pages 545–6 of Bruno, Burmeister, and Sheshinski (1966) and Theorem 5 on page 279 of Burmeister and Dobell (1970). But this fact is irrelevant to the discussion at hand.

23 And even when the technology is such that marginal products do not exist, the marginal productivity conditions, (4.7.3), may be replaced by more general *inequalities* which serve to bound equilibria factor prices from above and below.

24 The reader interested in this extension can easily construct his or her own proof using the methods in Cass (1973).

25 See note 2.

26 Also see Dorfman, Samuelson, and Solow (1958, pp. 253–4), Bruno, Burmeister, and Sheshinski (1966, pp. 544–5), and Samuelson and von Weizsäcker (1971, pp. 1192–4).

27 An empirical test involving only a knowledge of $\left[\dfrac{a_0}{a}\right]$ has been given by Parys (1976).

28 See Brown and Chang, (1976), Brown (forthcoming), and Burmeister (forthcoming).

29 Morishima (1973, pp. 179–96) has stated all the fundamental objections discussed below, although his treatment is sympathetic to the Marxist approach. The interested reader is referred to Morishima's book for a viewpoint opposing that expressed here.

30 When joint production exists, there can be many steady-state equilibria price vectors at the same profit rate, depending upon the pattern of final demand for commodities; see Burmeister and Kuga (1970).

31 Sraffa (1960, p. 22); also see Burmeister (1968a, pp. 83–7) and Miyao (1977).

32 Even this conclusion is incorrect if one does not assume that constant returns to scale prevail. Given fixed quantities of inputs and outputs, a_{ij} coefficients are defined, and *both* r_a^* and w^s depend upon these a_{ij} coefficients. If quantities change and the a_{ij}'s are *not* constant, in violation of constant returns to scale, the new quantity system will define new coefficients, say b_{ij}'s, for which a new relationship

$$r = r_b^*(1 - w_b^s)$$

is valid. Thus without the assumption of constant returns to scale, the validity of Sraffa's fundamental results, equation (4.9.7), depends crucially upon the unrealistic assumption that *all* quantities are frozen at given levels. These matters have been discussed in more detail by Burmeister (1977a).

33 See Theorem 4A.5 in the appendix to this chapter.

34 Meek (1967, p. 177).

35 Also see Burmeister (1968a, 1975a), and where the economic significance of Sraffa's exercise has previously been called into question.

36 Suppose that we observe two economies, 1 and 2, with Sraffa real wages $w_1^s > w_2^s$. We then can conclude that the real wage rates in terms of *every* commodity are higher in economy 1. This fact follows because $w_1^s > w_2^s$ implies from (4.9.7) that $r_1 < r_2$; but since $d(W/P_i)/dr < 0$ for all $i = 1, \ldots, n$, it must be the case that $(W/P_i)_1 > (W/P_i)_2$ for all $i = 1, \ldots, n$.

Note, however, that Sraffa's *particular* real wage plays no essential role in the argument above. For *any* consumption vector c, the real wage

$$w \equiv \frac{1}{pc}$$

has the property that

$$\frac{dw}{dr} = \frac{d(1/pc)}{dr} = \frac{-(dp/dr)c}{(pc)^2} < 0$$

because $dp/dr > 0$.

Note also that if there exist many alternative techniques, then there will exist a different Standard Commodity for each technique. However, Sraffa's real wage must be calculated using different consumption weights for each different technique, and generally, no welfare conclusions are possible when changes in an index also involve changes in the weights used to calculate that index.

Likewise, if constant returns to scale is *not* assumed, then whenever *any* output changes, new unit input coefficients are determined. Accordingly, without constant returns there is a different technique – and hence a different Standard Commodity – for every different output configuration!

37 The neo-Austrian approach is adopted by Hicks in his book *Capital and Time: A Neo-Austrian Approach* (1973). A paper by Cass (1973) provides a superb exposition of the Wicksell model and its relationship to the neoclassical one-sector model studied in Chapter 3, and von Weizsäcker (1971) provides a modern survey of Austrian capital theory. For a more complete critique of neo-Austrian models, the reader is referred to Burmeister (1974).

38 Hicks (1973, p. 15).

39 This and other portions of this section are excerpted from Burmeister (1974).

40 The original "von Neumann model" was presented in von Neumann (1945–1946).

41 Truncation is *not* implied by the conventional free disposal assumption, namely that if a net output vector

$$y \equiv \{(-a^1, b^1), (-a^2, b^2), \ldots, (-a^T, b^T)\}$$

is feasible, then any vector $y' \leqslant y$ is also feasible. In other words, free disposal implies that less or as much output may be produced with additional input, but it says nothing about what can be produced with *less* input.

42 Hicks (1973, pp. 19–23) calls this result a "Fundamental Theorem."

43 Of course, some – but not necessarily all – lawsuits may be avoided if a firm legally is allowed to dissolve.

44 Similarly, costless inputs – such as the air workers breathe – can be ignored when describing the feasible technology.

45 See Hicks (1973) and Arrow and Levhari (1969). Flemming and Wright (1971) have proved more general results when $r^t \neq r$ for all t and when there is a net cash flow after the truncation period. Sen (1975) has proved further generalizations.

46 Although the condition that the maximized present discounted value of a process be a decreasing monotonic function of r is sufficient for the uniqueness of the internal rate of return (assuming existence), it is clearly not a necessary condition. Thus a process might have a unique positive internal rate of return despite the presence of shutdown costs. See Arrow and Levhari (1969).

47 See Exercise 4.3.

48 Von Weizsäcker (1976) defines the "average period of production," an index of "roundaboutness," as "the 'centre of gravity' of the value flow of outputs on the time axis minus the centre of gravity of the value flow of inputs" (p. 217). This index is used for the special case considered in Exercise 4.4.

    For another attempt to define an index of "roundaboutness," not satisfactory on the basis of the criteria given below – conditions (4.10.12a) and (4.10.12b) – see Yeager (1976) and Yeager and Burmeister (1978).

49 In nondifferentiable cases where there are switch points between neo-Austrian processes, (4.10.12a) and (4.10.12b) are replaced by

$$\frac{\Delta c}{\Delta \tau} > 0 \qquad\qquad (4.10.12a')$$

and

$$\frac{\Delta \tau}{\Delta r} < 0 \qquad\qquad (4.10.12b')$$

where the finite changes are evaluated as the changes occurring as a switch point is crossed and the economy changes processes.

50 Exercise 4.4 provides an illustration of this result.

51 The reader interested in this problem may wish to glance ahead to Chapter 5 (Section 5.8, in particular).

52 Strictly speaking, von Neumann (1945–6) did not allow either primary factors such as labor or final consumption, but this detail has no consequence for our discussion. The example discussed here could be presented within the framework of Malinvaud's pioneering work (1954, 1962), but the von Neumann method has more structure and its economic interpretation is better suited for our purposes here.

53 The various activities exhibit constant returns to scale, and thus, in a steady-state equilibrium, the scale of operations is limited by the available fixed labor supply. Accordingly, letting

$$x = \begin{bmatrix} x_1 \\ x_2 \\ x_3 \end{bmatrix}$$

denote the *intensity vector* for the scale of operation of activities 1, 2, and 3, the labor constraint is

$$A_0 x = L;$$

by setting $L \equiv 1$, we interpret all quantities as per capita magnitudes. The steady-state output equation, dual to the price equation (4.10.19), is then

$$Ax \leqslant Bx - C \qquad \text{(with } C \geqslant 0, \ x \geqslant 0, \text{ and } x \neq 0)$$

where C is the vector $\begin{bmatrix} 0 \\ 0 \\ c \end{bmatrix}$ and c is the per capita magnitude of the consumption good (commodity 3).

54 Additional economic insights can be derived from the alternative method; see, for example, Exercise 4.5.

55 The neo-Austrian approach implies that the von Neumann input and output matrices must have a very specialized and restrictive pattern of zero elements.

56 Presumably a "fictitious" capital good is one that need not exist in a physical sense. If this meaning is intended, it is dubious whether or not the concept is useful in capital theory. Consider the common example of a wine-aging process. Suppose that plentiful grape juice is free, but it takes 1 unit of labor working 1 time period to prepare grape juice for aging. Without further labor inputs, aging for 2 additional time periods yields 1 unit of wine. In the notation of the neo-Austrian model, this production process is represented by

$$(a_t, b_t)_{t=0}^n = \{(1, 0), (0, 0), (0, 1)\}$$

where $a_0 = 1$ is the initial input of labor and $b_2 = 1$ is the final output of wine at the end of the third period. Since raw grape juice is free, labor is the only factor of production with a positive price.

As before, suppose that this process is started at calendar time $\tau = 0$. Consider time $\tau = 2$, the end of the second production period. At time $\tau = 2$ the grape juice has been aged for one time period. Do we require any "fictitious" capital good? The answer is clearly *no* because "grape juice aged for one period" is a perfectly well-defined commodity that exists in a physical sense and could, in principle, be traded in a competitive market.

Sometimes a model is formulated with the implicit (or perhaps explicit) assertion that some "fictitious" goods do not exist. Thus consider the example where a^1 workers produce one "machine of type 1" in the first period. Must some "machine of type 1" exist? Suppose not. The a^1 workers are employed for one time period (from calendar time $\tau = 0$ to $\tau = 1$), and assume there is an explosion (any physically destructive natural disaster will serve for my purposes) at time $\tau = 1$. Is the destruction of workers the *only* conceivable eventuality that would harm the production process, that is, one that would diminish the feasible future stream $\{(a^t, b^t)\}$ for $t > 0$? In every realistic case imaginable, the a_0 workers must produce *some* physical commodity that is in existence at time $\tau = 1$ and could, in principle, be destroyed by an explosion. We are free to name this commodity "a machine of type 1."

57 Bernholtz, Faber, and Ross (1978) have analyzed a two-period neo-Austrian model with heterogeneous capital goods using similar methods, but their primary results do not require neo-Austrian concepts. We establish more general propositions in Chapter 5. Moreover, their definition of "roundaboutness" is in terms of the total supply of consumption goods in the two time periods and in general is not related in any obvious way to the traditional notion of "an average period of production"; see Definition 2.5 on page 42 of Bernholtz, Faber, and Ross.

58 Most notably, see Harcourt (1972, 1974).

59 Harcourt (1975) and Hahn (1975).

60 Hahn (1975, pp. 363–4). The interested reader is also referred to Blaug (1974) and Burmeister (1975). Blaug (pp. 85–86) concludes his book with sentiments very similar to those of Hahn:

Anyone who has been attentive to the recent resurgence of the neo-classical research programme in regional analysis, urban economics, applied welfare economics, cost-benefit analysis, the economics of education, labour economics, the economics of time, the economics of search and information, the economics of crime, the economics of fertility, the economics of marriage, the economics of private property rights – the list is really endless – can hardly doubt that there is life yet in the concepts of maximisation, equilibrium, substitution and all other tricks of the trade of mainstream economics. Cambridge UK, however it tries, cannot get along without these ideas and in that lies the overwhelming superiority of the neo-classical tradition in economic thought.

61 See Hahn (1975, p. 342).
62 See Hahn (1975, p. 346).
63 See, for example, Miyao (1977).
64 See note 2.
65 This theorem first appeared in Burmeister (1968a).
66 This index is based on von Weizsäcker (1976); see note 48.

Chapter 5. Properties of dynamic paths

1 Uniqueness up to a constant of proportionality follows from the concavity properties of (5.2.4) under the assumption of no-joint production. Note that if we select one of the primary factors, say the first, as ''labor'' and normalize quantities by setting $\ell_1 = 1$, then the normalized or per capita vector $(k_1^*, \ldots, k_n^*)$ is unique.
2 Some readers may find it hard to believe that reputable economists have made such mistakes. Rather than refer the interested reader to errors, I refer them to Samuelson (1975, pp. 309–63), where he correctly criticizes this type of mistake.
3 Observe that Assumption 5.3 implies Assumption 5.1.
4 The interested reader is referred to Bliss (1975, pp. 244–6) and to Cass (1972a, 1972b).
5 The dot denotes the inner product of two vectors (e.g., $x \cdot y = \sum_{i=1}^n x_i y_i$).
6 Bliss defines *production prices* in an alternative manner and makes the observation that ''the definition of equilibrium prices is purely a formal one and as such is independent of any particular institutional interpretation in terms of price-guided behaviour'' (1975, p. 213).
7 This theorem is proved by Bliss (1975, pp. 227–8) in a slightly different context.
8 Also see Malinvaud (1962).
9 Readers interested in pursuing this technical question in detail are referred to the paper by Kurz (1969), and the work by Bliss in the context of a linear production model serves as an excellent introduction; see Bliss (1975, pp. 244–6).
10 In other sections of this chapter k^t and ℓ^t are column vectors with elements $k_1^t, \ldots, k_n^t$ and $\ell_1^t, \ldots, \ell_m^t$, respectively.

11 Any form of technological change has been excluded by assumption.

12 Selecting the point $(\bar{c}^t, \bar{c}^{t+1}) = (0, \frac{7}{6})$ would yield the weaker result $\frac{3}{4} \leqslant p^t/p^{t+1}$.

13 In fact, our assumption that $\ell^t = 1$ implies that $w^t > 0$, so that (5.6.12) may be strengthened to a strong inequality.

14 The reader should note that, owing to the assumed short-run efficiency property of path P, condition (P.4) is implied provided that either (1) capital can be stored, or (2) capital is "productive" in the sense that more of it makes possible extra consumption at some finite future time; for then assuming that (P.4) does not hold, one can construct a contradiction to the short-run efficiency of P.

15 The concept of the rate of return was introduced in Solow's *Capital Theory and the Rate of Return* (1963), with important results added in "The Interest Rate and Transition between Techniques" (1967, pp. 30–9). Some of the subsequent papers dealing with this subject include "The Black Box Rate of Return" by Nell (1975); "On the Rates of Return on Investment" by Nuti (1974); "Switches of Technique and the 'Rate of Return' in Capital Theory" (1969) and "Again on Capital Theory and Solow's 'Rate of Return'" (1970) by Pasinetti; and "On The Rate of Return: Reply to Pasinetti" by Solow (1970). The most elegant critique of the rate of return concept is given in Chapter 10 of Bliss (1975, especially pp. 230–40).

16 This definition allows for many consumption goods with $c^t = (c_1^t, \ldots, c_n^t)$, and none of the results in this section are invalidated by our simplifying assumption that c^t is a scalar.

17 Figures 5.8a and b are drawn with a time period so short that the curves appear continuous. This detail is of no consequence for the issue at hand. In a continuous-time formulation the social rate of return is defined as a number ρ satisfying

$$\sum_{t=0}^{\infty} [c(t) - \bar{c}(t)]e^{-\rho t} \, dt = 0,$$

analogously to equation (5.8.2). See Burmeister and Long (1977, especially pp. 306–12), where issues closely related to those discussed in this section are examined for a continuous-time model.

18 A more complete and technical discussion of these observations is contained in Burmeister and Long (1977) and in von Weizsäcker (1976, especially p. 223).

19 Von Weizsäcker (1976) uses the term "simple investment" equivalently.

20 Note that $\sum_{s=1}^{\infty} (c - \bar{c}^s) < 0$ since $\bar{c}^s > c$ for all $s > s'$, where s' is some finite time. Thus

$$\sum_{s=1}^{\infty} \frac{c - \bar{c}^s}{(1 + \rho)^s} < 0 \qquad \text{for } \rho < r.$$

21 For example, the interested reader is referred to Benveniste (1976a, 1976b), Benveniste and Gale (1975), Mitra and Majumdar (1976), Majumdar, Mitra, and McFadden (1976); and Mitra (1979). The most comprehensive results appear in the recent paper by Benveniste and Mitra (1978).

Chapter 6. Descriptive and optimal models with heterogeneous commodities

1 That is, take any multisector model and make the extraordinarily restrictive assumption that the heterogeneous capital goods are *always* used in fixed proportions (e.g., one shovel and one rake); this multisector model will then behave as a one-capital-good model with a fixed basket of heterogeneous capital goods serving as "aggregate capital" (e.g., one shovel plus one rake defines 1 unit of "capital").

2 Of course, there remains the question of the degree of decentralization which is possible in an economy that wishes to follow an optimal path. Such questions of economic planning will not concern us here.

3 The turnpike theorem was first stated in Samuelson (1960) and Dorfman, Samuelson, and Solow (1958, chap. 12); other references are given in note 48.

4 In Section 3.6 it was assumed that saving out of rental income was $s_r q_1 K_1$, whereas here we assume depreciation is taken into account with saving out of *net* rental income given by $s_r(q_1 - p_1\delta_1)K_1$; this distinction, however, is not relevant to our discussion.

5 The reader interested in exploring a two-sector, one-capital-good model with $s_c \neq 1$ is referred to Shell, Sidrauski, and Stiglitz (1969, pp. 15–26).

6 Alternatively, we could define a regular saddlepoint in terms of characteristic roots. Thus consider the Jacobian matrix of (6.2.10) given by

$$J = \begin{bmatrix} f_k(\bar{k}, \bar{p}) & f_p(\bar{k}, \bar{p}) \\ k_k(\bar{k}, \bar{p}) & k_p(\bar{k}, \bar{p}) \end{bmatrix}.$$

The point $(\bar{k}, \bar{p})$ is a *regular saddlepoint* if the characteristic equation

$$\det [\lambda I - J] = 0$$

has n characteristic roots with negative real parts and n characteristic roots with positive real parts. The equivalent geometric explanation stated in the text is somewhat easier to interpret for most students who are not familiar with differential equation systems.

7 Kuga (1977) also requires some technical assumptions which, although mathematically important, are not central for the economic conclusions we reach.

8 These results have been proved by Burmeister, Caton, Dobell, and Ross (1973).

9 The stability question was first raised by Hahn (1966).

10 See Burmeister, Caton, Dobell, and Ross (1973), Caton and Shell (1971), and Shell and Stiglitz (1967).

11 The longest time horizon on December 18, 1978, was for silver in June 1981.

12 Of course, one may be able to buy a contract for the future delivery of a certain machine tool at a specified price, but there is no market in which such contracts are traded.

13 It is suggested that the reader interested in *stochastic stability* see, for example, Arnold (1973), Friedman (1975, 1976), Gihman and Skorohod (1970), and Lukacs (1975).

14 That is, if we could observe repeated trials from the same initial condition (k^0, p^0) *not* on the convergent manifold, the ratio of the number of convergent paths to the number of nonconvergent paths would approach zero as the number of trials approached infinity.

15 See Burmeister and Turnovsky (1978) and Burmeister (1976c).

16 The interpretation of p_{1i}^{*t} and p_{2i}^{*t} as anticipated and unanticipated components of actual price change is clearer when an explicit stochastic mechanism is introduced. The interested reader is referred to Burmeister, Flood, and Turnovsky (1979, pp. 10–16). An alternative method for introducing forecast errors due to an information lag has been analyzed by Gray and Turnovsky (1978), but unfortunately this approach results in differential-difference equations that are mathematically more difficult than our simple differential equations.

17 *Perfect foresight* means that the entire path p_i^t is known; *perfect myopic foresight* requires only that the instantaneous rates of change are known.

18 See Burmeister and Graham (1974, 1975).

19 See Burmeister and Turnovsky (1978).

20 Becker (1977) shows that $\lim_{t\to\infty} (\hat{p}^t e^{-\gamma t}) = 0$, which together with assumptions assuring that k^t is bounded imply the transversality condition (6.3.26). The reader interested in mathematical details is referred to the references cited in this section.

21 The necessity of the transversality condition under assumptions satisfied by this model has been proved by Benveniste and Scheinkman (1980). An analogous result for discrete-time optimization problems was proved by Weitzman (1973).

22 For an early use of the perfect-foresight competitive equilibrium concept, see Brock (1974, 1975).

23 Becker (1977) shows that the initial price vector is

$$\hat{p}^0 = \int_0^\infty \hat{q}^s e^{-\hat{R}(s)}\, ds$$

where

$$\hat{R}(s) \equiv \int_0^s \hat{r}^\theta d\theta.$$

The portfolio equilibrium condition in vector form is

$$\dot{\hat{p}}^t + \hat{q}^t = \hat{p}^t \hat{r}^t$$

where $\hat{r}^t = \gamma - (d/dt)[\log \hat{u}'(c^t)]$; integration of the latter yields

$$\hat{p}^t = \int_{s=t}^\infty \hat{q}^s e^{(-\int_t^s r^\theta d\theta)}\, ds \equiv \int_{s=t}^\infty \hat{q}^s e^{-[\hat{R}(s)-\hat{R}(t)]}\, ds,$$

which confirms the expression above for $\hat{p}^0$ since $\hat{R}(0) = 0$ and $e^{\hat{R}(0)} = 1$. Becker's proof shows that the improper integral defining $\hat{p}^0$ exists (i.e., that it is convergent in every component, $\hat{p}_1^0, \ldots, \hat{p}_n^0$.

These results demonstrate that the *efficient market hypothesis* holds for perfect-foresight competitive equilibrium paths in that the price of a capital asset is always equal to the present discounted value of its future rentals. Accordingly, along such a path economic agents need only make *myopic* decisions involving $\dot{p}^t$, p^t, $\dot{q}^t$, and $\hat{r}^t$. Since these myopic decisions satisfy the portfolio equilibrium condition, all one need do is assure the economy *starts* in the proper place by selecting the proper initial price vector. Becker's development of this idea (in the work cited above) confirms the earlier work of Burmeister and Dobell (1969a) for a model with one capital good.

24 Becker (1979) has constructed a similar model with one capital good having multiple steady-state equilibria, some stable and some unstable.

25 See Becker (1978a, 1978b).

26 Pontryagin (1962) is the classic reference, and Magill (1977) cites a comprehensive list of references to both the mathematics and economics literature. Chapter 11 of Burmeister and Dobell (1970) offers an introductory survey and shows how optimal control solutions may be derived using elementary economic principles.

27 As we shall see, the Hamiltonian is used to solve optimal control problems, and in many applications it has an interpretation such as "the value of output." An elementary exposition of control theory is contained in Chapter 11 of Burmeister and Dobell (1970).

28 These necessary conditions are also sufficient given the concavity of the production functions.

29 The reader should be careful to note and remember that the notation for prices in this section differs from the notation in previous sections of this chapter. A notation similar to most of the optimal control literature has been selected here.

30 Moreover, ordinary net national product is maximized at the prices $Q = (Q_1, \ldots, Q_n)$, where $q = u'(c)Q$. See Exercise 6.6.

31 Sufficiency of the transversality condition was proved by Mangasarian (1966), as well as by Burmeister and Dobell (1970, pp. 418–19). Necessity and sufficiency has been proved by Benveniste and Scheinkman (forthcoming).

32 The vector of *current utility prices* is q; the analogous *discounted utility prices* defined by

$$p \equiv qe^{-\gamma t}$$

are called the *adjoint* or *dual variables*. The discounted value Hamiltonian is a function of p and k, and (6.4.24a) and (6.4.24b) may also be expressed as

$$\dot{p} = -\frac{\partial H(p, k)}{\partial k} \equiv -H_k(p, k)$$

and

$$\dot{k} = +\frac{\partial H(p, k)}{\partial p} \equiv +H_p(p, k).$$

The mathematical structure of optimal control problems in economics arises because $\hat{H}(q, k)$ is *convex* in q and *concave* in k, implying that the matrices $\hat{H}_{qq}$

and $\dot{H}_{kk}$ are negative semidefinite and positive semidefinite, respectively. When $\dot{H}(q, k)$ is *strictly* convex in q and *strictly* concave in k, $\dot{H}_{qq}$ and $\dot{H}_{kk}$ are negative and positive definite, respectively. An excellent analysis of the geometry of Hamiltonians is provided by Magill (1977, especially pp. 190–5).

33 Since det $\bar{J}$ is equal to the product of the characteristic roots of $\bar{J}$, this condition is equivalent to det $\bar{J} \neq 0$ and no purely imaginary roots. The condition can be assured by assuming a technology and a utility function such that $u(c)$ is a strictly concave function of $\dot{k}$ and k; see Levhari and Liviatan (1972).

34 See Kurz (1968) and Levhari and Liviatan (1972).

35 Michael Magill has provided a comprehensive analysis of the local stability properties of rest points to optimal capital accumulation problems, and the interested reader is referred to Magill (1977).

36 If there were more than n roots with negative real parts, the dimension of the (local) convergent manifold would be larger than n. In such circumstances *uniqueness* of an optimal path would be violated; given a k^0 sufficiently close to k^*, there would exist several values of p^0 and several associated paths satisfying the necessary and sufficient conditions for an optimal solution. All such paths must assign the same value to the criterion function, and hence one is indifferent among them on economic grounds. Often such nonuniqueness arises because there are, for example, "red machines" and "blue machines" which are perfect substitutes. By aggregating such commodities, the technology becomes more concave and a unique optimal path may result.

   Note that the foregoing argument depends both upon strict concavity and upon the condition $\gamma \geqslant 0$. If $\gamma < 0$ (see pp. 248–9 for a discussion of why this case can arise), more than n roots with negative real parts may exist. Even though more than one path converges to the rest point in this case, only one of them is optimal because only one path satisfies the transversality condition [equation (6.4.22)] with q_i approaching zero faster than $e^{-\gamma t}$ diverges [so that $\lim_{t\to\infty} (q_i e^{-\gamma t}) = 0$, $i = 1, \ldots, n$].

37 This point shall be further elaborated upon later in this section.

38 See Exercise 6.7.

39 An entire book is devoted to this problem; the reader is referred to Cass and Shell (1976a).

40 See Brock and Scheinkman (1976).

41 The limit inferior, sometimes called the lower limit, is denoted by *lim*.

42 Also see Burmeister and Dobell (1970, pp. 383–90), Koopmans (1965), and Magill (1977).

43 See Liviatan and Samuelson (1967).

44 Consider the problem $\max_{c_i} u(c_1, \ldots, c_n)$ subject to given $p_i > 0$, $i = 1, \ldots, n$, and given $M \equiv \Sigma_{i=1}^n p_i c_i$. The utility function is termed *normal* if the solutions to this utility maximization problem have the property that, for any given p_i's,

$$\frac{\partial c_i}{\partial M} \geqslant 0 \qquad \text{for all } i = 1, \ldots, n.$$

The proposition asserted in the text is proved by Brock and Burmeister (1976).

45 Ryder and Heal (1973) and Sutherland (1970) have generated optimal limit cycle behavior by including past consumption and the capital stock, respectively, as arguments of the utility function.

46 See Benhabib and Nishimura (1979).

47 Note that these results prove that price stabilization is not always desirable, for it may be *optimal* to have fluctuating prices. This observation is pursued by Burmeister (1978).

48 See Chapter 10 of Burmeister and Dobell (1970) for a review of the traditional turnpike theorem originally stated by Samuelson (1960). Consumption turnpike theorems were first proved by Cass (1965, 1966) and Samuelson (1965). An elegant treatment of more recent developments is provided by McKenzie (forthcoming, 1980).

49 See, for example, Samuelson (1976b, pp. 3–13), who invokes poetic license to describe the qualitative behavior as that of an "oscillatory saddlepoint" (p. 9).

50 Economic applications are found in Brock and Mirman (1972, 1973), Dana (1974), Jeanjean (1974), Levhari and Srinivasan (1969), Mirman and Zilcha (1975, 1976), and Radner (1973). Also see Bismut (1975) and Brock (1978). An excellent introduction to mathematical techniques which serves as a good source of other references as well can be found in Fleming and Rishel (1975).

51 This model is taken from Section 1.2 of Dasgupta and Heal (1974, pp. 9–18).

52 A complete analysis of the model sketched here is provided by Dasgupta and Heal (1974). Related questions of exhaustible resources are examined in the Symposium Papers found in the *Review of Economic Studies,* Symposium, 1974; Long (1974, 1975, 1977); Weinstein and Zeckhauser (1975); and comments on this article by Cropper, Weinstein, and Zeckhauser (1978). A comprehensive treatment of the technological conditions that allow sustained or growing consumption despite exhaustible resources is contained in Cass and Mitra (1980).

53 See Chakravarty (1962).

54 The numerical computations of Burmeister, Caton, Dobell, and Ross (1973) indicate that there is cause for genuine concern; see, in particular, pages 93–94.

Chapter 7. Introduction to stochastic models

1 Some of the relevant literature is cited in note 33 on page 295.

2 Note that $P^* = e^{p*} = e^{-b} > 0$.

3 See, for example, Burmeister, Flood, and Turnovsky (1980). This work examines genuine saddlepoint equilibrium in the two-dimensional space of the price level and employment.

4 Brock and Magill (1978) have shown how stochastic control theory can be applied to continuous-time economic models, and their techniques could be used to solve the type of problem sketched here. For discrete-time economic models, see, for example, Samuelson (1969).

5 See, for example, Sargent (1977) and Sargent and Wallace (1973).

6 The relevant papers by Brock (1974, 1975) are both based upon a representative-individual approach. Becker (1978b) admits heterogeneous preferences, but not in the context of a monetary model.

7 A continuous-time version of the model presented in this section, together with a more complete analysis, can be found in Burmeister, Flood, and Turnovsky (1979).

8 See, in particular, Quandt's work on this subject (1978).

9 See, for example, Carlton (1979). Likewise, McCallum (1980, Section VII) has provided a rationale for slow price-adjustment mechanisms which are consistent with maximizing behavior on the part of economic agents.

10 The proofs for the more difficult continuous-time formulations are contained in Burmeister, Flood, and Turnovsky (1979). Also see note 14 below for an important qualification.

11 The interested reader is referred to Lukacs (1975).

12 One such example can be found in Burmeister, Flood, and Turnovsky (1980). Burmeister (1980) contains a more complete discussion of some of the issues introduced here, and the question of stochastic determinacy is also examined.

13 Burmeister and Turnovsky (1978) have proved this result for a deterministic model with heterogeneous assets and they also demonstrate that the assumption of adaptive expectations with ''slow'' rates of adaptation plays a role identical to ''slow'' speeds of market adjustment. The adaptive expectations hypothesis is subject to the compelling criticism that it implies the unreasonable conclusion that economic agents do not use all the information available to them.

14 McCallum (1980) argues that the type of specification used for the price adjustment equation (7.3.2) is inappropriate on economic grounds. In section VII of McCallum (1980) alternative specifications such as

$$\frac{p(t + 1) - p(t)}{\alpha} = m(t) - m^d(t) + E_t \left[\frac{\bar{p}(t + 1) - \bar{p}(t)}{\alpha} \right] + \mu(t)$$

are suggested, where

$$m(t + 1) - \bar{p}(t + 1) = m^d(t + 1) - p(t + 1).$$

Clearly the issue is only of significance when $0 < \alpha < \infty$ and sluggish price adjustment does prevail. In the sluggish-adjustment case, alternative specifications for (7.3.2) – of which (7.4.1) is but one example – do influence the dimension of the convergent manifold for expectations and hence are relevant for the contradiction question.

Suppose, for example, that some variable $x(t)$ is predetermined with $E_t x(t) = \bar{x}$, and suppose that the difference equation generating $E_t x(t + h)$, $h = 0, 1, 2, \ldots$ is second order. Even though $E_t x(t) = \bar{x}$ is predetermined, one is still free to choose a value of $E_t x(t + h)$ for exactly one value of $h = 1, 2, 3, \ldots$. The type of contradiction discussed in the text may be avoided since the assumption that $E_t x(t + h)$ converges with $\lim_{h \to \infty} E_t x(t + h) = x^*$ is equivalent to setting $E_t x(t + h)$ at x^* for $h = \infty$.

15 Papers in which such issues are addressed include Feiger (1978), Green (1978), Grossman (1975a, 1975b), Grossman, Kihlstrom, and Mirman (1977), Grossman and Stiglitz (1978), and Kihlstrom and Mirman (1975).

BIBLIOGRAPHY

Adams, F. G., and Klein, S. A., eds. *Stabilizing World Commodity Markets*. Lexington, Mass.: Heath, 1978.

Arrow, Kenneth J. "Optimal Capital Policy, The Cost of Capital, and Myopic Decision Rules." *Annals of the Institute of Statistical Mathematics* 16 (1964).

Arrow, Kenneth J., and Intriligator, Michael D., eds. *Handbook of Mathematical Economics*. Amsterdam: North-Holland, forthcoming, 1980.

Arrow, Kenneth J., Karlin, S., and Suppes, P., eds. *Mathematical Methods in the Social Sciences, 1959*. Stanford, Calif.: Stanford University Press, 1960.

Arrow, Kenneth J., and Levhari, David. "Uniqueness of the Internal Rate of Return with Variable Life of Investment." *Economic Journal* 79 (September 1969).

Atkinson, Anthony B. *The Economics of Inequality*. Oxford: Clarendon Press, 1975.

Becker, Robert A. "A Simple Dynamic Model of Equilibrium with Heterogeneous Capital Goods." Discussion Paper. Bloomington: Indiana University, October 1977.

"The Existence of a Perfect Foresight Competitive Equilibrium in a Simple Dynamic Model of Capital Accumulation with Heterogeneous Households." Discussion Paper. Bloomington: Indiana University, February 1978a.

"A Note on the Long-Run Steady State in a Simple Dynamic Model of Equilibrium with Heterogeneous Households." Discussion Paper. Bloomington: Indiana University, February 1978b.

"A Simple Dynamic Equilibrium Model with Stable and Unstable Long-Run Equilibria." Discussion Paper. Bloomington: Indiana University, March 1979a.

"The Equivalence of a Fisher Competitive Equilibrium and Perfect Foresight Competitive Equilibrium in a Multi-sectoral Model of Capital Accumulation." Working Paper. Bloomington: Indiana University, 1979b.

Benhabib, Jess, and Nishimura, Kazuo. "The Hopf Bifurcation and the Existence and Stability of Closed Orbits in Multi-sector Models of Optimal Economic Growth.'' *Journal of Economic Theory* 21 (December 1979).

Benveniste, Lawrence M. ''A Complete Characterization of Efficiency for a General Capital Accumulation Model.'' *Journal of Economic Theory* 12 (April 1976a).

''Two Notes on the Malinvaud Condition for Efficiency of Infinite Horizon Programs.'' *Journal of Economic Theory* 12 (April 1976b).

Benveniste, Lawrence M., and Gale, David. ''A Short Proof of Cass' Theorem on Overaccumulation.'' Discussion Paper. Berkeley, Calif.: University of California at Berkeley, April 1974.

''An Extension of Cass' Characterization of Infinite Efficient Production Programs.'' *Journal of Economic Theory* 10 (April 1975).

Benveniste, Lawrence M., and Mitra, Tapan. ''Characterizing Inefficiency of Infinite-Horizon Programs in Non-smooth Technologies.'' Discussion Paper. Rochester, N.Y.: University of Rochester, 1978.

Benveniste, Lawrence M., and Scheinkman, José A. ''Duality Theory for Dynamic Optimization Models of Economics: The Continuous Time Case.'' *Journal of Economic Theory,* forthcoming (1980).

Bernholtz, Peter, Faber, Malte, and Ross, Winfried. ''A Neo-Austrian Two-Period Multisector Model of Capital.'' *Journal of Economic Theory* 17 (February 1978).

Bismut, Jean-Michel. ''Growth and Optimal Intertemporal Allocation of Risks.'' *Journal of Economic Theory* 10 (April 1975).

Blaug, Mark. *The Cambridge Revolution: Success or Failure?* London: The Institute of Economic Affairs, 1974.

Bliss, Christopher. *Capital Theory and the Distribution of Income.* Amsterdam: North-Holland, 1975.

Brock, William A. ''Money and Growth: The Case of Long-Run Perfect Foresight.'' *International Economic Review* 15 (October 1974).

''A Simple Perfect Foresight Monetary Model.'' *Journal of Monetary Economics* 1 (April 1975).

''An Integration of Stochastic Growth Theory and the Theory of Finance.'' Discussion Paper. Chicago: University of Chicago, February 1978.

Brock, William A., and Burmeister, Edwin. ''Regular Economies and Conditions for Uniqueness of Steady States in Optimal Multi-sector Economic Models.'' *International Economic Review* 17 (February 1976).

Brock, William A., and Magill, Michael J. P. ''Dynamics under Uncertainty.'' Discussion Paper 324. Evanston, Ill.: Northwestern University, June 1978.

Brock, William A., and Mirman, Leonard J. ''Optimal Economic Growth and Uncertainty: The Discounted Case.'' *Journal of Economic Theory* 4 (1972).

''Optimal Economic Growth and Uncertainty: The No-Discounting Case.'' *International Economic Review* 4 (1973).

Brock, William A., and Sheinkman, José A. ''Global Asymptotic Stability of Optimal Control Systems with Applications to the Theory of Economic Growth.'' *Journal of Economic Theory* 12 (February 1976).

Brown, M. ''The Measurement of Capital Aggregates – A Post Reswitching

Problem." In *The Measurement of Capital,* ed. by Dan Usher. Chicago: University of Chicago Press, forthcoming, 1980.

Brown, M., and Chang, W. W. "Capital Aggregation in a General Equilibrium Model of Production." *Econometrica* 44 (1976).

Brown, M., Sato, K., and Zarembka, P., eds. *Essays in Modern Capital Theory.* Amsterdam: North-Holland, 1976.

Bruno, M., Burmeister, E., and Sheshinski, E. "The Nature and Implications of the Reswitching of Techniques." *The Quarterly Journal of Economics* 80 (August 1966). Reprinted in *Readings in Mathematical Economics,* vol. 2, ed. by Peter Newman. Baltimore: Johns Hopkins University Press, 1968.

Burmeister, Edwin. "On a Theorem of Sraffa." *Economica* 35 (February 1968a).

"The Role of the Jacobian Determinant in the Two-Sector Model." *International Economic Review* 9 (June 1968b).

"Synthesizing the Neo-Austrian and Alternative Approaches to Capital Theory: A Survey." *Journal of Economic Literature* (June 1974).

"Comment: This Age of Leontief . . . and Who?" *Journal of Economic Literature* 13 (June 1975a).

"Review of Mark Blaug's *The Cambridge Revolution: Success or Failure?*" *The Economic Record* (September 1975b).

"Many Primary Factors in Non-joint Production Economies." *The Economic Record* (December 1975c).

"Critical Observations on the Labor Theory of Value." Discussion Paper. Charlottesville: University of Virginia, August 1976a.

"Real Wicksell Effects and Regular Economies." In *Essays in Modern Capital Theory,* ed. by M. Brown, K. Sato, and P. Zarembka. Amsterdam: North-Holland, 1976b.

"Specifications of Adaptive Expectations in Continuous Time Dynamic Economic Models." *Econometrica* 44 (September 1976c).

"The Irrelevance of Sraffa's Analysis without Constant Returns to Scale." *Journal of Economic Literature* 15 (March 1977a).

"On the Social Significance of the Reswitching Controversy." *Revue d'Economie Politique* (March–April 1977b).

"Is Price Stabilization Theoretically Desirable?" In *Stabilizing World Commodity Markets,* ed. by F. G. Adams and S. A. Klein. Lexington, Mass.: Heath, 1978.

"On Some Conceptual Issues in Rational Expectations Modelling." *Journal of Money, Credit, and Banking* (forthcoming, November 1980a).

"Comments on Capital Aggregation." In *The Measurement of Capital,* ed. by Dan Usher, Chicago: University of Chicago Press, forthcoming, 1980b.

Burmeister, Edwin, Caton, Christopher, Dobell, A. Rodney, and Ross, Stephen. "The 'Saddlepoint Property' and the Structure of Dynamic Heterogeneous Capital Good Models." *Econometrica* 41 (January 1973).

Burmeister, Edwin, and Dobell, A. Rodney. "Guidance of a Developed Free-Market Economy." *Record of the IEEE Conference on Systems Science and Cybernetics.* Philadelphia, October 1969a.

"Disembodied Technological Change with Several Factors." *Journal of Economic Theory* 1 (1969b).

Mathematical Theories of Economic Growth. New York: Macmillan, 1970.

Burmeister, Edwin, Flood, Robert P., and Turnovsky, Stephen J. "Rational Expectations and Stability in a Stochastic Monetary Model of Inflation." Discussion Paper. Charlottesville: University of Virginia, October 1979.

"Dynamic Macroeconomic Stability with or without Equilibrium in Money and Labor Markets." Discussion Paper. Charlottesville: University of Virginia, February 1980.

Burmeister, Edwin, and Graham, Daniel A. "Multi-sector Economic Models with Continuous Adaptive Expectations." *Review of Economic Studies* 41 (July 1974).

"Price Expectations and Global Stability in Economic Systems." *Automatica* 2 (1975).

Burmeister, Edwin, and Hammond, Peter J. "Maximin Paths of Heterogeneous Capital Accumulation and the Instability of Paradoxical Steady States." *Econometrica* (May 1977).

Burmeister, Edwin, Jackson, John, and Ross, Stephen A. "The Evaluation of Simple and Optimal Decision Rules with Misspecified Welfare Functions." In *Applications of Control Theory to Economic Analysis,* ed. by J. D. Pitchford and S. J. Turnovsky. Amsterdam: North-Holland, 1977.

Burmeister, Edwin, and Kuga, Kiyoshi. "The Factor-Price Frontier, Duality and Joint Production." *Review of Economic Studies* (January 1970).

Burmeister, Edwin, and Long, Ngo Van. "On Some Unresolved Questions in Capital Theory: An Application of Samuelson's Correspondence Principle." *Quarterly Journal of Economics* 91 (May 1977).

Burmeister, Edwin, and Phelps, Edmund. "Money, Public Debt, Inflation, and Real Interest." *Journal of Money, Credit, and Banking* 3 (May 1971).

Burmeister, Edwin, and Turnovsky, Stephen J. "Capital Deepening Response in a Model with Many Capital Goods." *American Economic Review* (December 1972).

"Price Expectations, Disequilibrium Adjustments, and Macroeconomic Stability." *Journal of Economic Theory* 17 (April 1978).

Carlton, Dennis W. "Contracts, Price Rigidity, and Market Equilibrium." *Journal of Political Economy* 87 (October 1979).

Cass, David. "Optimum Growth in an Aggregative Model of Capital Accumulation." *Review of Economic Studies* 32 (July 1965).

"Optimum Growth in an Aggregative Model of Capital Accumulation: A Turnpike Theorem." *Econometrica* 34 (October 1966).

"Distinguishing Inefficient Competitive Growth Paths: A Note on Capital Overaccumulation and Rapidly Diminishing Future Value of Consumption in a Fairly General Model of Capitalistic Production." *Journal of Economic Theory* 4 (April 1972a).

"On Capital Overaccumulation in the Aggregative, Neoclassical Model of Economic Growth: A Complete Characterization." *Journal of Economic Theory* 4 (April 1972b).

"On The Wicksellian Point-Input, Point-Output Model of Capital Accumulation: A Modern View (or, Neoclassicism Slightly Vindicated)." *Journal of Political Economy* 81 (January–February 1973).

Cass, David, and Mitra, Tapan. "Persistence of Economic Growth despite Exhaustion of Natural Resources." Working Paper. Pasadena, Calif: California Institute of Technology, 1980.

Cass, David, and Shell, Karl. "Introduction to Hamiltonian Dynamics in Economics." *Journal of Economic Theory* 12 (February 1976). Reprinted in *The Hamiltonian Approach to Dynamic Economics,* ed. by David Cass and Karl Shell. Philadelphia: University of Pennsylvania Press, 1976a.

   The Hamiltonian Approach to Dynamic Economics. Philadelphia: University of Pennsylvania Press, 1976b.

Caton, Christopher, and Shell, Karl. "An Exercise in the Theory of Heterogeneous Capital Accumulation." *Review of Economic Studies* 38 (1971).

Chakravarty, S. "Optimal Savings with Finite Planning Horizons." *International Economic Review* 3 (September 1962).

Chilosi, Alberto, and Gomulka, Stanislaw. "Technological Condition for Balanced Growth: A Criticism and Re-statement." *Journal of Economic Theory* 9 (1974).

Cropper, M. L., Weinstein, M. C., and Zeckhauser, R. J. "An Elaboration, Correction, and Extension." *Quarterly Journal of Economics* 92 (May 1978).

Dana, R. A. "Evaluation of Development Programs in a Stationary Stochastic Economy with Bounded Primary Resources." In *Mathematical Models in Economics,* ed. by J. Los and M. Los. Amsterdam: North-Holland, 1974.

Dasgupta, P., and Heal, G. M. "The Optimal Depletion of Exhaustible Resources." *Review of Economic Studies,* Symposium (1974).

Debreu, G. *Theory of Value.* New York: Wiley, 1959.

Diamond, Peter A. "Disembodied Technical Change in a Two-Sector Model." *Review of Economic Studies* 32 (April 1965a).

   "Technical Change and the Measurement of Capital and Output." *Review of Economic Studies* 32 (October 1965b).

   "National Debt in a Neoclassical Growth Model." *American Economic Review* 55 (December 1965c).

Dorfman, Robert, Samuelson, Paul A., and Solow, Robert M. *Linear Programming and Economic Analysis.* New York: McGraw-Hill, 1958.

Eatwell, John. "Mr. Sraffa's Standard Commodity and the Rate of Exploitation." *Quarterly Journal of Economics* (November 1975).

Feiger, George M. "Divergent Rational Expectations Equilibrium in a Dynamic Model of a Futures Market." *Journal of Economic Theory* (April 1978).

Feinstein, C. H., ed. *Socialism, Capitalism, and Economic Growth.* New York: Cambridge University Press, 1967.

Fisher, Irving. *The Rate of Interest.* New York: Macmillan, 1907.

   The Theory of Interest. New York: Macmillan, 1930.

Fleming, Wendell H., and Rishel, Raymond W. *Deterministic and Stochastic Optimal Control.* New York: Springer-Verlag, 1975.

Flemming, J. S., and Wright, J. F. "Uniqueness of the Internal Rate of Return: A Generalization." *Economic Journal* (June 1971).

Friedman, Avner. *Stochastic Differential Equations and Applications,* vol. 1. New York: Academic Press, 1975.

Stochastic Differential Equations and Applications, vol. 2. New York: Academic Press, 1976.

Gale, David. "On Optimal Development in a Multi-sector Economy." *Review of Economic Studies* 34 (January 1967).

"Dynamic Behavior of a Simple Neoclassical Model with Wealth and Capital Unequal." *Journal of Economic Theory* 15 (1977).

Garegnani, P. "Switching of Techniques." *Quarterly Journal of Economics* 80: "Paradoxes in Capital Theory: A Symposium" (November 1966).

Gihman, I. I., and Skorohod, A. V. *Stochastic Differential Equations.* New York: Springer-Verlag, 1970.

Gomulka, Stanislaw. "Technological Condition for Balanced Growth: A Note on Professor Whitaker's Contribution." *Journal of Economic Theory* 13 (December 1976).

Gray, Malcolm R., and Turnovsky, Stephen J. "Expectational Consistency, Informational Lags, and the Formulation of Expectations in Continuous Time Models." Discussion Paper. Canberra: Australian National University, April 1978.

Green, Jerry. "Value of Information with Sequential Futures Markets." Discussion Paper. Cambridge, Mass.: Harvard Institute of Economic Research, July 1978.

Grossman, Sanford J. "On The Efficiency of Competitive Stock Markets Where Traders Have Diverse Information." *Journal of Finance* (May 1975).

"The Existence of Future Markets, Noisy Rational Expectations and Informational Externalities." *Review of Economic Studies* (October 1977).

Grossman, Sanford J., Kihlstrom, Richard E., and Mirman, Leonard J. "A Bayesian Approach to the Production of Information and Learning by Doing." *Review of Economic Studies* (October 1977).

Grossman, Sanford J., and Stiglitz, Joseph E. "On the Impossibility of Informationally Efficient Markets." Discussion Paper 259. Palo Alto, Calif.: Institute for Mathematical Studies in the Social Sciences, Stanford University, April 1978.

Hahn, F. H. "Equilibrium Dynamics with Heterogeneous Capital Goods." *Quarterly Journal of Economics* 80 (1966).

"Revival of Political Economy: The Wrong Issues and the Wrong Argument." *The Economic Record* (September 1975).

Harcourt, G. C. *Some Cambridge Controversies in the Theory of Capital.* Cambridge, England: Cambridge University Press, 1972.

"The Cambridge Controversies: The Afterglow." Paper presented at the Fourth Conference of Economists, Canberra, Australia, August 1974.

"Decline and Rise: The Revival of (Classical) Political Economy." *The Economic Record* (September 1975).

Heckscher, E. "A Note on South Sea Finance." *Journal of Business and Economic History* 3 (1930).

Hicks, John. *Value and Capital,* 2d ed. Oxford: Clarendon Press, 1946.

Capital and Time: A Neo-Austrian Approach. Oxford: Clarendon Press, 1973.

Hirsch, Morris W., and Smale, Stephen. *Differential Equations, Dynamical Systems, and Linear Algebra.* New York: Academic Press, 1974.

Jeanjean, P. "Optimal Development Programs under Uncertainty: The Undiscounted Case." *Journal of Economic Theory* 7 (1974).

Kac, Mark. "Some Mathematical Models in Science." *Science* 166 (November 1969).

Kaldor, N. "Capital Accumulation and Economic Growth." In *The Theory of Capital,* ed. by F. A. Lutz and D. C. Hague. New York: St. Martin's Press, 1961.

Keynes, J. M. *The General Theory of Employment, Interest and Money.* London: Harcourt Brace, 1936.

Kihlstrom, Richard E., and Mirman, Leonard J. "Information and Market Equilibrium." *Bell Journal of Economics* (1975).

Koopmans, T. C. "On the Concept of Optimal Growth." *The Econometric Approach to Development Planning.* Chicago: Rand McNally, 1965.

Kuga, Kiyoshi. "General Saddlepoint Property of the Steady State of a Growth Model with Heterogeneous Capital Goods." *International Economic Review* 18 (February 1977).

Kurz, Mordecai. "The General Instability of a Class of Competitive Growth Processes." *Review of Economic Studies* 35 (April 1968).

"Tightness and Substitution in the Theory of Capital." *Journal of Economic Theory* 1 (October 1969).

Levhari, David, and Liviatan, Nissan. "On Stability in the Saddlepoint Sense." *Journal of Economic Theory* 4 (February 1972).

Levhari, David, and Samuelson, Paul A. "The Nonswitching Theorem Is False." *Quarterly Journal of Economics* 4: "Paradoxes in Capital Theory: A Symposium" (November 1966).

Levhari, David, and Srinivasan, T. "Optimal Savings under Uncertainty." *Review of Economic Studies* 36 (1969).

Liviatan, N., and Samuelson, Paul A. "Notes on Turnpikes: Stable and Unstable." *Journal of Economic Theory* 1 (December 1967).

Long, Ngo Van. "International Borrowing for Resource Extraction." *International Economic Review* 15 (February 1974).

"Resource Extraction under the Uncertainty about Possible Nationalization." *Journal of Economic Theory* 10 (February 1975).

"Optimal Exploitation and Replenishment of a Natural Resource." In *Applications of Control Theory to Economic Analysis,* ed. by J. D. Pitchford and S. J. Turnovsky. Amsterdam: North-Holland, 1977.

Los, J., and Los, M., eds. *Mathematical Models in Economics.* Amsterdam: North-Holland, 1974.

Lu, Yung-Chen. *Singularity Theory and an Introduction to Catastrophe Theory.* New York: Springer-Verlag, 1976.

Ludwig, Arnold. *Stochastic Differential Equations: Theory and Applications.* New York: Wiley, 1973.

Lukacs, Eugene. *Stochastic Convergence,* 2d ed. New York: Academic Press, 1975.

Magill, Michael J. P. "Some New Results on the Local Stability of the Process of Capital Accumulation." *Journal of Economic Theory* 15 (June 1977).

Majumdar, Mukul, Mitra, Tapan, and McFadden, Daniel. "On Efficiency and Pareto Optimality of Competitive Programs in Closed Multisector Models." *Journal of Economic Theory* 13 (August 1976).

Malinvaud, E. "Capital Accumulation and Efficient Allocation of Resources." *Econometrica* 21 (April 1953).

"Efficient Capital Accumulation: A Corrigendum." *Econometrica* 30 (July 1962).

Mangasarian, O. L. "Sufficient Conditions for the Optimal Control of Nonlinear Systems." *Journal Society for Industrial and Applied Mathematics* 4 (1966).

McCallum, Bennett T. "Rational Expectations and Macroeconomic Stabilization Policy: An Overview." *Journal of Money, Credit, and Banking* (forthcoming, November 1980).

McFadden, Daniel. "The Evaluation of Development Programmes." *Review of Economic Studies* 34 (January 1967).

McKenzie, Lionel. "Optimal Economic Growth and Turnpike Theorems." In *Handbook of Mathematical Economics,* ed. by Kenneth J. Arrow and Michael D. Intriligator. Amsterdam: North-Holland, forthcoming 1980.

Meek, Ronald L. *Economics and Ideology and Other Essays.* London: Chapman & Hall, 1967.

Mirman, Leonard J., and Zilcha, Itzhak. "On Optimal Growth under Uncertainty." *Journal of Economic Theory* 11 (1975).

"Unbounded Shadow Prices for Optimal Stochastic Growth Models." *International Economic Review* 17 (1976).

"Characterizing Optimal Policies in a One-Sector Model of Economic Growth under Uncertainty." *Journal of Economic Theory* 14 (April 1977).

Mitra, Tapan. "A Note on Efficient Growth with Irreversible Investment and the Phelps–Koopmans Theorem." *Journal of Economic Theory* 18 (June 1978).

"Identifying Inefficiency in Smooth Aggregative Models of Economic Growth: A Unifying Criterion." *Journal of Mathematical Economics* 6 (March 1979).

Mitra, Tapan, and Majumdar, Mukul. "A Note on the Role of the Transversality Condition in Signalling Capital Overaccumulation." *Journal of Economic Theory* 13 (August 1976).

Miyao, Takahiro. "A Generalization of Sraffa's Standard Commodity and Its Complete Characterization." *International Economic Review* 18 (February 1977).

Morishima, Michio. "Refutation of the Nonswitching Theorem." *Quarterly Journal of Economics* 80: "Paradoxes in Capital Theory: A Symposium" (November 1966).

Marx's Economics. Cambridge, England: Cambridge University Press, 1973.

Nell, Edward J. "The Black Box Rate of Return." *Kyklos* 28 (1975).

Newman, Peter, ed. *Readings in Mathematical Economics,* vol. 2. Baltimore: Johns Hopkins University Press, 1968.

Nuti, Domenico Mario. "On the Rates of Return on Investment." *Kyklos* 27 (1974).

Parys, Wilfried. "A Simple Criterion for Equal Value Composition of Capital." Mimeograph, 1976.

Pasinetti, Luigi L. "Changes in the Rate of Profit and Switches of Techniques."
  Quarterly Journal of Economics 80: "Paradoxes in Capital Theory: A Symposium" (November 1966).
  "Switches of Technique and the 'Rate of Return' in Capital Theory." *Economic Journal* 79 (September 1969).
  "Again on Capital Theory and Solow's Rate of Return." *Economic Journal* 80 (June 1970).
  "The Unpalatability of the Reswitching of Techniques – A Comment on Burmeister, Krelle, Nuti, and von Weizsäcker." Discussion Paper. Rome: Universita Cattolica del Sacro Cuore, 1977.
Phelps, Edmund S. "Second Essay on the Golden Rule of Accumulation." *American Economic Review* 55 (September 1965), pp. 793–814.
Pitchford, John D. *Population in Economic Growth*. New York: American Elsevier, 1974.
Pitchford, John D., and Turnovsky, Stephen J., eds. *Applications of Control Theory to Economic Analysis*. Amsterdam: North-Holland, 1977.
Pontryagin, L. S. *Mathematical Theory of Optimal Processes,* trans. by K. N. Trirogoff. New York: Wiley, 1962.
Quandt, Richard E. "Tests of the Equilibrium vs. Disequilibrium Hypotheses." *International Economic Review* (June 1978).
Radner, R. "Optimal Stationary Consumption with Stochastic Production and Resources." *Journal of Economic Theory* 6 (1973).
Ramsey, F. P. "A Mathematical Theory of Saving." *Economic Journal* 88 (December 1928).
Robinson, Joan. "The Production Function and the Theory of Capital." *Review of Economic Studies* 21 (1953–1954).
  "Response" to Comments by Samuelson and Solow. *Quarterly Journal of Economics* 89 (February 1975a).
  "The Unimportance of Reswitching." *Quarterly Journal of Economics* 89 (February 1975b).
Ryder, H., and Heal, G. "Optimal Growth with Intertemporally Dependent Preferences." *Review of Economic Studies* 40 (January 1973).
Samuelson, Paul A. "Abstract of a Theorem concerning Substitutability in Open Leontief Models." In *Activity Analysis of Production and Allocation,* ed. by T. C. Koopmans. New York: Wiley, 1951.
  "Intertemporal Price Equilibrium: A Prologue to the Theory of Speculation." *Weltwirtschaftliches Archiv* 79. Hamburg: Hoffman & Campe Verlag, 1957. Reprinted in *The Collected Scientific Papers of Paul A. Samuelson,* vol. 2, ed. by Joseph E. Stiglitz. Cambridge, Mass.: The MIT Press, 1966.
  "An Exact Consumption-Loan Model of Interest with or without the Social Contrivance of Money." *Journal of Political Economy* 66 (1958).
  "Efficient Paths of Capital Accumulation in Terms of the Calculus of Variations." *Mathematical Methods in the Social Sciences,* ed. by K. Arrow, S. Karlin, and P. Suppes. Stanford, Calif.: Stanford University Press, 1960.
  "A New Theorem on Nonsubstitution." *Money, Growth and Methodology,* vol. 20. Lund, Sweden: CWK Gleerup, 1961. Reprinted in *The Collected Sci-*

entific Papers of Paul A. Samuelson, vol. 1, ed. by Joseph E. Stiglitz. Cambridge, Mass.: The MIT Press, 1966.

Economics: An Introductory Analysis, 6th ed. New York: McGraw-Hill, 1964.

"A Caternary Turnpike Theorem Involving Consumption and the Golden Rule." *American Economic Review* 55 (June 1965).

The Collected Scientific Papers of Paul A. Samuelson, vol. 1, ed. by Joseph E. Stiglitz. Cambridge, Mass.: The MIT Press, 1966a.

The Collected Scientific Papers of Paul A. Samuelson, vol. 2, ed. by Joseph E. Stiglitz. Cambridge, Mass.: The MIT Press, 1966b.

"A Summing Up." *Quarterly Journal of Economics* 80: "Paradoxes in Capital Theory: A Symposium" (November 1966c).

"Indeterminacy of Development in a Heterogeneous Capital Model with Constant Saving Propensity." In *Essays on the Theory of Economic Growth,* ed. by Karl Shell. Cambridge, Mass.: The MIT Press, 1967. Reprinted in *The Collected Scientific Papers of Paul A. Samuelson,* vol. 3, ed. by Robert C. Merton. Cambridge, Mass: The MIT Press, 1972.

"Lifetime Portfolio Selection by Dynamic Stochastic Programming." *Review of Economic Studies* (August 1969). Reprinted in *The Collected Scientific Papers of Paul A. Samuelson,* vol. 3, ed. by Robert C. Merton. Cambridge, Mass.: The MIT Press, 1972.

The Collected Scientific Papers of Paul A. Samuelson, vol. 3, ed. by Robert C. Merton. Cambridge, Mass.: The MIT Press, 1972.

"Trade Pattern Reversals in Time-Phased Ricardian Systems and Intertemporal Efficiency." *Journal of International Economics* 5 (1975). Reprinted in *The Collected Scientific Papers of Paul A. Samuelson,* vol. 4, ed. by H. Nagatani and K. Crowley. Cambridge, Mass.: The MIT Press, 1977.

Economics, 10th ed. New York: McGraw-Hill, 1976a.

"The Periodic Turnpike Theorem." *Nonlinear Analysis, Theory, Methods and Applications,* 1 (1976b). Reprinted in *The Collected Scientific Papers of Paul A. Samuelson,* vol. 4, ed. by H. Nagatani and K. Crowley. Cambridge, Mass.: The MIT Press, 1977.

The Collected Scientific Papers of Paul A. Samuelson, vol. 4, ed. by H. Nagatani and K. Crowley. Cambridge, Mass.: The MIT Press, 1977.

Samuelson, Paul A., and Solow, Robert M. "A Complete Capital Model Involving Heterogeneous Capital Goods." *Quarterly Journal of Economics* 70 (November 1956).

"Comments" to Joan Robinson. *Quarterly Journal of Economics* 89 (February 1975).

Samuelson, Paul A., and von Weizsäcker, C. C. "A New Labor Theory of Value for Rational Planning through Use of the Bourgeois Profit Rate." *Proceedings of the National Academy of Sciences, U.S.A.* 68 (June 1971). Reprinted in *The Collected Scientific Papers of Paul A. Samuelson,* vol. 3, ed. by Robert C. Merton. Cambridge, Mass.: The MIT Press, 1972.

Sargent, Thomas J. "The Demand for Money during Hyperinflation under Rational Expectations: I." *International Economic Review* 18 (February 1977).

Sargent, Thomas J., and Wallace, Neil. "Rational Expectations and the Dynamics of Hyperinflation." *International Economic Review* 14 (June 1973).

Sen, Amartya. "Minimal Conditions for Monotonicity of Capital Value." *Journal of Economic Theory* 11 (December 1975).

Shell, Karl, ed. *Essays on the Theory of Optimal Economic Growth.* Cambridge, Mass.: The MIT Press, 1967.

Shell, Karl, Sidrauski, M., and Stiglitz, J. E. "Capital Gains, Income and Saving." *Review of Economic Studies* 36 (January 1969).

Shell, Karl, and Stiglitz, Joseph E. "The Allocation of Investment in a Dynamic Economy." *Quarterly Journal of Economics* (1967).

Smith, Adam. *The Wealth of Nations,* ed. by Edwin Cannan. New York: Modern Library, 1937.

Solow, Robert M. *Capital Theory and the Rate of Return.* Amsterdam: North-Holland, 1963.

"The Interest Rate and Transition between Techniques." In *Socialism, Capitalism, and Economic Growth,* ed. by C. H. Feinstein. New York: Cambridge University Press, 1967.

"On the Rate of Return: Reply to Pasinetti." *Economic Journal* 80 (June 1970).

Sraffa, P. *Production of Commodities by Means of Commodities.* Cambridge, England: Cambridge University Press, 1960.

Stigler, George J. "The Success and Failures of Professor Smith." *Journal of Political Economy* 84 (December 1976).

Sutherland, R. S. "On Optimal Development in a Multisector Economy: The Discounted Case." *Review of Economic Studies* (October 1970).

Swan, T. W. "Golden Ages and Production Functions." In *Growth Economics,* ed. by A. K. Sen. Baltimore: Penguin, 1970.

Thom, René. *Structural Stability and Morphogenesis: An Outline of a General Theory of Models,* trans. by D. H. Fowler. Reading, Mass.: W. A. Benjamin, 1976.

Usher, Dan, ed. *The Measurement of Capital.* Chicago: University of Chicago Press, forthcoming, 1980.

Uzawa, H. "Neutral Inventions and the Stability of Growth Equilibrium." *Review of Economic Studies* 28 (1961).

"Time Preference, the Consumption Function, and Optimum Asset Holdings." In *Value, Capital and Growth,* ed. by J. N. Wolfe. Chicago: Aldine, 1968.

Varian, Hal R. "Catastrophe Theory and the Business Cycle." *Economic Inquiry* 17 (January 1979).

Velapillai, K. "Irving Fisher on 'Switches of Technique': A Historical Note." *Quarterly Journal of Economics* (November 1975).

von Neumann, J. "A Model of General Economic Equilibrium." *Review of Economic Studies* (1945–6). Reprinted in *Readings in Mathematical Economics,* vol. 2, ed. by Peter Newman. Baltimore: Johns Hopkins University Press, 1968.

von Weizsäcker, C. C. "Existence of Optimal Programs of Accumulation for an Infinite Time Horizon." *Review of Economic Studies* 32 (April 1965).

Steady State Capital Theory. New York: Springer-Verlag, 1971.

"Substitution along the Time Axis." In *Essays in Modern Capital Theory,* ed. by M. Brown, K. Sato, and P. Zarembka. Amsterdam: North-Holland, 1976.

Weinstein, M. C., and Zeckhauser, R. J. "The Optimal Consumption of Depletable Natural Resources." *Quarterly Journal of Economics* 89 (August 1975).

Weitzman, M. L. "Duality Theory for Infinite Horizon Convex Models." *Management Science* 19 (1973).

Whitaker, John K. "Harrod-Neutral Technical Progress and the Possibility of Steady Growth." *Rivista Internazionale di Scienze Economiche e Commerciali* 17 (1970a).

"Neoclassical Economic Growth and the Consumption Function." *Oxford Economic Papers* 22 (November 1970b).

"Balanced Growth." Discussion Paper. Charlottesville: University of Virginia, October 1977.

Yeager, Leland B. "Toward Understanding Some Paradoxes in Capital Theory." *Economic Inquiry* (September 1976).

Yeager, Leland B., and Burmeister, Edwin. "Continuity and Capital Reversal: Reply." *Economic Inquiry* (January 1978).

Zeeman, C. "Differential Equations for the Heartbeat and Nerve Impulses." In *Towards a Theoretical Biology,* vol. 4, ed. by C. H. Waddington. Chicago: Aldine, 1968.

INDEX

Numerals in italics refer to pages on which terms are defined.

323